CH

GOODEI____AM'S

TEN BODIES
TWO BIKES

AND

A BOIL

–

LANDS END
TO
JOHN O'GROATS
CYCLE RIDE

The names, characters, places and incidents in this book truly existed, although their uses have been altered to ensure confidentiality for those concerned.

Buy at www.lulu.com
Visit www.landsend2johnogroats.co.uk

To Bike Buddy for giving me a tale to tell.

I am truly sorry.

Other Books by Chris Gooderham:

The Soul Collector

Wicked Rhymes

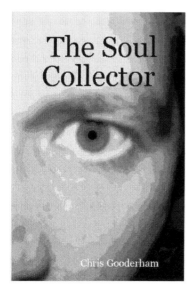

www.dateofdeath.co.uk

Buy at www.lulu.com

PROLOGUE

They say the day you are born is the day you start your journey towards death. They also say half the people who have existed on this planet are still alive today. Whether that's true or not, with a global population of more than six and a half billion expanding rapidly and causing an exponential rise in aggression and rudeness levels in the world, is irrelevant. For there is no mistaking the truth - however politically correct we are forced to be and despite the ever-increasing number of human rights activists knocking at our doors, this world is full of a huge number of arseholes.

We all know one. We've all met them. The dickhead who tailgates you on the road or cuts you up to gain a crucial second. The shop assistant who has no intention of being polite or courteous. The gang of youths standing on the street corner jeering and shouting as normal folk go about their everyday lives. The scrounger who sits on his arse all day and expects the rest of us to pay for his Sky TV. They're everywhere, and they're increasing in numbers. Soon the world will be overrun with arseholes and there is absolutely nothing you can do about it. That is unless of course the rules change.

What if the laws of the country didn't apply? What if you were free to settle the score? What if you could do whatever you wanted and nobody could stop you? Welcome to my life.

My name is Matthew Moore and I am free. Last year I discovered I was about to die. Last year I uncovered the most uncomfortable and embarrassing ailment known to man – a boil on my butt. I tried to ignore it. I tried to pretend it would go away, but it didn't. One Tuesday morning, I strolled into my local GP surgery embarrassed by a lump and strolled out with a death sentence. What started out literarily as a pain in the arse, turned into a living nightmare that would rip my world apart.

My boil is not an ordinary boil – it's poison. At the age of twenty-seven I was diagnosed with an inoperable, irreversible boil on my backside that was slowly sucking the life from my body and within a year I would be dead.

But things change. My name is Matthew Moore and this is my story. A death sentence doesn't have to be a death sentence; it can be the key to unlocking your chains. If you know you're going to die you are free. If you know you're going to die there is no need to save for the future, there is no need to build a career, or look after the garden. If you know you're going to die you don't need to do anything except be selfish. And I am selfish.

Perhaps you've heard of me. My name is Matthew Moore, does that ring any bells? It should do. I've met the arseholes and I've readdressed the balance. I've lifted myself up from the lowest point of my life and I've fought back. I'm everything you want to be. I may be dying, I may be on the brink of extinction, but I've done what you can only dream of doing. I am the vigilante leading this world to a better future.

I have helped you and you must remember that. No need for thanks. I ask only one thing from you. When I finally leave this world, you must remember me. If I am truly to live forever you must recall my actions and speak of me for generations to come. That is my only reward, but to me it is reward enough.

Now let me tell you my story. Let me take you back twelve months to the start, where every good story should start - in the beginning.

IN THE BEGINNING

'It's made of poison sir. I assure you, you will die!'
I woke in a cold sweat, the words reverberating through my mind. How could I be dying from a bloody boil? How could I be dying at the age of twenty-seven?

It was such a shock to suddenly realise I wasn't immortal. Prior to that I'd always assumed I would live forever, then at the age of twenty-seven, death suddenly took one giant leap towards me.

The boil on my bum had existed for a couple of weeks before I finally decided to see a doctor. I'd been reluctant. I'd been too embarrassed. Surely it was nothing to worry about and would soon just slip away. Surely, at such a young age it couldn't be anything more serious. How wrong I was! Within forty-eight hours, the doctor had sent me to a specialist, given me tests and I'd been diagnosed. My backside had been prodded and poked more times than a homosexual rabbit.

The boil was not a boil; it was a door - a door to my body. A door used by a small, slim worm that had nibbled at my arse, cut itself an opening, and come in. The worm had entered my body, made itself at home (with no invitation I can tell you) and to make matters worse the bloody thing had laid eggs while it was there. I didn't even know worms laid eggs, but obviously this one did! Now the eggs had hatched, and the worms from those eggs and laid more eggs. The worms were taking over my body, slithering through my blood stream, and making their way through my insides. They were overrunning me, and there was nothing the doctors could do about it.

Up until this point the doctors confidently told me there'd only been one other reported case of worm infestation in the world and that man had died within twelve months of the symptoms occurring. Furthermore, he'd been saved the embarrassment of being bitten on the bum, since his worm had entered through a leg. Jammy bastard!

This one case told them important facts, which they took great delight in passing on to me. My worms were slowly reproducing inside me and I was dying. One minute I was the Highlander and would live forever, the next minute the tall ugly bloke who killed Sean Connery was holding my severed head aloft in his arms. Now what was he called in the film? Oh yes – the Kurgan!

My reaction to finding out about the killer worm from outer-my-arse, was to sit on the sofa and sulk. I thought this was a pretty good reaction really. It didn't hurt anybody and I was comfortable.

What are you supposed to do when you find out you're dying?

My wife looked after me like I was an invalid. I was a spoilt kid again - a teenager, who couldn't be bothered to do anything. When asked a question I just grunted. Why should I care what was for dinner? I'd be dead soon!

I started to think I might be better putting myself out of the misery. I started to hate everything and everyone. I hated doctors, I hated work, I hated my family and I hated my cat. The cat seemed to know I hated it because it kept coming and sitting on my lap. Then it would turn around and around until settling in the perfect position for me to have a full-face view of its arse. Even the cat knew my problem, and was screaming at me, 'Look, I don't have a boil on my butt!'

Could I really live like this for the last year of my life? I'd been given twelve months to live, but all I really wanted to do was spend the twelve months feeling sorry for myself, curled up like a child sulking my life away. That was until the day I changed my mind.

My young daughter came up to me and asked a question that will stay with me forever (well twelve months anyway).

'Daddy, why don't you play with me anymore?'

I was numb with shock. My small baby daughter, who was only three years old, was asking why I didn't play any more. At the time I just wanted to turn away from her and cry, but I suddenly realised what being a parent was all about. It's nothing to do with bringing your children up right, it's nothing to do with getting them to eat good food or making sure they go to bed at a sensible time. Being a parent is simply protecting your children from the pain they will soon feel as adults. Being a parent is about lying to your children so they don't understand the real meaning of life. Lying to them so they don't realise that one day we will all die.

I looked my little princess in the eyes, and while fighting back the tears, rolled myself off the sofa. She took hold of my finger in her tiny hand and carefully and gently led me back to life. She gave me the courage to continue the fight. She gave me the courage to switch off the television and stop watching any more episodes of Richard and Judy. About time really, those two were driving me mad.

I knelt on the floor next to a large box of Lego and, with my daughter, rebuilt my life. I'd been given a jolt. Not a very pleasant jolt, but one that sent shock waves through my whole body. I had been given a shot to say, 'Get on with it buddy, or it will be too late,' and I suddenly realised what I had to do - I had twelve months to make something of myself.

After building the grandest princess Lego tower ever built, I sat down in the dining room, pulled out a pile of paper and started to make notes. My wife had gone to work, my eldest daughter was at school, and my little girl was at home with her daddy on the odd day when she wasn't at pre-school. Everyone else was continuing with their lives as if nothing had changed; now it was time for me to sort out mine. I started to write.

I needed to make my plans, and I needed to do it quickly. Time was short. I'd always had this theory that I should live every day as if it was my last, and then I couldn't be disappointed when it was. Well, I now knew when my last one was coming. I had a trump card in the game of life. I knew my life was coming to an end, and whatever anybody else did to me they couldn't take that away.

When you are told you have a year to live, things are suddenly put into perspective. When your children fight it no longer matters. When you burn the toast it no longer matters. When you hear a dripping tap in the middle of the night, it no longer matters. Things become clearer. Not to begin with, I grant you, but eventually things become so much clearer.

I'd never really done anything exciting in my life. Okay, I'd done all the normal things. I'd been to college, I'd started work, I'd got married and I'd had two children. Well okay, I suppose, I should say I had my wicked way, and then my wife had two children. But even before I was diagnosed I was just getting to the stage in my life when I wanted to achieve things. I was fed up of going to work, getting home, sitting on the sofa, watching television, going to bed, getting up and going back to work. I wanted to do something that I could be proud of. Perhaps my body had known for a while what was going to happen and was trying to give me a kick-start. Unfortunately I'd ignored the signs and had just carried on in my normal haphazard manner. Well if my body hadn't managed to give me the kick, the doctors certainly had and I wasn't going to spend the last twelve months of my life sitting in a chair sulking or complaining about what a bad lot I'd been given.

I wanted to use the information properly and to do so it was essential nobody else knew what was wrong with me. The doctors couldn't make me better, but they could get rid of the symptoms, particularly early on. They had lanced my boil, and drugged me up so I couldn't feel the pain and to my amazement it had actually worked. Physically, at that moment, I felt better than I'd felt in years, and I could finally sit down again without wincing. My problems were mental.

The first thing I wrote on my list was to get back to work. I'd been away for a good few days and it was time I made a comeback. The second item on the list was to resign from work. How brilliant would that be? I'd been dreaming for months about going and telling my boss to shove his job up his arse. Well now I could. I then had a second thought, crossed out resign and replaced it with 'made redundant.' This would take some careful manipulation, but I wasn't going to miss out on six years worth of redundancy pay.

Of course I could have continued to work and claimed the death-in-service award, but that seemed a little sick. After all, what use would the money be to me when I was dead? Perhaps it was meant for my wife and children, but hell, I knew I only had a year to live, why would I want to spend half of that time sitting at a desk doing the same mundane crap I'd been doing the rest of my working career. Not for me. Death-in-service would just have to disappear. I continued to write.

I was going to write down everything I wanted to achieve in my last year - a kind of wish list. It was going to take some careful thought, but I was determined to get it right. I needed to become someone, and to do that I needed to set some big aims and reach them.

What would you do if you had twelve months to live? Would you go to Amsterdam and sleep with some prostitutes? Would you go to Las Vegas and blow all your money on slot machines? Would you throw yourself out of an aeroplane and sky dive? Well I didn't want to do any of these things. I wanted to do something I could be proud of, something people could remember me for. Besides I'm afraid of heights. How stupid is that? A man, who has a gang of worms slowly eating him from the insides, is afraid of heights in case he dies. Even if I was dying from Colonic Worm Infestation, I still didn't want to shorten what little life I had left by throwing myself out of a plane. In some ways having a fixed end date made the thought of risking my life even more worrying.

For the next few nights I stayed awake. I couldn't get to sleep because I was too busy trying to fine-tune my list. It had to be perfect. In order to work it had to be just right. Nobody could know the plan until the last piece was in place otherwise the whole plan would be ruined. It had to be right, and I continued to adjust it until it was perfect. Besides, I wouldn't get a second chance.

Finally at half past three on Sunday morning I sat back in the dull glow of my study and looked at what I'd achieved. The list was complete. The jigsaw created, all I needed to do now was fit the pieces in and I would become someone.

The following morning I announced to my wife and children I was going to cycle from Lands End to John O'Groats. I said I'd do it for charity, but that was really just a front - I was doing it for me. I wanted to prove to myself I was still capable of such a feat. I wanted to prove I could sit on a bike saddle for three weeks despite the boil on my bum. I also wanted to cycle the length of the country to prove I was still young and fit, and because once I'd done it nobody could take it away from me.

My work colleagues obviously knew I'd been ill, but they didn't know how bad it was. They knew I'd been a little under the weather, but not that the grim reaper was making his way towards my soul. My plan was they would now see me as a recovered man, and I knew in order to make my recovery look truly real I needed to return on my bike.

I'd been cycling to work for a few years by now, and people were used to seeing me arrive by bicycle. I was worried it would really hurt when I sat on the saddle, but it would raise too many eyebrows if I started to drive, and besides if I was going to survive three weeks of cycling I needed to check I could still do it.

The cycling was easy, but the first day at work was hard. Everybody wanted to know how I was and if I was feeling better now. I just shrugged my shoulders and said I was fine, but I wasn't very convincing. I'd never been particularly good at lying - another thing that needed to change.

One day back at work and I was already fed up. I couldn't spend the last year of my life as if it was any other year. I needed to do all those amazing things I'd always dreamed of. I needed to get away from the rat race and start living properly. I needed to get on with the plan. I needed to get out of work quickly, and, the only way to do it was to persuade my employer I was surplus to requirements. Not an easy task when you've spent the last six years trying to prove you're indispensable.

The second day at work gave me the opportunity to put my plan in motion. We had a meeting; a video conference, with my boss at the other end of the conference call. It was a big meeting, with most of the top executives, and a few minor employees like myself who had been invited along because of our specialist knowledge of the area.

Video conferences are very strange. There was a group of us sitting in a semicircle starring at a large television screen. In the television we could see another group of people sitting in a semicircle starring back at us. When you have a video conference you don't talk to people at your end of the conference, you only talk to the folk at the other end, and if I'm honest, you don't talk, you shout. That way you're sure the microphone picks up what you have to say so the images at the other end can hear you, and it doesn't seem to matter that everyone at your end are covering their ears

The call started. My boss, Gordon was a stuck up git. He liked the sound of his own voice. He liked to give his opinion on everything, but unfortunately he never had anything worthwhile to say. He spoke loudly and annoyingly, he would shout to drown out anybody else who might want to talk, and he would look down at anybody who dared disagree with him. In fact nobody disagreed with him. He was the Sales Director, but, in reality, was too narrow minded to be a real director. He was just a salesman who'd risen to the top too quickly. He smoked non-stop, drank to excess and his best friend was his mobile phone, which he liked to hold in his hand at all times, even in meetings.

Gordon would sit in a meeting, staring at his mobile phone, far too rude and self-important to switch it off. This meeting was no different from all the others. He was waiting for his phone to ring, and I knew when it did I would get my opportunity.

I stared at the screen, my eyes fixated on the small electronic device in his hand, willing it to ring, and when the phone call eventually came he did what he always did. He pushed his chair back, lifted the phone to his ear and stood up. For some reason he had to walk when he was talking on his mobile. Perhaps it was to prove to everyone how wonderful his phone was because it was truly mobile.

I watched as he walked backwards and forwards, chatting to the person at the other end. The rest of us just stopped, because we knew it was pointless continuing while Gordon strode around the room. He was far too important to leave out (and his constant talking would have been just too annoying), so we would just have to wait until his lordship had finished. We waited patiently.

After a few minutes Gordon strode back to his seat and sat down. No apology, no thank-you for waiting. The ignorant bastard just sat down and expected things to continue as normal. I'd seen this happen so many times before and had always willed myself too speak, but was too afraid of the repercussions. Not today. Today I was going to attack.

'Don't you think you owe us all an apology?' I asked.

Gordon looked up at the screen and sneered at me. 'What?' he replied.

'I said, don't you think you owe us all an apology?'

The room was silent. Everyone was waiting for the fireworks to erupt, and erupt they most certainly did.

'Who the fuck do you think you're talking to, you little pile of shit?' Gordon most eloquently remarked. He always resorted to bad language when he was pushed into a corner. This was something I'd been relying on, for amongst the congregation listening to our little conversation was non-other than the Personnel Director.

'I'm talking to the annoying Sales Director who thinks it's acceptable to hold up twelve members of staff so he can talk nonsense to some prat on the other end of his mobile phone.' I quickly quipped.

The room sucked in a deep breath as one, and then fell silent waiting for a reply, but Gordon just got up from his chair and walked towards the exit. 'I'll deal with you later Moore,' he threatened as he stepped through the door.

Strangely we didn't really achieve a great deal in that meeting. At least, nobody else achieved much, but I believe I achieved everything I'd set out to. Just a few minutes after the end of the meeting, as I sat back down at my desk, my phone rang. It was Gordon, what a surprise!

'How dare you speak to me like that? You had no right to confront me. I will not put up with anybody talking to me in that way, especially someone who works for me. You will not talk to me again like that, do you hear? There will be repercussions - you mark my words. You will not get away with this.'

I decided to fight fire with fire, 'I won't have you swear at me. I think it is rude and vulgar and I won't put up with it from anybody, particularly someone in your position. You can threaten me as much as you like, but I will not be bullied. I will not be spoken to as if I have just slipped on to the pavement from the back of a dog's arse. I think you'll find that Steve will back me up if you'd like to take this further.' (Steve, being the Personnel Director, who unfortunately had about as much backbone as a jellyfish.) However I knew what would happen, and I just needed to press the right buttons. Gordon hung up. I waited for the next call, and it came within half an hour. It was Steve.

'Can you come downstairs please Matthew?'

I was on my way at a quick pace. I waved at colleagues on the way down and told them I was on my way out. This was a certainty. I entered the room as Steve put the phone down, I assume to Gordon again. He ushered me towards a chair, and sat in the next one himself.

Steve, the spineless wonder, told me the position I was in. Gordon had suddenly decided I was of no further use to the company. That I was surplus to requirements and should leave with immediate effect. I had three months' notice on my contract, but I would take that as garden leave. I was free to go.

Of course I pretended to object. I disputed the decision. I tried to persuade Steve that Gordon was just getting rid of me because I'd remonstrated with him. Steve agreed, but he could do nothing about it. I knew however, what they were doing was illegal, and that Steve would have to agree a good sum for me to leave. Three months notice, tax-free. Six-years service at two weeks per year, tax-free. That totalled twenty-five weeks pay, tax-free, and that was his first offer.

By the time I left his office, Steve had been on the phone to Gordon a further three times, and my settlement had increased gradually from twenty-five weeks pay up to forty weeks pay. The grand total of twenty-four thousand pounds given to me as a cheque there and then. I snatched the money, signed a little agreement to say we had parted in good faith and left the office. I was to go to my desk, collect my personal belongings and leave the company, and to ensure I did nothing untoward Steve came with me.

The trouble is Gordon and Steve had forgotten what a whiz I was with computers. They'd forgotten I was the statistician, and had all the data about the company for the last sixteen years. I knew everything there was to know, and what's more, I'd compressed this information until it sat neatly within one very large e-mail. I approached my desk for the final time, Steve following a few steps behind, doing his best not to make a scene in front of the remaining workforce. I knew my instructions – clear your desk and walk out the door. I stepped up to the computer, hit the 'Enter' key and watched my last e-mail whiz out the company. I moved the mouse, pressed delete and the e-mail and all its contents vanished from the screen. Then I turned to Steve and I smiled. A smile that hid the fact all the data held on my computer had just been deleted and sent to every one of our main competitors. What a shame!

I got home that night and told my dear wife I'd resigned. I'm not sure why I didn't tell her about the redundancy money. I'm not a greedy man, and I certainly didn't want to rob her of her inheritance, but for now, I wanted the money to be mine, just in case I needed it. I then told her more about my cycling feat. I was going to go in August, which at the time was six weeks away. I was going to plan everything down to the minutest detail from train travel to accommodation. I also told her I wanted to find someone to cycle with me. I needed a cycling partner, a Bike Buddy.

I was still fairly new to bikes so I needed someone who knew how to mend a puncture. I needed someone who could read a map. I needed someone who could look after me and protect me from the dangerous folk I would meet on the way, but above all, I needed someone I could get on with for three weeks solid. We would be living and breathing as one, together all day and all night, relying on each other when everyone else was gone, going through highs and lows together, joy and stress. I thought long and hard about who might fit the bill, but alas I could think of nobody and in the end I was forced to settle for a much less flexible partner. A man stuck in his ways, who was unfit and unkind, who could turn any pleasant experience into a catastrophe at the touch of a button. A man close to my heart, but also close to forcing my insanity. None other than my father-in-law; John - my new Bike Buddy. I decided he was easy prey. I could persuade him to come with me, no problem.

'How about a new challenge?' I asked him that evening.

My big advantage was Bike Buddy was drunk, and I was not. After dampening down the magnitude of the challenge, I think I put it as, 'A little jaunt on the bikes,' and after the tenth pint he finally agreed. I got him to sign on the dotted line, just in case he tried to back out when sober.

Despite the high level of alcohol in his blood, I was still not sure why he agreed to come on my mad expedition. Perhaps because he'd toured Devon and Cornwall as a kid and wanted to prove he could still do it. Perhaps because he didn't think I'd survive on my own. Perhaps because he wanted a real challenge in his life. Or perhaps he had an inkling that somehow this trip was very important to me. I was sure my wife hadn't told her father my diagnosis, but he seemed to know something, perhaps just enough to make him curious. Or maybe, like me, he was just a little mad.

As he said yes, I finally realised why I'd chosen him. Despite all the unnatural goings-on in my body, I still considered myself fairly young and fairly fit. I was twenty-seven years old when we set off from Lands End. Bike Buddy on the other hand was fifty-seven. He ran a building firm, and was big, over six-foot, and weighing in at, actually I don't know how much he weighed, but let's say around seventeen stone. He had high blood pressure and was forced to take beta-blockers everyday of his life or he'd die. He had a knackered knee, which had been operated on a few years earlier, and he had an obsession with food. I realised at that moment what a stupid plan this really was – because one of us could easily die. The only consolation was, despite all that had happened, it probably wasn't going to be me.

PLANNING, PLANNING AND MORE PLANNING

When you say you're going to cycle from Lands End to John O'Groats the first thing people say is, 'Why are you starting at the bottom and going up? Isn't it uphill?'

I'm sorry, but that is a really stupid question. If you start at sea level one end and finish at sea level the other end, funnily enough you will go up as much as you go down.

Rather than reply with simple sarcasm, I more politely explained the wind normally blew from the south-west in the British Isles, and therefore should help more than it hinders if we started at the bottom. I also added that it seemed like a good idea to get the worst part of the journey over at the beginning - Devon and Cornwall. They are by far the hilliest parts of the country and the plan was to get them out of the way early on. Strangely enough, after the umpteenth question, I resorted to simple sarcasm.

We decided to go in August, because the weather would be nice, and that was important. I didn't tell Bike Buddy I had to go fairly soon otherwise my arse would swell up and my insides would turn to compost thanks to an army of mutant worms. It was probably best he didn't know.

I bought every map I could find - National Cycle Routes, Ordnance Survey Touring Maps, Landranger maps, road atlases, CTC recommended routes, wall maps, pocket maps, in fact anything I could find with part of our journey on it. The theory was the more information I had the more chance I had of finding a flat route. If Ordnance Survey showed the road as hilly, perhaps another map might not – some chance. Over a couple of days I ploughed through them all, picking the best bits from each, until eventually I'd pieced together our route.

If we went straight up the motorways from Lands End to John O'Groats the total distance would be just shy of 900 miles. For some reason we didn't fancy cycling straight up the hard shoulder of the motorway, so Bike Buddy and I opted for a more relaxed, and hopefully quieter route. It's never very pleasant cycling on main roads, let alone motorways (apart from the fact cycling on motorways is also illegal) so we wanted to avoid them and instead the idea was to stick to the National Cycle Routes as much as possible.

I looked at my plans and smiled, then I started adding up the mileage - moving up from Lands End to Bristol, across from Bristol to Worcester, on to Nottingham and Derby, across to the east coast via York and Middlesbrough, then up through Sunderland, Newcastle, Berwick-upon-Tweed, into Scotland via Edinburgh, Montrose, Aberdeen, Inverness, up to the north coast at Tongue and along to John O'Groats. I sat and looked at my effort with a sense of pride. We'd done it. We'd made it to John O'Groats. Well we'd done it on paper anyway.

Okay, now for the mileage, how much further than 900 miles was it going to be, perhaps another 50, perhaps 100, maybe even 110?

Some chance, my route worked out at just over 1,700 miles. Ouch! I added the numbers up again. Yep, 1,700 miles - that's nearly double. We could go up and down for 1,700 miles. Surely that couldn't be right, surely I'd made a mistake. I checked the numbers again. Nope, 1,700 miles, no mistake, no double counting.

I lay in bed that night wondering what I'd done wrong. One suggestion came to mind - maybe I'd done it in kilometres rather than miles. Unfortunately not!

Okay, so we'd given ourselves three weeks to complete the trip. That worked out at about 90 miles per day if we took a day off each end for travelling. We would never make it! I reckoned we could manage around 50 a day. Any more and we'd collapse with exhaustion before the finish line. Time to get the maps out again.

Right, what do we have to do? We have to start at Lands End, we have to finish at John O'Groats, and that's pretty much it really. The National Cycle Route from Lands End to Bristol wasn't bad. I cut off corners when they looped for no reason. I cut corners with the roads and with the map measurer. This seemed like a good idea at the time. Rather than wobble the map measurer round every bend I occasionally pushed it straight across a corner. Psychologically the route would add up to a lower number, I'd worry about the extra miles when we got there. Surely there would be a way to cut corners while cycling anyway, just take the racing line round bends.

After a lot of corner cutting, I added up the mileage again - wait for it - this time it totalled 1,093 miles, oh and a half. Not bad, and pretty accurate hey? I was so confident of my distance measuring skills that I could measure to the nearest half a mile. That last half a mile was important, that could be the half mile when the wheels exploded and we hurtled into the sea at breakneck speed. My 1,093 and a half even included the cycle from the train station in Penzance to Lands End and the cycle from John O'Groats to the train station in Wick to come home. An average mileage of 57 per day. Still more than I'd hoped, but not bad, not bad at all! (Remember this moment. Remember the corners I cut, and it may explain some of the problems ahead. This is the time you should say, 'Don't cut corners Matthew.' Then you can say, 'I told you so,' in a few pages' time.)

As this was going to be my biggest adventure ever, I wanted to plan everything down to the minutest detail. So, having plotted the route, totalled the mileage, the next stage was to plan the stopping off points. Where could we stay overnight?

Bike Buddy and I had already discussed this. We'd decided to carry all our own equipment with us, but avoid the heavy pots, pans and tents required for camping, and stay in Bed and Breakfasts instead. Train times meant we could travel down to Penzance on Saturday morning, cycle to Lands End and back in the afternoon and stay in Penzance overnight. That was my starting point.

I started phoning. Penzance was a nightmare. 'Sorry we're full up' seemed to be the standard response. This was the first place I'd tried. I had twenty-one Bed and Breakfasts to book and I couldn't even get the first one sorted out. If they were all like this it was going to be horrendous. How on earth could I book all these places if they were already full? The tenth Bed and Breakfast in Penzance offered me hope, a dim light at the end of the tunnel. I managed to book two single rooms. We were on our way, and thankfully, from then on it got easier.

When I asked a lady in Glastonbury whether she had a couple of single rooms for the night she told me, 'Of course not, they're all doubles. Why don't you phone someone with singles?'

I pulled the earpiece away from my head and stared at the receiver. Was she really telling me off for asking if she had a room for the night?

I replied quickly and smartly, 'If I'd known you only had doubles do you think I'd have wasted my time phoning you? You strange and sad little old lady.'

Then I quickly hung up the phone, and prayed she wouldn't ring back.

Stupid idea this 1471 by British Telecom. If you suddenly feel the urge to shout at someone down the phone, they can always find out who you are, or at least know your phone number. I've had to change my phone number at home more than a dozen times in the last year because of the stupid 1471. I know what you're going to say, 'Why don't you set up your phone to withhold the number?' It's a good point, and when I'm through with my Colonic Worm Infestation I'll look into it.

After three nights spent solely on the phone I'd booked all our Bed and Breakfasts. The strangest was a lady in Blackburn who was curious about our route because everyone else seemed to go east from her, not west. She tried to persuade me to change my whole route because of what she thought we should do. When I refused she became quite odd and abrupt. If I'd had a choice I would have chosen another Bed and Breakfast to stay in. Unfortunately, there weren't any others around. Instead I made a mental note that she was unpleasant and should be dealt with by Bike Buddy if at all possible.

As I moved up the country the strangest thing happened. The further north I went, the more people seemed to trust me. Our first two overnight stays down in Cornwall wanted full payment up front. Slowly as I worked my way up the country the deposits reduced, until I got to Scotland when most didn't want anything other than my name. This was strange because the further north I went the more unlikely it was that these people actually knew me. Maybe that wasn't strange after all. Perhaps the people who trusted me the most were the ones who knew me the least. Perhaps I was an untrustworthy kind of person, although I still thought it was strange. After all, there was more chance of us getting to Penzance than there was of getting to Somerset. There was more chance of us getting to Somerset than of getting to Cumbria and so on up the country. If we were going to fail we would be letting everybody down from that point onwards, yet they trusted me. The mad fools! They obviously didn't know how unfit Bike Buddy was, or that my body was being sucked to death by a mass of fast growing worms.

The most worrying problem started to appear before me as I booked the accommodation - around a third of the Bed and Breakfasts couldn't supply two single rooms, and I was left with a twin. Normally such details are not too concerning, but then usually you're not sharing a room with Bike Buddy. The guy snores like a pneumatic drill, and I've always been a light sleeper. It became obvious that with a drill in the bed next to me I wouldn't get any sleep. I would have cycled for eight hours, be completely exhausted, but I still wouldn't be able to get to sleep. Even the thought of having a snoring Bike Buddy next to me stopped me getting any sleep for three nights. I would be tired before I even started on this cycle tour. Bike Buddy was going to snore me to death!

Having planned everything, including all the Bed and Breakfasts, Virgin Trains suddenly decided to change their timetable and cancel the early Saturday morning train to Penzance. A rapid change of plan meant we decide to travel down on Friday instead, stay in Penzance on Friday night, have a leisurely cycle on Saturday to Lands End and back and stay in the same Bed and Breakfast on Saturday night.

Sorted! In fact better than sorted. When I booked the train tickets it just so happened the Friday night train was about half the price of the Saturday train. Bargain! But then, why was that? Why should a train journey's price be determined by what time of day you go? Do fuel costs increase on Saturday? Is there more resistance on the tracks on Saturday, causing the train to use more energy? Perhaps drunken louts walk home on a Friday evening after a night out, and piss on the tracks. The urine then dries and makes the tracks all sticky. These sticky tracks then slow the train and make the running costs higher. Perhaps they have to pay drivers and conductors double time on Saturday? Actually, there might be something in that. Perhaps Virgin Trains just think people who travel on Saturday have more money. Perhaps Saturday travellers are train-spotters who don't care how much they pay. Perhaps it's just another British rip-off. Anyway, from my point of view I'd saved some money, so why should I care?

The only thing to sort out now was what to take and what to wear. Bike Buddy and I decided to take a couple of cycle tops each, one yellow and one orange. Both so bright they defied the law of physics which states, 'Light doesn't bend round corners.' With these t-shirts on, light not only bent round corners, but actually sped up. You could see us coming at least three hours before we arrived. They also had 'Lands End to John O'Groats – Cyclists On Tour' emblazoned across the backs. This was so people knew what we were doing, so we could take on hero status for a few weeks, and to encourage passers-by to part with money for charity. The more people who knew we were cycling for charity, the more we could raise. Actually, I think it was mainly for the hero status.

Apart from the t-shirts, I decided I didn't really need much else. A couple of pairs of cycle shorts (with padding), one pair of boxer shorts (for three weeks – please don't tell any of the ladies), two pairs of socks, a waterproof top and a pair of cycle trousers to double up as my 'Going out on the town' gear. My, I was going to look sexy at night.

The most crucial entry in my panniers was definitely going to be the Sudocrem. This is the cream used by parents on their young babies to help soothe nappy rash. Being a father of two, I was convinced of the benefits this cream would have on my nether regions. I was to lather my backside with Sudocrem every morning to help stop the risk of butt blisters. Three weeks on a bike, seven hours per day, seven days per week. That's around a 150 hours on a bike saddle. My arse was really going to hurt! My arse would have hurt even without the boil, but despite it being lanced, the boil was still going to make my arse hurt even more.

Despite my attempt to keep things down to a minimum, I remained deeply concerned about the weight of my panniers. I cut weight wherever I could, small tubes of toothpaste, a tiny roll-on deodorant stick, and a sawn-off toothbrush. I took a disposable camera, because it was lighter than my proper camera. I could simply post it off to be developed when I finished it and buy another one. Of course, if I'd felt the weight of Bike Buddy's panniers at this stage I might not have been quite so worried.

Talking of cameras, I should point out that I'm not great when it comes to taking photos. My wife photographs everything that moves. I don't! I prefer to see things through my own eyes, rather than through a lens. I prefer to record things in my mind, rather than on a piece of photographic paper. Wedding photographers annoy me! Having said that, ours was excellent, but as a general rule, they annoy me. They need to realise they're at a wedding to record the day, not as the main attraction. Guests don't want to stand around for two hours waiting to have their photos taken, they want to get inside and eat the food.

Another thing I can't stand is a set of twenty-four photos, when there are only four different pictures and six copies of each. Praise the Lord for digital cameras when you can pick and choose the ones to keep. Unfortunately, at the time, they didn't make disposable digital cameras, but I would use the disposable camera sparingly; one picture every time we stopped, nothing more and nothing less.

I also decided to take a diary, and to fill it with Post Office stamps from any Post Offices we passed en-route. Not sure whether the Post Offices were allowed to stamp books willy-nilly, but there would be no harm in asking.

That's it! I pushed what I wasn't going to wear into my panniers and placed them on the bathroom scales. Just over a stone. Not bad, I thought.

One other area of concern leading up to the start day was my bike. It wasn't the best bike in the world. It wasn't the most expensive bike in the world, and although I'd used it to cycle to work quite a lot, it wasn't really designed for long distances. It was just a run-of-the-mill hybrid bike. Bike Buddy's bike, on the other hand, was spectacular. He'd had it built around his body – moulded to his shape, which is probably why it was such a peculiar design. But, however many concerns there were about Bike Buddy's body, there were no concerns about his bike. It was built to survive. My bike was not.

I took the bike in for a service, and at the same time decided to change the gears on the back. This was something I was particularly proud of. I'd never really used my easiest gear, but decided that I would like to put an even easier one on, better known as a 'Granny gear.' The name comes from the fact that, however steep the hill, when in this gear, even your granny could keep the bike moving.

I was a little embarrassed asking for a granny gear in a shop, but I bucked up the courage to go and make the purchase. I made out it actually was for my granny. Not sure they believed me, but then I was fairly sure I would never actually need this gear. After all, I was a young, fit, strong, stud. Despite my Colonic Worm Infestation, I wouldn't need a gear designed for an old age pensioner, particularly a female old age pensioner, but I wanted it anyway, just in case. A kind of security blanket, like my old blanky when I was a child. The new gear was so big it was almost the same diameter as the wheel itself. Hills were now a thing of the past. No problem, let me at them.

The bike was clean and sparkly new, the panniers were packed, and I was ready for the off. Or just about! Funny how you suddenly become very aware of every slight niggle. My left knee started to ache a little – would I have to cancel the ride? My bike was making a rubbing noise – would I have to cancel the ride? My hair needed a cut – would I have to cancel the ride? Luckily Bike Buddy was going through the same trauma.

Despite all my planning there remained three major uncertainties on our trip - would the drugs keep the numbness in my arse at bay long enough for me to finish the trip, would my 'thrown together' bike hold together long enough to make the distance, and would Bike Buddy's body hold together long enough to ensure he survived? Apart from that we were fairly confident of success.

DAY 0: BIKES, TRAINS AND AUTOMOBILES - GETTING TO PENZANCE

The day arrived. Day 0, as I shall call it because we wouldn't be doing any cycling. I spent the morning at home packing and re-packing, weighing my panniers and re-weighing my panniers. I then spent a good hour holding each of my children and an hour hugging my wife. I was scared. I was scared I wouldn't see them again. I was scared I would panic when lying in bed alone at night. I was scared I was using up some of the precious time I had left to do a crazy feat. I was scared my wife thought I was selfish for leaving her when there was so much to worry about, but she didn't show it, and I hope she understood. I would have loved to take my family with me, but I couldn't put them through it.

Just after lunch, we got in the car and drove to Bristol Parkway railway station, arriving just before 4pm. The train wasn't due until 5.11pm, but we didn't want to risk the whole tour by getting stuck in traffic and missing the train.

Needn't have worried. In an unusual twist all the trains were delayed that day. Every single one. Was it flooding that caused this problem? No. Perhaps thunderstorms taking out power cables? No. The wrong type of leaves on the track? No, don't think so. So what caused every train into and out of Bristol Parkway to be delayed on the 10th of August that year? I believe it was the curse. The curse of the long distance cyclist. The curse of anyone who has tried to plan a trip around train times. The curse of British Rail, the company deregulated years earlier, but whose ghost still lives on in the tracks. The ghost that comes alive during night or day, up through the sleepers and pulls back every train like a lead-weight dragging on the wheels, slowly grinding the whole system to a standstill.

Our train was twenty minutes late. Considering it had already travelled from Glasgow to Bristol, I considered twenty minutes was not too bad.

Bristol Parkway station was very smart, as if sparkly new and thrown together from a plethora of corrugated iron sheets. Bright yellow beams broke up the shining metal, and an enclosed glass walkway took us from one platform across to the other. All in all the place was clean and tidy, but unfortunately the guards working there didn't know anything about trains. As we'd been advised by others taking bikes on trains, we asked the platform guard which end of the platform to stand in order to put our bikes in the guard van when the train arrived.

'Dunno' was the reply.

'The opposite end to First Class,' the other guard helpfully butted in.

'Which end's First Class?' I asked hopefully.

'Dunno,' the first guard replied, 'It depends which way round the train arrives. Look out for the number one sign in the window.'

How helpful I thought, and how glad I was that I'd taken the time to ask.

We made the decision to stand in the middle of the platform, to make a run in either direction doable before the train departed. The train arrived, and the first class coaches sailed past us. We knew instantly we should head for the rear of the train.

If you've ever tried to put a bike in a guard van on a train, you'll know what a joke it is. When the train came to a standstill, we were informed the guard van was already full.

'But I've paid for the bikes,' I said, 'they have tickets.'

'Oh, you'd better try to get them in then,' he said.

We stepped onto the train, the train left the platform, and we spent the next half-hour rearranging the guard van. We moved seven other bikes and a full-boxed set of band equipment. None of the other items had tickets to travel, yet they'd been allowed in regardless. They'd been allowed in despite the fact I'd booked, in advance, two bikes to travel on this very train. Obviously nobody bothers to check the bookings.

Eventually we squeezed our bikes in between a snare drum and a rusty Raleigh racer. We left the guard van quite rapidly, but then realised soon after we hadn't locked our bikes up. Anybody could just step into the guard van and walk off with them, or the bikes could be destroyed, smashed between boxes of drums before we even arrived at the start. It was obvious to me that our tour was going to be over before we'd even stepped onto the platform at Penzance and this made the journey down the country tense and stressful.

Less than satisfied we walked through the train to take up our seats. What a nightmare! The train was packed. Luckily, we'd reserved seats, but unfortunately the joker who'd designated them to us had decided to put them at the opposite end of the train to the guard van and we weren't even in first class. I can imagine him now, looking at his computer screen and sniggering to himself, 'How can I make this as difficult as possible? I know, I'll put the bikes in carriage one, and then give them seats in carriage twenty-eight.' Ha, bloody ha. If I ever saw his smirking face again, I'd ram the palm of my hand into his nose so hard he'd be sniffing through the top of his head for the rest of his life. Actually, I wouldn't – I'm not a vicious man. Besides I couldn't remember what he looked like, just his Cheshire cat smile.

It took us forty minutes to get to our seats, which were already taken, but thankfully by a couple of burly gentlemen. The aisles were packed with people, the whole train was heaving. There was no way anybody else could fit on, so we very calmly walked up to the gents and said, 'Oi stupid, can't you read? It says reserved, you know, reserved for someone else. Well it's us they're reserved for, so shift your arses.'

I didn't mind asking them to move, I would have felt very guilty if they'd been elderly ladies. I'm not saying it would have stopped me, I'm just saying I'd have felt guilty.

The gents stood up and we relaxed into our seats. At least, we relaxed as much as we could, when we had two very disgruntled men standing over us, peering down on us as if we were the scum of the earth. Besides we had to stare out the window at every station to ensure nobody was walking down the platform with our bikes. Nobody did, or at least not that we saw.

As we travelled through the countryside I started to dream of what lay ahead. I looked at the scenery in a different light. I looked at how flat it was and how many steep hills were scattered around. We would be cycling quite close to the railway line on a number of sections of the route. The railway would touch our lives again, but we would see the trains from the outside. As the afternoon turned to evening and the evening to dusk, the sun dropped below the horizon and the light was gone. I wouldn't know what Devon and Cornwall looked like until I met them on my bike. Perhaps that was just as well!

As it arrived at the penultimate stop to Penzance the train had caught up its twenty minutes, and was expected to arrive on time. We slowly made our way down the train towards the guard van, carriage twenty-seven, carriage twenty-six, carriage twenty-five. The place was now deserted. All the passengers had abandoned us long ago, and we were alone. As we moved from carriage to carriage, nineteen, eighteen, seventeen, the ghost of British Rail continued to haunt us. It switched the lights off in the carriages we vacated as soon as we stepped into the next one. Very spooky! How did it know where we were?

As we moved through the gap between carriages nine and eight, I decided to test the ghost. Bike Buddy was in front, and as I followed I only pretended to step into carriage eight. As I lifted my trailing leg off the ground the lights went out in carriage nine. I stopped, and quickly laid my foot back on the ground in the dark coach. The lights remained off. Perhaps the ghost was pretending not to see. I took a step back into nine, and the lights remained off. I slowly walked through nine on my way back to ten. The lights remained off. Even as I reached ten and started to step through the gap the lights remained off. I peered over my shoulder and saw Bike Buddy disappearing into seven. As he did so the lights from eight went out as well. My God, I was soon going to be left completely in the dark. I turned once more, and started running through nine, then eight towards Bike Buddy. I leapt into seven, just as the lights from seven started to dim. Bike Buddy was nearly in six, could I make it before the ghost's spindly fingers pulled me back into the darkened carriages. I ran, the adrenaline pumping through my veins, my heart thumping against the wall of my chest. I dived for six, and slid into the feet of Bike Buddy just as the lights in seven went out. I was safe. Bike Buddy was there to save me. He looked down at me as I lay at his feet, then tutted to himself, and carried on walking. Perhaps he was starting to have doubts about my sanity. Perhaps he was right to have doubts.

Penzance station at nine thirty-five pm was deserted. The bikes were still in the guard van, and they appeared unscathed. A miracle! Thank-you ghost of British Rail for keeping our bicycles safe and sound!

We cycled down the deserted platform, making sure our pride and joys were still mobile –thankfully they were.

It was dark, as you'd expect for 9.35pm even in August. We hadn't thought to bring any lights for our bikes, so we had to push them through Penzance to the Bed and Breakfast.

I was certain when I booked the Bed and Breakfast he'd told me it was near the station. 'A stone's throw from the beach,' had been his exact words. Perhaps he meant near as in you can travel it in less than an hour by fighter-jet. This was a long walk. It was a stone's throw from the beach, but only if you hurled the stone from a scud missile launcher.

Penzance at night was glowing with neon tubes. We wandered along the seafront for a while, slowly pushing our bikes along the path. The amusement arcades were alive with the sound of money chinking, electronic music playing and teenagers laughing and shouting. The beach was deserted, but the sea glistened under the stars. A cold wind blew off the sea, from the south. This was a good sign; a southerly wind was a good sign.

We found the Bed and Breakfast at 10.15pm. The outer door was still open so I walked in, rang the bell for attention and was swiftly greeted by the proprietor. He seemed a little confused to see two luminous yellow men on his doorstep, but kindly informed us we could leave our bikes in the front room - the lounge. I lifted my bike onto my shoulder and lugged it up the steps into the hallway, then carefully negotiated the fire extinguisher, before landing it with a thump in the lounge. Bike Buddy unfastened his panniers and then did the same. The bikes were safely locked away, ready for the great day.

The owner showed us to our rooms; two singles next door to each other on the top floor. Bike Buddy strained to move his body up the stairs and I started to get worried. Bike Buddy could hardly walk, how was he going to cycle up the country? He eventually hauled himself into his bedroom, and I was sure that was where he would want to stay, but no. Food was more important, and after unpacking our minimal luggage, we met back out in the hall. It had been a long journey and all this pushing bikes around had made us both hungry. We asked for directions to the local chippy and then walked up the main street to get chicken, chips and some coke.

Sitting on the wall outside the library eating our food made me laugh. How was this for preparing for the big day? You can't beat chicken and chips and a diet coke for nutritional value. Only in Britain would someone order chicken and chips and a diet coke. As if the diet bit was going to make amends for the over indulgent, over calorific, fat-dripping chicken and chips.

As we ate I decided we should be good to our bodies from now on, today was the last day of overindulgence. After downing the greasy grub, I wiped my hands on the greasy paper, which seemed to make them even greasier, but it didn't matter. I automatically moved, and wiped my hands down my trouser legs, then I realised these trouser legs had to survive three weeks without being washed and before even getting on my bike I'd covered them in chip grease. Good start Matthew!

With filled stomachs and covered in grease, we trudged back to the hotel ready to call it a night. When we arrived the door was still open, our bikes were still safe in the lounge, and it was time to get some rest. I wished Bike Buddy a good night and retired to my room.

As I lay in my bed that night I started to think about things. This is something I'd started to do most nights. When you've been told you are dying, you spend a lot of time thinking, especially at night as the shadows creep across the land and the country falls asleep, you start to feel alone and isolated. At home I could comfort myself with being in bed with my wife. When at home, I could hug her in the middle of night as the thoughts drifted through my brain, and the very touch of her body next to mine would be enough to ease my suffering (and make me horny).

Death is not a pleasant thing to consider, and I mean really consider. We talk of death all the time, but not real death. As a society we've grown immune to death because we see it so often on the television, in magazines and in newspapers. Death has become an entertainment; we enjoy seeing people die, provided we believe they deserve to die.

Did I deserve to die? Had I done something in the way I lived my life that justified my premature demise? I didn't think so, and twenty-seven just seemed far too young to die. It wasn't fair.

I have a theory that we spend our lives worrying about things because when we haven't got anything else to worry about we start worrying about own mortality. Death is so scary, we instantly think of something else to worry about instead. I tried to move my thoughts away from death for I had nobody to hug that night to take the nightmares away. Tonight I was alone, and alone I was scared.

I tried to worry about bicycles. It was hard work, but I tried. Would we succeed or would we fail? Would we return home with our heads held aloft, or hung below our bellies? If Bike Buddy failed, would I fail with him, or would I continue alone? Despite my desperate need to make something of my life before it finally finished. Despite this being my one great aim for my life to give people something to talk about after I was gone, I realised I couldn't continue alone if Bike Buddy stopped. I couldn't leave Bike Buddy on his own in failure; I would have to stop with him. Either we both succeeded or we both failed. Besides, I didn't have the map holder on my bike, so how could I continue alone? Perhaps if he gave up just a few days from the finish line I could finish without him. It would seem a shame to cycle one thousand miles and not make it. Only time would tell.

I felt uneasy, and a little bit scared, but I was looking forward to starting on my bike the next morning, and at just after 1.00am I drifted off to sleep.

DAY 1: JOURNEY TO THE END OF THE EARTH –
PENZANCE TO LANDS END AND RETURN

The breakfast was excellent. A bit of cereal to start, followed by a cooked breakfast of sausage, bacon, hash brown, tomato, mushrooms and a poached egg (thought having a fried egg was going too far). Some toast, orange juice, coffee, more toast and we were ready for the off. Well, ready to go back to our rooms for the final act before departing. This would quickly become our ritual. Refuel with breakfast before dumping the equivalent undigested waste out the other end (sorry, was that a little too much detail?).

At 8.30am we really were ready for the off. Panniers half-empty, after discarding anything not required for the short trip to Lands End and back. After all, we'd be staying in the same Bed and Breakfast again that night; different rooms, but the same Bed and Breakfast, so why carry anything we wouldn't need during the day?

The cruise down into Penzance was nice and easy, and Penzance looked different in the daylight. The neon lights were gone, the glistening sea was no longer glistening. Penzance looked dull, boring and on the verge of being dead. Perhaps that was a little unfair as it was a dull day, the air was full of moisture and the sun was hidden away behind the clouds.

The cycle along the sea front towards Lands End was very pleasant, and Bike Buddy and I laughed and joked as we merrily cycled along. We crossed over a bridge, turned the corner and suddenly came face to face with our first hill. Actually describing it as a hill is a bit of an understatement. It was more like a wall. Just outside Penzance, a vertical column of tarmac going up into the sky. I wondered whether we'd see the giant when we reached the top.

Up we went, higher and higher, into lower and lower gears, until there were none left. I was in the granny gear and we'd only cycled a mile and a half. 'Oh my God, I'm going to die!' My lungs wanted out - they were pushing hard against the inside of my ribcage, and my heart was thumping so violently I could feel the pulse in my neck. Bike Buddy stopped halfway up the hill and decided to walk the rest, but I was determined not to be defeated by the first hill on our quest. I kept going, at a pace slightly slower than that of a snail, dragging my body and metal machine up into the skyline.

Eventually the brow arrived and like a mountaineer summating on Everest I sucked in oxygen, bent double and waited for Bike Buddy to appear. When he did we just nodded to each other that we were okay, without a word being spoken.

A few minutes later, and when breathing returned to being a subconscious act controlled by my body without the need of reminder from my brain, we hauled ourselves back onto our bikes and set off once more.

The road to Lands End was quiet. We'd chosen country lanes wherever possible and were glad, but there was one problem with country lanes – they're used by country folk.

Round one corner we suddenly came face to face with a bloody big tractor. This was no ordinary tractor, this one had eight huge tyres, two in every place you'd normally expect to find one. The tractor driver sat up in the sky, amongst this massive mound of heaving metal. He didn't even see us, but I can tell you for certain that I saw him. I saw the whites of his eyes, and the freckles on his face. I saw the tattoo on his arm, the front right tyres of the tractor, the number plate, the front axle and the ditch.

Lifting myself out of the hedgerow, I glanced behind and saw Bike Buddy also in the ditch, heaving himself onto his knees. He was cursing a little more than me, while desperately trying to haul himself out of the trench.

After pulling myself back onto the road, I offered a hand to Bike Buddy, and strained with all my might to lift him clear of his muddy grave. Bike Buddy weighed a tonne. I thought my arm was going to pop out of its socket and Bike Buddy would land on his arse back in the ditch with my right arm still in his hand. My God, he was heavy, but I couldn't leave him in a ditch on the outskirts of Lands End, so I pulled and tugged. Bike Buddy clung to my arm and pushed with his feet, and finally arrived on the road covered from head to toe in mud and leaves.

We brushed ourselves down, made a few ungentlemanly comments, climbed back on our bikes and carried on our way thankful that we'd survived the ordeal and our bikes had survived also. We were blissfully unaware that this encounter would be the first of many more near misses on our adventure.

Our prayers for south-westerly wind had worked and the wind was gusting almost gale force from the south-west. If it stayed like this for whole three weeks we would have no problems getting to John O'Groats. In fact our biggest problem would be stopping at junctions. Unfortunately, for the first few miles of our journey, we were heading straight into it. The wind blew in our faces, the gusts buffeting us, shoving us across the road, and then back. We tried to keep in a straight line, but it was difficult because there was no protection from the wind now we'd climbed out of Penzance. Nothing to stop its constant howl around us, and the cycling was intense, but I wasn't going to complain because I knew once we turned around this wind would be extremely helpful. Long may it last!

We followed the National Cycle route as it wound its way towards Lands End. Criss-crossing the main A roads, and jumping from junction to junction in a bid to intersect with the last signpost in England. Just as we approached Lands End the National Cycle route turned off road and onto a gravel track specifically designed for the job. I smiled at the start of this route, so pleased to escape the motorised vehicles that kept flying past us in our slow progression forward. We'd avoided main roads, but as we got closer to Lands End these minor roads themselves got busier, as everyone wanted to make a sudden effort to get to the end of the world.

The off-road track itself began with fine gravel and slowly turned into sand. From a distance this track had looked perfect, but close up it was anything but. Have you ever tried to cycle on thick sand? I don't recommend it. The bike won't go the way you point it, the tyres slip, you can't get any power from the back wheel and you basically trudge along at little more than walking pace. The route designers had also decided to add a little interest, by putting particularly thick layers of sand on any short steep climbs or descents. These thicker layers were probably a result of the constant howling wind sweeping the sand into dunes just waiting to catch a passing cyclist unawares. I had to disengage my feet from the pedals at rapid pace on a couple of occasions as the bike slipped away, and I needed to plant my feet on the ground to avoid falling sideways onto the gravel. Thank-you Sustrans for making this part of the National Cycle route so bloody difficult to cycle on.

I suppose I should have pointed out before this stage that I have clipless pedals. These were a strange and new phenomenon for me only a couple of months earlier when I first decided to attach them to my bike.

When you use clipless pedals you have cleats on the bottom of your shoes that clip into the pedals and hold your feet in place as you cycle. (Actually, why are they called clipless pedals when you have to clip your feet in? Surely they should be called clip-in pedals, or something equally sensible.) Anyway, the use of such pedals raises an issue. Clipping in and out is fine when you're cycling along a straight, long road and you can plan ahead, but not so good when you need to put your feet down at short notice. I'd already fallen off my bike with these pedals on. During the first week I wore them, I was coming up to a major roundabout and thought I could go straight across without stopping. At the last minute, I realised I had to stop, but couldn't undo my feet. The bike came to a standstill, my feet stopped moving, my body started to lean to the left and very slowly I collapsed sideways, landing on my shoulder in the middle of the road.

Picture the scene, it's 8.30am the roads are packed with people going to work or dropping kids off at school. One of the busiest roundabouts on the outskirts of Worcester, and there at the junction is a guy dressed in a luminous yellow cycle top, lying on his left side in the middle of the road, still attached to his bicycle. It was actually quite dangerous, most of the drivers were too busy laughing to remember to brake, but the worst part was I couldn't get out of the pedals to pick myself up. I was trapped, like a beached whale. Luckily a passing pedestrian stopped and lifted me back upright. If that was you, thank-you very much. I apologise for not stopping to say thank-you at the time, but all the laughter was doing my head in.

Anyway, on these cycle tracks short notice was definitely the way forward. I decided to cycle unclipped. I was loose again, free from my feet restraints. If this was what National Cycle Routes were like, perhaps we should have stuck to the roads?

We arrived in Lands End at 10.30am and were bitterly disappointed with the place. Not much there really, just a tourist attraction. Of course, people have the mistaken belief that Lands End is the most southerly point on the British mainland. Sorry, that honour goes to The Lizard. Thinking about it, Lands End has done pretty well for itself, considering it isn't the most southerly point. It is the most westerly point of England, and the reason people travel from Lands End to John O'Groats is because it's the greatest distance between two points on the mainland, but on its own, Lands End is pretty insignificant.

The owners of the land at Lands End have turned it into a tourist attraction, like a miniature Alton Towers built in a wind tunnel. Visitors have to pay to get in, but this has to be charged as a parking fee, because there's a public right of way to the end which means they can't charge an actual entry fee (at least that's my understanding of the situation). As cyclists we didn't have to pay. After all we didn't want to park our bikes anywhere, we just wanted to hit the water, turn around and cycle back.

On our way to the water, we rolled up to the tourist office and asked to sign the book for 'End-to-enders.' This was a term I found highly amusing. I wasn't sure I could go into a pub, stand on the bar and declare myself as an 'End-to-ender.' I'd be a little embarrassed, and probably find a lot of blokes standing with their backs against the wall. Who came up with such a camp name?

The book to sign was halfway through the end-to-end museum, which I suddenly pictured as row upon row of naked men lying top to toe. Not a pleasant thought.

When we entered the museum I was relieved to find it was actually to do with folk who had travelled from Lands End to John O'Groats, or vice-versa, using one form of transport or another. People had done it walking backwards, hopping, on a pogo stick, and even on a motorised toilet.

What persuaded that guy to convert his toilet into a car? Was he sitting on it at the time and suddenly thought, 'I know I'll strap an engine to this dunny and drive it up the length of the country.' I wonder what his wife thought, 'Of course dear, I'll be able to hold on until you get back.' He must have been completely bonkers. Mind you, it would cut down on the number of toilet stops he'd have to make. I wonder whether he could only flush when he was moving, like on a train? What the hell would you think if you stepped out of your door and saw a guy pottering (excuse the pun) past on a motorised toilet? There's nought stranger than folk!

We signed the book, and then made our way back to the tourist office, which also was pretending to be a Post Office. This was the first Post Office we'd passed, and was the prime time for me to get my book stamped for the first time. Unfortunately, it was at that point I realised there was a slight hitch to my plan. Firstly, it wasn't a real Post Office, so they didn't have a Post Office stamp, and secondly, I'd left my diary in the Bed and Breakfast in Penzance. In my eagerness to lighten the load for today's journey, I'd left my diary in the hotel. What a bummer! I couldn't believe how stupid I'd been.

Thinking quickly, I got them to stamp a blank piece of paper with a 'Lands End' stamp (but not a real Post Office stamp), which I planned to glue in my diary at a later date. I was an idiot! Maybe people wouldn't believe me now. Maybe I'd ruined the whole journey by being a prat. Maybe I should just go home. Maybe I was just trying to think of excuses to give up and go home, and I should stop making a fuss, get on my bike and start pedalling.

We bought some postcards, wrote them and posted them in the post box. After letting the postcard drop I suddenly had a horrible feeling it might have been a pretend post box as well, but it seemed real to me.

Finally, we made our way to 'The signpost' to have our photos officially taken and took one final look at the sea. I was disappointed not to be able to actually touch the sea, but the death drop cliff kind of put me off. I thought about giving Bike Buddy a shove and seeing what happened, but then I realised I might have to hang around while they recovered his broken body, and I really wanted to get on my bike. They say, on a clear day you can see the Isles of Scilly from Lands End. Today we could hardly see each other, let alone anything else, and besides the wind continued to tell us to get going. It desperately wanted to push us back to Penzance, so we climbed on our bikes and turned around

As we drifted back up through the mini-Alton Towers, Bike Buddy and I made a pact that we wouldn't drink alcohol until we reached John O'Groats. This was a bigger deal for Bike Buddy than it was for me, since I only drank the occasional pint of beer or glass of wine, whereas he consumed a number of units in any hour, night or day. I didn't tell Bike Buddy the real reason I made this pact; the fact I was drugged up so much I dare not drink any alcohol or the drugs may freak and cause my body to react badly, and Bike Buddy didn't ask.

In a final act before leaving Lands End for good, we made a quick toilet stop, and as we stood outside shaking our hands dry before putting them on our beautiful bikes, I heard a couple of tourists talking about us, so I stopped shaking and listened. We were wearing our 'End-to-end' t-shirts and must have looked the part if nothing else, and I heard one woman say to her young daughter, 'Look at them, honey, they've just cycled from John O'Groats.'

I wish! Read it again love.

I walked up to her, and asked her to repeat what she'd just said. I then turned around and asked her to read the back of my t-shirt. 'Read it out loud,' I said, 'say the words in the order they are printed.'

'Lands End to John O'Groats,' she stuttered.

'That's right – to John O'Groats, not from.' I replied, 'Would you like to sponsor us?'

Funnily enough, she didn't seem keen, so I tutted and went back to my bike.

Cycling out of Lands End I suddenly felt like life was worth living. The thoughts of death that had haunted me the previous night had disappeared, and I felt contented and at one with my machine. We were finally starting; we were finally going in the right direction and getting somewhere. Every turn of the pedal from now on would take us closer to our goal (apart from all the wrong turns we would make).

Cycling from Lands End was much easier than cycling towards it. The wind continued in the same direction. It was a miserable day, grey skies and drizzle, but somehow that didn't matter. If I knew then what we had in front of us, I think I would have stopped pedalling, climbed off my bike and phoned for a taxi to take me home, but at Lands End at least we had fresh legs, and hope in our hearts.

Back onto the country lanes, and the cars seemed to have vanished so that the bottom tip of Cornwall was almost deserted in parts. We stopped in St. Buryan for lunch. A local pub serving local food, and sitting pleasantly opposite the village church. I ordered a cheese ploughman's and then received a mound of cheese the size of Bike Buddy's belly. Bike Buddy's alcohol free pact lasted precisely eight miles. He looked at what the pub could offer him and without even thinking ordered his first pint of lager.

We chatted about the poor weather, we chatted about the mound of cheese in front of me, and we chatted about Bike Buddy's inability to live without alcohol. We then chatted about which way we could get back to Penzance without having to go down the death-drop hill we'd cycled up this morning. We decided on a slight detour, which would take us down to Mousehole where we could join the coast and cycle along by the sea back to Penzance. Seemed like a good idea at the time.

Back on our bikes, with my arteries freshly clogged from the cheese mountain I'd consumed, we were on our way again. As planned, just before Penzance we turned off the normal route to visit Mousehole. Unfortunately this road was also a very steep descent, perhaps even steeper than the one to Penzance, and this time it almost ended in disaster.

This was so very nearly the end of my tour. In fact this was so very nearly the end of my life. Just as I was losing the battle with my bike to stop it descending at break-neck speed a young lady decided to walk out from her driveway without looking. I screamed. She stopped and stared. I screamed. She looked in disbelieve. I screamed, braked harder, swerved left, then right and just brushed the front of her toes as I plummeted by, and then I screamed again.

As the hill stretched out into a more gradual descent I pulled harder on my brakes and brought the bike to a standstill. I'd learnt that in order to save one's brake blocks on a sharp descent one pumps the brake levers rather than constantly keeping them on. I had pumped like I'd never pumped before. In fact I was pump-exhausted and ready to drop. My hands ached, by arms ached and I was still screaming.

Bike Buddy came to a standstill next to me. 'That was close,' he said. My mouth was still open, but the screams had subsided.

I'd devised the pump-braking technique after Bike Buddy had informed me the biggest problem facing touring cyclists was the risk of overheated wheel rims exploding on sharp descents. At the time, I have to admit I hadn't been overly pleased to learn this bit of news, whether it was factual or not, but now I'd come to a standstill I was curious to know whether my newfound method of pump-braking had helped. I touched the rim of my front wheel. Not a wise thing to do when you've just fallen down a hill at the speed of sound. I burnt my finger, the skin melted onto the rim of the wheel, and with a quiet whine I quickly peeled my finger off the white-hot metal. I guess pump-braking didn't work that well after all! Mind you I had now way of knowing what the rim would have been like if I'd kept the brakes on constantly – probably a lot hotter. I sucked my burnt finger, climbed back on my bike and together with Bike Buddy slowly drifted along the road into Mousehole.

Mousehole is a working fishing village. The roads are narrow and windy, and packed with tourists. We didn't bother to stop, deciding to drift aimlessly along the coast to Newlyn and then gently back to Penzance for an early finish.

We arrived back at the Bed and Breakfast at around one-thirty, hauled the bikes back into the lounge, took our half-empty panniers back to our rooms and had a cup of tea (well actually I had coffee, because I don't really like tea.)

After a quick rest we decided to wander round town to find a good restaurant for the evening. We needed to celebrate the fact we'd now accomplished half of our target. In other words, we'd been to Lands End, now all we had to do was get to John O'Groats and the job was done.

Having collected up my diary, I decided to get my first stamp actually in the book, and headed for the Penzance Post Office. Unfortunately, my efforts were hampered by the fact it was Saturday and therefore the Post Office was closed from 1pm. Maybe this 'Getting the book stamped' idea wasn't such a good one after all.

With our thoughts set on the task ahead, Bike Buddy and I purchased some drinks ready to fill our water bottles the next day. A mixture of water and fruit juice seemed to be the drink of choice and we were comfortable that we were now treating our bodies as the temples they deserved to be for the long journey ahead.

Penzance was a bustling little town. Okay, it was Saturday, but the streets were packed with locals and tourists. The weather was still grotty, and people had obviously decided to go to the shops for the day, although the choice of shops appeared to be fairly limited this far down the country.

We decided not to do any shopping ourselves. Something told me carrying a dozen carrier bags up the country wasn't the best idea, and, besides, Bike Buddy said he hated shopping because 'he wasn't a girl.'

Our evening meal was at a cosy Italian restaurant on the seafront called Ginos. We were so early we had to wait for the owner to open up. He looked at us a little concerned. Not sure whether it was my luminous yellow t-shirt, the fact I had metal cleats on the bottom of my shoes which clicked when I walked, or the lycra shorts which made him concerned. I didn't care, and proudly pushed my back into people's faces so they could read what we were attempting to do. Nobody seemed that interested, but I felt proud.

Bike Buddy and I decided to continue our new plan of treating our bodies as temples and ordered pasta with salad and garlic bread. A gorgeous lasagne! Bike Buddy's body temple plan had a slight variation to mine, and he ran it alongside a new pact of drinking alcohol whenever we stopped the bikes. Sticking to his plan, he downed two pints of lager.

Just as we were making our way out, the restaurant filled up with a dozen young ladies and I seized the opportunity to show them what a stud I was as I left the room. I considered going back in to ensure they'd read the back of my shirt, but thought that a little unsubtle, and Bike Buddy's continual desire to hobble everywhere was kind of ruining the effect.

Back in the hotel, Bike Buddy and I started to pack our panniers ready for the next day. I was bewildered by the amount of clutter Bike Buddy had decided was essential for his journey. When fully loaded, the back wheel of his bike couldn't be lifted off the ground. I persuaded him to unload and scatter his belongings on the floor in front of us. I had to get him to send some items home or he wouldn't make it down the road, let alone to John O'Groats.

Bike Buddy resisted. He wasn't keen to let any of his 'vital supplies' go, but after much negotiation he finally agreed to send back one of his two sets of nail clippers - the heavy-duty pair lined with lead seemed a little excessive to me, particularly as we would be staying at home in just seven day's time. How long could a person's fingernails grow in seven days? Perhaps he had some hideous nail-growing disorder that meant his nails grew three or four inches overnight and unless he scythed them off every morning he wouldn't be able to hold his handlebars. This was a risk I was willing to take, so the lead-lined nail clippers went on the 'discard pile.'

Next on the 'discard pile' was a large bottle of talcum powder. This also seemed excessive to me. Besides, if we were to spread Sudocrem over any area that might come into contact with the saddle, adding talcum powder to this cream would surely lead to some kind of floury, sticky mess. Now picture this floury, sticky mixture being joined for eight hours a day by warm, moist conditions and an excess of sweat, and this would lead to a rather nasty smelling dough. Not a pleasant thought, so the talc was placed on the 'discard pile.'

For some reason Bike Buddy had decided to bring three jackets with him. One was a thin jacket for those 'not so cold' days. One was a warmer, waterproof jacket and the final one was a cycling cape. Did he really need all three? I didn't think so. I'd brought just one, and while Bike Buddy wasn't looking I slipped the thin jacket onto the discard pile.

I managed to persuade Bike Buddy that carrying four t-shirts as well as two sweatshirts was a little over the top, and he eventually relinquished one thick t-shirt. Also onto the 'discard pile' went four packs of energy sweets, leaving Bike Buddy with only about a dozen, and hundreds upon hundreds of energy bars. For some reason Bike Buddy was of the opinion that despite cycling the length of Great Britain we might not come across any shops that could sell us food or sweets.

The pile of discards was quite weighty, and we placed them in an old carrier bag and strapped them up with duct tape (remember this moment – this could be critical – the moment when we use a lot of the tape we were carrying specifically to repair a burst tyre). Unfortunately with the Post Office now closed and highly unlikely to open in the morning (as it was a Sunday) we decided to ask the owner of the Bed and Breakfast to kindly post the parcel back home for us, but that could wait until the morning.

We spent the rest of the evening studying the maps of our journey. The actual maps we were going to take had been a constant source of discussion prior to the off. The Ordnance Survey Landranger maps are wonderful for seeing where to go. Unfortunately we would need thirty-four to complete the journey. Since these would fill our panniers completely and the weight would be enough to bring us to a grinding halt, we decided on another method. Bike Buddy had spent many an evening photocopying snippets from the maps we would use, a bit from Ordnance Survey, a bit from CTC, a bit from Sustrans. I have to admit we didn't get permission to do this, but for anyone reading who feels the urge to see me in prison, I can categorically declare that the copies were destroyed the moment we arrived home. As such, no photocopies exist, and there is no proof they were ever created. (Apart from this book obviously, but you don't want to listen to me I'm clinically insane.)

Finally we had our own set of maps. Each day was drawn on a single piece of paper, carefully marked and then laminated against the elements. In case we got lost we also took along just three Travelmaster maps, covering the whole country. Just a shame we hadn't thought to bring a compass, but more of that later.

That evening's discussion centred around which part of the journey would be the most difficult. I'd heard from a number of sources that Devon and Cornwall were by far the worst. Bike Buddy was unconvinced, mainly because of a little hill we had to go up in Scotland called Drumochter Pass. This was the highest part of our journey, but to make matters worse it was also a dual carriageway. Sustrans had very kindly pointed out on their route that this was 'extremely dangerous.' Their advice was to take the train.

How could we take the train? It's kind of cheating a little. Bike Buddy had already convinced himself. His mother had told him not to take risks. If the pass truly was that bad, he would go by train. I told him there was no way I was going on a train, otherwise we might as well take the bloody train all the way up and save ourselves three weeks. On that note I left him in his room with his thoughts and wandered across the landing to my room with my own thoughts.

The first days cycling had only really been half a days cycling. We'd covered 26 miles, just two miles further than originally planned, and mainly because of our detour to Mousehole. We'd been in the saddle for three and a half hours, which gave us an average speed of just over seven miles per hour. Obviously this was not the true average speed of our cycling, which would have been much higher. I mean, obviously, we don't cycle that slowly. This is simply the distance travelled divided by the time taken. There is no allowance for the numerous times we stopped to look at the map and work out which way to go, and believe me – that happened a lot.

DAY 2: ONE MAN AND HIS DOG – PENZANCE TO ST. COLUMB MAJOR

Down for breakfast at 7am, we asked the owner about our discard parcel, and he very kindly agreed to post it home for us. We paid him generously what we thought would be the postage (leaving him at least fifteen pence for his trouble).

After another full English breakfast Bike Buddy and I went to our rooms to continue our morning rituals. These rituals now had added zest with the application of Sudocrem all over our backsides. Despite Bike Buddy and I now becoming very close friends these rituals remained in the privacy of our own bathrooms.

It was raining! In fact, it was probably better described as drizzling. Lots of drizzle, the kind that grabs hold of you and slowly seeps through your clothes until it eventually finds your skin. You know, wet rain - not the other type of rain. (What on earth is 'the other type of rain'? One day on a bike and I was already turning quite peculiar.)

We left the hotel at 8am, gave our bikes a very quick rub down with the rag and sprayed lube over any bits that might be expected to move. Content that we were finally moving, we stepped over our bikes and pushed off into the rain.

Despite the weather we had a good morning's cycle, but got very wet, very quickly. The road was flat for the first ten to fifteen miles and I began to think the talk of Devon and Cornwall being the hilliest was a crock of shite. The wind was on our backs and we were making good progress, fairly zipping along the promenade, and continuing beside the sea for many miles.

Beware the morning of good cycling! Good ride in the morning – cyclist warning! If only we knew then what was still to come.

The National Cycle route was great. Well, most of the time. It had this annoying tendency to zigzag everywhere. At first I assumed this was to avoid any really difficult hills, or busy roads, but after just one days cycling I started to realise it zigzagged specifically to find the difficult hills.

If you ever cycle this route you will find Sustrans have put down little arrows marking the route as you go, which are extremely helpful. However, because Sustrans also sell maps for each route, they have this little trick to ensure you've paid your money; they make having a map a necessity rather than a luxury.

'How do they do that if there are route markers?' I hear you cry.

Ah, well, what they do, you see, is they take a few of the route markers away. Clever isn't it? Just when you're building up confidence in the direction you're going - boom, you've missed a turning and are going the wrong way. Just as you get to a really busy stretch going through a major town – boom, the route signs vanish and leave you stranded like a canoeist with no paddle. This is particularly annoying in towns. We got lost in Hayle, with shoppers looking at us in disbelieve as we circled round them again and again, before finally coming across what might be a route out.

The other trick Sustrans have is to leave the next sign just a little further on than you expect. Picture the scene, you've been cycling for ten miles with route signs every half-mile. Then suddenly, on a really long straight section you realise you've been peddling for at least three or four miles and haven't seen the next sign. What do you do? Stop and look at the map? Yes we seem to be going the right way! Double back on yourself? No, not quite yet, but let's go slowly in case we miss something. Then just as you come to almost a complete standstill – there it is, the next sign. The little buggers!

We came to another of many off-road cycle tracks, which unfortunately had been covered in gravel. Gravel is not good to cycle on. Not on a touring bike, with slick tyres and no suspension. The small ruts slowly hammer away at your backside, until they've worn a couple of holes in your butt cheeks. At that moment I wished I'd bought a suspension seat-post. As well as the pain in my derrière I was having great difficulty keeping upright with the tyres skidding on the wet gravel. Oh the fun!

We passed through Camborne and then on to Redruth, before climbing out of the town towards Gwennap Pit. The climb through Redruth was hard work, the road going forever upwards as we made our way back into the countryside. As we reached the top we could see for miles in all directions. Unfortunately, for some reason the locals had decided to use this area of Cornwall as a waste disposal site. The lane was scattered with broken glass, old settees, abandoned fridges and freezers and the occasional double bed. Why it was easier to drag an unwanted bed up to the top of Gwennap Pit to dump, rather than take it to the local tip, beats me. I'm sure the locals have a good reason. Perhaps they like to offer comfort to the local tramps; their own bed, settee and kitchen appliances. All they needed now was some electricity.

Just before Truro we stopped at a pub for lunch. To continue my cheese theme, I decided upon jacket potato with cheese, and a pint of fruit juice. Bike Buddy kept his alcohol pact intact with a pint of lager.

The lunch was sound, filled a gap, and before long we looked at our watches and decided it was time to get going again. Our first port of call after lunch was Truro. Truro was busy, even for a Sunday. The shops were open, and there were hoards of people drifting in and out aimlessly. We were cycling pretty aimlessly ourselves, having lost the cycle route once again, but were still able to take in the wonders that Truro had to offer. Apparently Truro is famous for an eighteenth century dwarf known as Black John. Black John's party trick was to tie mice together by their tails, swallow them whole and then haul them back out again still alive. Now that was a neat party trick. That one would get the girls wowing - or throwing up at least.

I wondered what the mice thought of it all? I wondered if they lined up to be his accomplice, saying to their girlfriends, 'Watch this love, I'm going to dive down that dwarf's throat, spew in his stomach and then drag myself back up again, and what's more, I'm going to do it all while tied by the tail to my brother, Mortimer.'

What a neat mouse party trick that would be!

What was that phrase I said earlier? Good ride in the morning – cyclists warning! Here it comes. The afternoon was what we'd been expecting from Cornwall. Very hard work, with steep climbs reducing our cycling speed at times to just three miles per hour. Find a happy gear, find a happy gear! The good old granny gear was back in use, and was starting to become a bit of a favourite for me.

The biggest problem in Cornwall was whoever had designed the roads forgot about all the small streams. Just when we got to the top of a staggeringly steep climb, we realised the road dropped instantly back down again. Why did it do this? Because there was a stream at the bottom, and we had to get down to a little wooden bridge to take us across the water.

Personally I would have preferred to bunny hop along the top of the hills. Call me fussy, but I like to get some reward for my climbing. If I'm going to struggle up the side of a mountain I like to stay high for a while before slowly descending at speed. In Cornwall this just doesn't happen - ever! We went up and down, up and down, up and down. The ups were granny gear climbs, the downs were bare-knuckle brake-pumping death drops. What made it worse was we'd chosen to cycle on tiny back-lanes covered in wet grass and moss. We couldn't see where the road went and couldn't see what was round the corner, so we had no option but to brake. This meant we started every new climb at almost a standstill. I would descend with my brakes pumping away, cross the wooden bridge, hit the next climb and start dancing on the pedals like an extra out of Michael Jackson's Thriller video.

Remember the near miss with the tractor, and the woman in Mousehole? You ain't seen nothing yet. Just before Zelah, after cycling many miles on quiet country lanes, we suddenly came to a junction with the A30. The traffic was horrendous, cars coming from both directions as well as a car by the side of us and four lined up to come out from the opposite junction. We wanted to go straight on, and sat patiently hoping someone would let us out. Eventually the car coming up the hill from the left flashed his lights to let us go. The car from the opposite junction waved us on. I went to go. Just as I pushed my feet down on the pedals I glanced up the main road to the right and saw a white Vectra hurtling towards me. In a panic I grabbed for my brakes and just managed to stop myself as the car whizzed about an inch past my front tyre.

Obviously Mr Vectra was in a hurry and was determined not to be slowed by some idiot on a bike. I wonder what his reaction would have been with me lying on his front windscreen. Perhaps Vectra's have very good windscreen wipers and he would have simply wiped me away! Personally, if I ever get killed by a car, I hope I make such a mess that the driver has to at least stop and give it a wipe with a cloth. I'd feel a little robbed otherwise.

Slightly shaken by my experience, and just a little more wary, we continued on our way. This last part of the day was very difficult. Have you ever heard the phrase 'bonked?' No, not the type of bonking you do when you've met a nice girl and invited her back to yours for a coffee. And not the type of bonking you do with a tennis racket when you pretend it's a guitar. Actually I think that one's called gonking, or something like that. Anyway, bonking in cycling, I have come to learn, is when you hit the wall. When your legs won't turn the pedals anymore, and you just want to lean over to one side and fall onto the verge. I bonked big-style. Bike

Buddy bonked as well, and we had a major problem. We'd done 45 miles, which was already one mile more than it should have been, and there was no sign of St Columb Major. Okay, we'd missed a couple of turnings, but not too many, and as a result our minds told us we should be there and, very dangerously, informed our bodies they should be resting now. So they did!

We sat down outside a school on a wooden bench. Bike Buddy cracked open a packet of sultanas, and I cracked open my bottle of water. What a feast we had before us. We gorged ourselves on tiny pieces of dried fruit, sighed a few times, and then clambered back on our metal steeds.

Ten miles further on, and at around 4.30pm we rolled into the exotic delight that is St Columb Major.

Okay, I'm exaggerating a little. Exotic delight is probably a little over the top. To be honest this town was a dump! The armpit of the world! A new bypass had been built around the town and sucked the life from it. The area seemed to have died on its feet. The locals had obviously just celebrated something because there were banners across the road and empty beer cans and bottles strewn across the pavements. Perhaps they'd been celebrating the fact everyone had left. The place seemed deserted, apart from the local drunken yobs sitting on the bench outside the town hall. Maybe they'd been celebrating the fact someone had managed to find the local tip and brought back all their empty bottles.

The Bed and Breakfast was even worse. 'My God, we're going to die here,' was my first thought. I should have sussed something was up when the lady at the Bed and Breakfast had checked if they were taking over-nighters when I booked, but being a tad simple, the information had completed passed me by without a second's thought.

It was as much as the owner could do to let us in the door. We had no tea or coffee facilities, no television, no towels, no soap and no shampoo. The toilet, shower and bathroom looked as if they hadn't been washed for years. I particularly liked the strategically placed mould that gave the shower a unique appeal.

The owner told us the brewery was closing him down in a few weeks. It was obvious why! We had single rooms, with a shared, mouldy bathroom. The reward for our bikes for carrying us up from Lands End was to be chained up outside the pub, amongst the left over food, split rubbish bags and steaming piles of dog shit.

The first thing Bike Buddy liked when he arrived at a Bed and Breakfast was a cup of tea. Sorry mate, no tea at the Inn. The second thing Bike Buddy liked was a shower. At this Bed and Breakfast I wasn't sure having a shower was going to make us any cleaner, but I had one anyway, and Bike Buddy went without.

Just before showering, I thought, being a picky kind of guy, that it would be nice to have a towel. When I went to ask the owner he appeared at the door naked with his dog between his legs. Not sure what he was doing with the dog. I quickly mentioned the towels and then hid my eyes, but it was too late. I knew I would now be scarred for life. There are certain things you just do not want to see, and that was one of them. The owner closed the door, and came back a few seconds later with two towels, and the obedient dog. I wasn't about to wait and see anymore so grabbed the towels and tried to block from my mind what the towels might have rubbed against on their journey to my hand.

To my surprise, the Bed and Breakfast did serve food. I suppose I shouldn't have been so surprised, I mean, it was a pub after all. You know how Bike Buddy likes his food? Well, one thing I should point out is Bike Buddy likes his food cooked hygienically. He likes to feel when he goes to sleep at night he has a good chance of waking up the next morning. In this Bed and Breakfast the odds seemed to have switched dramatically in favour of the ever-lasting sleep. If we ate in the Bed and Breakfast it would likely be our last meal, and the end of our tour, so instead we decided to wander around the ghost town. One small supermarket, and everything else was closed. It was Sunday, but come on!

We eventually settled and got into another pub called the Ring of Bellz. Amazingly, we sat outside the Ring of Bellz for half an hour waiting for it to open, but when eventually the doors were unlocked, we peered inside and the place was packed. How did they all get in? Perhaps they'd come through the walls. Perhaps this really was a ghost town.

The Ring of Bellz was much better than we'd both expected, and a vast improvement on the rest of the town. The owners and workers inside were friendly enough, and we finally found ourselves able to relax.

Continuing my attempt to eat my way through the European cheese mountain, we both ordered chilli-con-carni with cheese. This was followed by apple and caramel flan. The meal was made better by our table position, at the bottom of the stairs leading to the bar. The waitress was very pretty and must have stayed fit by constantly climbing the stairs to take food to the bar. To start with I couldn't understand why Bike Buddy kept staring past me. We would be in the middle of a conversation and he would suddenly look over my right shoulder and stare into space – at least I thought he was staring into space. What he was actually doing was staring at the backside of the pretty waitress as she ascended the stairs. What a pervert! I couldn't believe it. He was my father-in-law after all. He was married to my mother-in-law. He shouldn't be having thoughts like that – yuck!

I told him I was disappointed in him. I told him I couldn't believe what a pervert he was. I told him to behave himself, and then I told him to move along so I could switch sides and sit next to him. A good position for watching! Bike Buddy was turning me into a pervert. Maybe I'd always been a pervert and he'd just brought me out of my shell.

A very satisfying meal, made all the better by the lack of guilt which normally accompanies any large eating extravagance. When you've been cycling for seven hours I think you can afford to eat well, and then I suddenly realised the reason Bike Buddy had agreed to come with me. He liked his food and he now had the perfect excuse to eat as much of it as he could find for three whole weeks. Never before had I seen someone so attune with their own stomach.

Back in my room, with no television, no games to play, no books to read I started to feel very depressed. I wrote in my diary about how depressed I felt and then I looked at today's map. We'd cycled ten miles further than planned, and I wanted to know why. Why, God damn you, why? And there it was, staring up at me. Despite having a degree in maths, I was obviously not as good at arithmetic as I thought. I had failed to learn in all my years at school and college how to take seventeen from seventy-one. Seven hours in the saddle and fifty-four miles on the clock, lugging luggage up the country - that was a hard days cycle.

The town was a hole and the Bed and Breakfast was a pigsty, and that made me feel bad. The badness turned sour and as I lay in bed, in the dark mouldy room, I started to feel very bitter. The arrogant bastard who ran the Bed and Breakfast was just a parasite on the planet, yet he didn't have Colonic Worm Infestation. He wasn't going to die in ten and a half months, he was very much alive. How was that fair? How could it be possible for such an arse to get away free whilst I suffered, and my family suffered? He needed to be taught a lesson. Oh, how I hoped he would be taught a lesson, but who was going to teach him it? Then something remarkable dawned on me; when you're dying the normal rules of the world just no longer apply. All the laws in this country are designed with the assumption that you do not want to die. When you know that whatever happens you are going to die, they no longer apply. Why should I care if I got reprimanded by the police, or arrested, when I knew I'd die before the court hearing? Why should I care what happened if I didn't pay my taxes? The more I thought about this, the more it intrigued me. I was free. The law couldn't hold me, the justice system didn't work for people like me. I was a law unto myself. In fact, as Judge Dredd once said, 'I'm not above the law – I am the law!'

This newfound knowledge was like a breath of fresh air to me. I could live my last year as a free man, doing whatever I liked. It was as if a weight had suddenly been lifted off my shoulders, and I realised, as a free man, I was the person to teach the Bed and Breakfast owner a lesson. I was the one who should show him how to respect his customers. I was the one to even up the score and make sure he suffered like I was suffering.

I turned over and set the alarm on my watch for 3am. I wanted to make sure everyone else was asleep when my punishment was being handed out.

DAY 3: THE DAY OF THE FLY – ST. COLUMB
MAJOR TO PYWORTHY

At 7.30am we were both awake, dressed, and waiting for our breakfast. There was no sign of the owner of the Bed and Breakfast, or his dog. I suggested to Bike Buddy that we make a quick escape before he woke. Not wanting to wait around half the day for him to appear, and not wanting to eat whatever it was he would cook for us that morning. Bike Buddy agreed.

'We're making a run for it,' Bike Buddy joked as we left the accommodation. Although as far as he was concerned it wasn't really a run as in 'must get away before he catches us and makes us pay' because I'd stupidly already paid in full when I booked (another thing I should have picked up on at the time – never trust anyone who doesn't trust you!) But Bike Buddy did feel like he was escaping before meeting his ultimate doom. Before the owner and his dog forced him to eat the devil's scrotum for breakfast and poisoned him into an early grave, forever destined to roam in the depths of despair with his stomach aching and throat bleeding.

Bike Buddy suggested I write a snotty letter to the owner when I got home, but after last night's fun, for some reason I didn't think it would do any good. I'm not sure he'd get to read it!

Something told me I was going to be punished for punishing the owner, and before we'd even left the town I started to have a bad feeling about the day. As we turned our bikes to leave the car park, Bike Buddy squealed like a little baby. I thought, perhaps, he'd broken his arm or something equally appalling, but it turned out he'd lost one of the stoppers from the end of his handlebars. About two hundred metres further on and he squealed again, this time even louder, and I feared for a minute that he would wake the local constabulary who would come stomping out to see what all the fuss was about. I looked at him and asked sarcastically whether he'd lost his dummy this time, but the look on his face made me a little concerned, and I realised he'd managed to split one of the links in his chain. Bummer!

We rolled to a standstill, Bike Buddy turned his bike upside down and took out his handy tool kit ready to set to work replacing his chain link. Thankfully we'd remembered to bring some spare links with us, and the breakage wasn't going to be a disaster.

It was at that moment I realised where we were; in the entrance to St Columb Major church. I'm not sure whether it's blasphemous to put oil all over the entrance to a church, but it seemed a little naughty at the time, and was certain it wouldn't gain me many points when I stood at the gates of heaven begging to come in.

Bike Buddy took ages with his chain, twisting his little tool and poking around with his little rod. I stood jumping from one foot to the other, desperate to make him work quicker but certain any encouragement from me would slow him even more. I wanted to get away from St Columb Major and the Bed and Breakfast as quickly as possible. I was a law-free man, but I wanted to finish my cycling challenge before anybody caught up with me and discovered the punishment I'd handed out to a man who so readily deserved it.

Half an hour later and we were ready to get on our way. 8.20am and we were finally leaving the armpit of the world.

Cycling was hard going in the morning, but then I'd always expected it would be. Thankfully, however, to start with I didn't even notice how hard it was because my mind was elsewhere, going over the previous night. I should have been tired, I'd been up most of the night, but for some reason adrenalin seemed to spur me on. I was on a high, and nothing could stop me now.

We struggled over the hills and on towards the Camel Trail, which was almost perfectly flat but ruined by a wet gravel surface making it highly treacherous. Sustrans resumed their route sign disappearing tricks, just when we needed them most. Although I soon realised, to be fair to Sustrans, the signs were actually there, but unfortunately bushes and undergrowth had overgrown to block the view. Then I thought I was going soft trying to be fair to Sustrans since the routes had only been open a few months and not much thought could have gone into potential organic growth.

Thanks to the hidden markers, we cycled two miles the wrong way, and then two miles to get back to where we'd started. If anything drained the energy from our legs it was going the wrong way, but at least this time the road was relatively flat.

At 11am Bike Buddy and I were starting to tire. We suddenly remembered we'd missed the most important meal of the day; breakfast, and agreed to stop at the next opportunity and have something to eat. Unfortunately the next opportunity just happened to be at the top of one of the hardest climbs so far. The hill dragged on and on, going ever higher and ever steeper until eventually we came to the little village going by the name of St Breward.

In St Breward was a Post Office (time to get my first real Post Office stamp) and in the Post Office was a coffee shop. Wonderful! Self-service, make your own coffee, buy some biscuits from a tin, and just what the doctor ordered. They even had an Internet café, but I decided not to send an e-mail to my ex-work colleagues - I was trying to forget them.

After breakfast, I sent my second postcard home, and then came the first bonus for the day - we were at the start of Bodmin Moor. We had climbed to the top and now had the luxury of many flat miles in open countryside and then a gentle decline.

What an eerie place Bodmin Moor is, and so quiet. The moor is a windswept expanse with a bleak character and strange lonesome feel. There were wind-bent trees, stone walls and nothing else but sheep and a ghostly mist. Nobody else ventured on the moors that day, and we were alone - two cyclists surrounded by the mist, the bent trees and the sheep. At that moment I was glad it was day-time. A night-time trip across the moors would not have been pleasant.

Stories continued in these parts of the beast of the moors - a black panther, lurking in the twilight, ready to strike at passing cyclists. Despite the daylight, the mist made everything murky and grey. There was a strange unwelcome feel about the moorland, and I started to recall An American Werewolf in London and how the two strangers were pounced upon by the great local beastie. At that moment I heard a howl behind me. Was it the werewolf, or the beast of the moors? Maybe it was just a dog, but I wasn't taking any chances. I'd seen enough horror movies to know the guy at the back always got killed first and I wasn't about to take any chances. I accelerated and whizzed past Bike Buddy. He could follow me.

As we descended from the summit, I checked over my shoulder to ensure Bike Buddy was still behind me. He'd escaped the beast of the moors despite being slow and resembling a nice juicy chunk of meat on a metal skewer. Something I was quite relieved about. I wasn't sure how I'd have explained to my wife that her dad was dead and had been eaten on the moors while I'd carried on cycling completely oblivious to his screams.

After crossing the moors we cycled through an old airfield, zigzagging along a serious of runways that seemed to go on forever. The roads were long and open, and for most of the cycle the wind was slightly in our faces, but as we turned from one runway to the next, the breeze changed to hit our sides, and then back into our faces once more. Oh how a few degrees can make all the difference!

After the airfield the hills started again and took us upwards toward Camelford. As we approached, locals tried to tell us Camelford was the site of Camelot and send us north to Slaughter Bridge to see the spot of Arthur's last battle. We ignored the blithering idiots and continued on our way to Hallworthy, where we found a pub in Wilsey Down, and decided at 1.30pm to stop for lunch.

You'll never guess what I had! Yes, I maintained my cheese eating exploits with a cheese ploughman's and I have to say it was delicious. I'm starting to think I should give up cheese, I've heard viscous rumours that it isn't particularly good for the old arteries, but then again I like it. Bike Buddy had started this annoying habit of ordering whatever I ordered. I always found this annoying when I went out with my wife and she decided to copy my order instead of thinking for herself, and now I knew why; she was like her dad. Bike Buddy didn't have a mind of his own, he relied on me to make decisions for him. That is until it came to ordering drinks when he always managed to decide which beer he needed at that precise moment.

While resting our weary legs, and looking at the afternoon's cycle ahead, a chill suddenly ran down my spine. I noted on Bike Buddy's drawn map, our destination was Pyworthy, but I also knew I'd booked a Bed and Breakfast in a place called Plyworthy. Shit! Were they the same place? What's an 'L' between friends? Perhaps five hundred miles! I told Bike Buddy my concerns and he went quite ashen, so I tried to calm him down.

'I'm sure it'll be fine. I'm sure it's the same place. Don't worry, we'll get an evening meal.'

The reassurance over food seemed to do the trick, and he started getting colour back into his chubby cheeks. After all, there was nothing we could do now. If it was the wrong place, I was sure we'd find somewhere else to stay, or perhaps a nice comfortable ditch to lie in.

After two and a half days cycling we finally left Cornwall. My God, that was a long county. Into Devon and on to Week St Mary and then Bridgerule. Tiny little villages, all looking the same, with a small school, a pub and a Post Office doubling up as the local shop. It was like cycling back in time, to the good old days when you could pop to the local shop in the village.

Unfortunately the rest of the country was slowly losing its local Post Offices and stores. For some reason people preferred driving five miles to the supermarket. That's fine for the weekly shop, but what happens when you run out of bread or milk and there's no longer a local shop to get it from? You have to get in your car again! We've all got into the habit of going out our front doors and straight into our cars. No wonder we're all getting fat!

As we entered Bridgerule the bonk was starting to gain on us again, so we pulled over at a Post Office in search of some rest and a Post Office stamp. The owner was very chatty and asked what we were doing, and when we replied, very kindly made us a cup of tea and had one herself.

We sat outside the store on some plastic garden furniture sipping hot tea on a scorching afternoon in August and I laughed. Only the English would do something so silly. The sun was beating down on our sweat-drenched bodies, sticking the flies to our faces and the t-shirts to our backs. It was difficult to imagine that very morning we'd been met with mist at the top of Bodmin Moor.

My leg was awfully itchy! Having said that, so was my neck! Pulling up my cycle shorts I noticed a very large red lump, and Bike Buddy confirmed the same had appeared on my neck. I'd been bitten twice by a bloody horsefly! What a little sod! To make matters worse I hadn't even had the opportunity to squash it.

I had no ointment in which to soak my bites and no ice to reduce the swelling, so I accepted the pain and asked the Post mistress about our destination. Thankfully she confirmed our Bed and Breakfast was in fact in Pyworthy and not Plyworthy so we were going the right way (phew!). To make things even better Bridgerule to Pyworthy was only about three miles, and those final miles flew past as I scratched my neck and leg, and wiped the dripping sweat out of my eyes. Within minutes we found our accommodation.

I realised, at that moment, that I was building an unwelcome reputation for choosing Bed and Breakfast's situated at the top of hills. Tonight's Bed and Breakfast was no exception. It was a fantastic place, with lovely views for miles, but it involved a short climb to get there. The owners had built the house themselves when they'd retired from farming, although the farm was still next door. They told us how they'd run the dairy farm, plus had up to sixteen people for Bed and Breakfast on any night – bloody hell, some people worked hard.

The accommodation was a couple of luxurious single rooms with en-suite bathrooms. The couple made us feel at home, giving tea and home-made ginger cakes on arrival. They offered to wash our clothes (probably because the stink was already getting difficult to bear), and even took Bike Buddy to a friend's house to collect more chain links (just in case he managed to break another one). They offered us a dip in their spar tub, but we declined since we didn't have any swimming trunks, and despite me becoming close to Bike Buddy, I didn't want to spend my evening lying naked with him in a bubble bath.

We went to the local pub for dinner, and gorged ourselves on chicken pie and chips. Again I ordered my meal first and Bike Buddy copied. I would need to keep any eye on this little arrangement. I found it quite distressing not having cheese, but knew I could make up for it the following day. After the pie and chips, and a large banana split for dessert I was feeling good. My stomach was nicely rounded, but I felt no remorse because I'd earned it. Besides, if there's one good thing about discovering your imminent termination, it's the fact you no longer have to look after your body for the future. All of a sudden I didn't give a damn if I put on a few pounds – it would just make the coffin heavier. We ordered some coffee, and relaxed into our chairs.

What is it with coffee after a meal? The fluid seems to seep into every remaining hole in your stomach, and then bloat it out like a balloon. The coffee made me feel very full. Uncomfortably full. In fact I was starting to feel so full there was a real risk I might actually pop.

'One more wafer thin mint sir?'

'Nah, I'm stuffed.'

From now on I would lay off the coffee.

With my stomach aching with the stress of keeping itself within my body, Bike Buddy challenged me to a pool tournament. We decided to turn the tournament into a full-blown championship the length of the country, and the first games would start tonight. Hampered by my own greed, Bike Buddy left the arena with a 2-1 lead, but there was still a long way to go.

As we wandered aimlessly back to the Bed and Breakfast I recalled the day. 53 miles cycled on a bike for more than seven hours. My backside was really starting to get sore. As I walked I could feel the welt rubbing against the lycra of my shorts. Mind you, we were staying with nice people tonight, and that would make things easier, but I couldn't help remembering the guy in St Columb Major. The arsehole who'd ruined our evening and our morning. The man who got exactly what he deserved.

After a prolonged chat with the owners of the Bed and Breakfast, I retired to my bedroom, undressed and jumped into the plump, soft bed. As I lay there gently scratching my still-itching leg and my still-itching neck, I recalled the day. A day that had started off in a pig-sty and ended beneath a soft duvet. The warmth of the bed surrounded me, gently caressing away my troubles, and I slowly drifted off to sleep.

The owner struggled to loosen the grip around his neck, but however much he struggled there was no way he could get the brake cable free enough to draw breath. The man was suffocating to death, and it was all in my hands. I pulled harder, crushing his fingers beneath the metal cord, and forcing his Adam's apple to squeeze in against his neck. The bastard had to die, because only through death would he feel the pain that I felt.

I didn't feel remorse for killing, I just felt relief. He needed to die, because he was a bastard and only in death could he give me what I craved. He needed to die so that I could live on forever. By his death, he would give me life. I pulled harder on the brake cable and his struggling subsided, slowly his body lost strength and he fell like a sack in my arms. He was dead and I knew I would now be free forever.

I woke with a start, sweat pouring down my forehead. Initially, I believed what I'd dreamt. I believed I'd killed the owner of the Bed and Breakfast at St Columb Major, and thought I was now doomed to be hunted down like a fox. I decided my life would never be the same again, people everywhere would see my face on the television and everyone would want me caught. I would be known across the country as a murderer and a dangerous man hated throughout the land, but what was interesting was I didn't care. In fact I was pleased. For a split second I actually felt like I'd made it as someone, a murderer perhaps, but at least I'd become known. As my dream had foretold, through the arsehole's death I had been reborn.

This thought stayed with me long after reality hit home and I remembered what had actually happened in St Columb Major. I hadn't killed him, but simply make him suffer. Suffer with severe stomach cramps when he finally made himself a cup of coffee with what he assumed were coffee granules. Little did he know I'd crumbled dried dog crap into the coffee jar for him to enjoy with his drink. I didn't think he'd smell it with the overwhelming aroma of coffee, and I hoped he wouldn't taste it, but I was certain he would feel it in his stomach when it finally entered his body. A little bit of toxoplasmosis to help him while away the day.

DAY 4: CLIMB EVERY MOUNTAIN – PYWORTHY TO TIVERTON

I t was no surprise to have a wonderful breakfast in the morning. I could see from Bike Buddy's eyes that he was sorely tempted to stay in Pyworthy for the rest of the three weeks. He would have been quite happy living in luxury for the entire trip, before catching a train home to rapturous applause for his intrepid journey. He would have known inside that he was a cheater, but he wouldn't care. However, I did care. I didn't want to cheat my way to John O'Groats, and I now had fresh hope in my heart that there were some lovely people to meet further up the country. I was sure St Columb Major was just a one-off. I was sure Pyworthy was what real Bed and Breakfast's were like, and we would be lucky from now on. I was certain I'd have no further need to feed my hosts dried dog crap, and everyone from now on would be a delight to meet. Beside, if we didn't get back on our bikes and resume our intrepid journey, we would never know.

A full English breakfast, the morning rituals completed, wipe down the bikes, tighten the brake blocks and by 8.30am we were on our way. As we set off, I realised this had been the day we were dreading. (Okay, it was just one of the days we were dreading, apart from all of Cornwall, all of Devon, Cumbria and the little jaunt up Drumochter Pass.) However, we also knew today would be a milestone; our last full day in the hills of Devon and Cornwall.

One advantage of booking Bed and Breakfast's at the top of hills is you get to go down at the start of the following day. Unfortunately the local farmer had decided to trim the hedge the previous evening, so we started the journey swerving across the road desperately trying to avoid the broken twigs and thorns. I felt certain I'd get a puncture in at least one tyre, while Bike Buddy actually carried his bike on his shoulder for the first mile – 'to save rubber on tyre!'

It was amusing watching this hulking great man carry his bike on his shoulder. I laughed a few times, and Bike Buddy looked at me scornfully. He would have said something sarcastic, but the strain of his bike meant he didn't have the breath to speak.

Thankfully we survived the thorns unscathed, and the first five or so miles into Holsworthy were relatively flat. Then the hills started. It's fair to say the hills in Devon are not quite as steep as they are in Cornwall, but they certainly go on for longer and reach higher into the sky.

We wound our way through delightful countryside, with the sun on our backs, enjoying the warm morning heat and fully aware that as the day drew on the temperature was going to turn up. Today was not only going to be hard cycling, but it was also going to be a scorcher.

After an hour and a half we approached a pretty little village going by the name of Sheepwash. This was definitely one I wanted the Post Office stamp from, so we stopped for a breather, and took the opportunity to increase our energy loads by devouring bananas, oat biscuits and fruit juice. We sat in the village green, surrounded by cobbled stones and thatched houses. It was only just past ten in the morning, but the sun was already warming up and taking its toll on our tired bodies. We restocked our water bottles, applied sun block, took a deep breath and climbed back on our bikes.

Delightful cycling! Not easy by any means, but the views and the places we passed through made it all worthwhile.

At Hatherleigh, which is an attractive little village set amongst the hillside, we stopped in a quaint little village store to buy some lunch. We didn't want to eat it yet, but were getting ready just in case the opportunity didn't arise again. A dear old lady came out from her bedroom to serve us in the shop. We could actually see her bed through the door.

We bought her last two pasties, a couple of cans of coke and her last two green apples. 'Much better than Tescos,' I thought to myself. It makes you feel warm inside to see into these people's lives. So quiet, so relaxing and such beautiful countryside!

On we cycled up more hills, and down into more valleys until we eventually came to another village, this one called Winkleigh. Here we sat to gorge on our feast. The pasties were good, the coke was coke, the apples were bloody awful.

They must have been in the shop for at least six years. The skin was old and wrinkly, the flesh dry and pappy. After all those nice things I'd said about the little old lady, she turned out to be a deceiver. At that moment I was certain she'd kept those two apples especially to sell to us. She probably saw us coming down the road, put the apples out, and then went into her bedroom to make herself look old and frail. I wondered how many other unsuspecting cyclists she'd poisoned in that way. I wanted to go back and give her a piece of my mind. I wanted to go back and force feed her something horrible, but I didn't want to cycle any further than I really had to - not in this sun. Besides, I'm not sure Bike Buddy would have understood my need for revenge, so I let it lie.

Feeling suddenly full, I allowed my apple to be eaten by the local waste paper bin, stretched my legs and nodded to Bike Buddy that it was time to go.

We had a decision to make this afternoon. Our route involved the use of the B3096 into Tiverton. After a few miles on this road we would leave it and then had the option of either rejoining it later all the way to Tiverton, or going a slightly longer route down country lanes. We looked at the maps, then decide to delay our decision until we'd encountered the B road for the first time.

Cycling for hour after hour, with nothing to occupy my mind other than which way to turn, how tired I felt, how much my backside was still hurting and when I might eventually meet my maker, I started to think about those little idiosyncrasies in life. Like, 'Why do they put indicators on Volvos?' Bike Buddy drove a Volvo, and I put it to him that next time he bought one he could reduce the price by cutting out all those unnecessary extras he never used, namely, indicators, dipped headlights and the rear-view mirror. Bike Buddy didn't seem to find this funny, but I was actually being serious (well semi-serious anyway).

Straight after lunch we joined the B3096 for about 25 miles towards Tiverton. What a wonderful road. It was fairly flat, undulated slightly, but nothing much. We picked our speed up and fairly whizzed along, and with just ten miles to go before Tiverton, we started to feeling particularly pleased with ourselves.

We turned off the B3096 for the first time and came across a little pub that Bike Buddy instantly grew attracted to. By now it was mid-afternoon, and the sun had been beating down on our backs all day. We'd eaten lunch outside, shaded only slightly by the branches of an old tree, and apart from that brief respite, the heat had been upon us all day. Stopping for a drink and some shade seemed sensible, and almost compulsory.

Bike Buddy continued to keep his 'must drink alcohol' pact and downed a pint of lager. I kept to the fruit juice. This drink was a real thirst quencher. All day in the saddle under the blazing sun, we were thirsty, and desperately needed protection from the heat. We sat quietly inside the pub while everyone else enjoyed the sunshine outside. It's amazing how people lead their lives differently. We'd been outside all day and needed shade, others had obviously been inside all day and needed sun. Each to their own!

A quick trip to the little boy's room told its own story. My backside was sore, very sore. The heat had made me sweat profusely inside my shorts and this had made a warm, moist area just ripe for blister growth. I looked in the mirror at my sun-dried face, and washed the thunder-bugs away with a few splashes of water. I was hot and tired, but I was having a great time. Little did I know what was about to come our way.

Remember that saying, 'Good ride in the morning – cyclists warning,' never has its use been more appropriate. At least today we'd managed to get to mid-afternoon before the devil himself came to spoil our day.

Having cycled the B road happily for so many miles it wasn't a difficult decision to rejoin it and canter along to Tiverton. Up until that point we hadn't encountered a car on the B road for about ten miles, and, looking at the map, it appeared to be much flatter than the minor roads surrounding it. Talk about making a bad decision!

As we pulled back out onto the road the devil rose and we were hit by an onslaught of motorised vehicles - cars, vans, caravans, buses, lorries. The entire population of Devon had decided to use this road today - now. To make it worse the road had also become very hilly. I don't mind traffic on roads provided I can keep up a reasonable speed. When I dropped to three or four miles per hour, life suddenly became very fragile. Today it was like cycling on glass.

We found Nomansland, but unfortunately so did everyone else. What a strange name for a village. If it really was no man's land, who had named it - perhaps the women? With so many cars and other motorised vehicles shaking its foundations it wouldn't be long before Nomansland disappeared into the land, man.

To make matters worse, the wind hit our faces for the first time in the day and the road to Tiverton became a long, tiring climb that was unpleasant and extremely hard work.

Bike Buddy had informed me during our previous drinks' stop that he'd been cycling blind all afternoon. The battery in his cycle computer had failed, and he now had no idea how far we'd travelled or how much further we had to go. Mine was working fine, but I felt it would spoil it for Bike Buddy if I was to give him any information that might help him work out where we were (despite the fact he was the map-reader). To be fair, passing information between cyclists is not easy when you have lorries whizzing past your head. It wasn't as if we could dawdle along side-by-side, exchanging pleasantries. So I kept my information to myself, and let Bike Buddy work it out from the shadows and the sun.

Despite this disability Bike Buddy did manage to keep us on the right road and we eventually arrived in Tiverton town centre, alive and glad to be within a 30 mile-an-hour zone at last.

Tiverton used to be a prosperous wool town, and is well worth a look. A splendid twelfth century castle overlooks the river Exe and there are a number of other particularly grand buildings. Unfortunately we needed to get a battery for Bike Buddy. Well, not actually for him – for his cycle computer, so the search was on for a bike shop.

Cycling round Tiverton was great fun, down one-way streets, into shopping arcades, down pedestrianised roads, trying desperately to find a cycle shop and leaving little old ladies scattered in our wake, then after many wrong turns, we finally came upon just the thing.

One battery later, and all we had to do was find the Bed and Breakfast. Ha, bloody ha! Someone had decided Tiverton was the prime sight for building houses on mountain tops. The Bed and Breakfast, we suddenly realised, was at the top of a seventeen percent hill. I don't believe for one minute that this road was only seventeen percent. Perhaps if we'd gone up the whole thing it might have flattened off later to give a miserly seventeen percent overall. The first part, however, the bit we had to cycle up, was more like forty-seven percent. This was not a road you could lay tarmac on, but more a wall you would grout. Neither of us could cycle this monster. In fact it was almost impossible to push the bike up, let alone cycle. This was one hill too many on a hot day after too many hills. My first failure as a cyclist on this tour, and I was determined it would be my last.

I comforted myself with the fact we had to descend this hill in the morning and therefore it wasn't really part of our route, but just a detour for the night. Then I suddenly lost all comfort, when I realised what I'd just thought - we had to cycle down this hill the morning. Tomorrow we would throw ourselves off the top of a cliff, which ended abruptly at the main road into Tiverton. There was no way I wanted to do that first thing in the morning with dew on the ground and moss on the road. I hated hills, but funnily enough, I believe I hated going down them more than going up.

My third 'Bed and Breakfast on a hill' out of four, was a splendid establishment, situated within a seventeenth century coach house, with large rooms and high ceilings. The owner brought us tea and biscuits on arrival in the garden, and Bike Buddy's pains slipped away. He was happy again. We'd cycled all day through the hills of Devon, only 52 miles, but 52 hard miles and five miles further than planned. Another eight hours on a bicycle saddle, and we were very, very glad to be in a place of rest for the next few hours.

After a few moments of relaxation in the garden, I decided it would be better to remove the dried fly remains off my body before they became a permanent feature, and headed for the bathroom. Again we would have the luxury of single rooms, this time with a shared bathroom, and as Bike Buddy filled his body with more tea and biscuits, I took the opportunity to run myself a bath and start scrubbing.

One good thing about cycle clothes is they dry very quickly. Since I was plastered with fly remains, and my clothes were in a similar state, I decided to bathe in my cycle-wear. After a long soak, I peeled off my lycra shorts and luminous yellow t-shirt and started to scrub them in the water. All this hot weather and hills made me very sweaty and it was good to feel marginally clean again.

As I scrubbed I couldn't work out why the brown thumbnail size marks on the back of my hands, wouldn't come off. More soap and scolding hot water, but the brown stains remained. After scrubbing for a while, and only being successful in turning the skin a bright red colour, I realised these marks were my cyclist's tan. Two small brown tan marks where my mitts fixed together and the sun got through. Holding my hands up before me, I suddenly became very proud of my cyclist's tan and realised I would have to work on it over the coming days, while the sun shone.

After rinsing my shorts and t-shirt I wrung them out, wrapped them in a towel and dried them as best I could. Then I strategically placed them on the heated towel rail and prayed they would be dry by the morning.

Funny, this Bed and Breakfast was nothing like I'd expected. I recalled asking the owner about an evening meal when I first booked and she asked me to phone her the day before if we wanted her to provide a meal. I'd done this, as requested, but she sounded very off. So much so I offered to cycle back to Tiverton town centre for a meal. Thank God she eventually agreed to cook, because I didn't want to go near that hill anymore times than I had to.

Having arrived, I now knew why she'd sounded off! The lady of the house had twisted her ankle playing tennis and was hobbling around with her leg bandaged up and the use of a crutch. How bad did I feel? I felt like I'd asked a cripple to dance a jig, or a blind person to read Teletext. However, despite my overwhelming feeling of guilt my appetite remained (well it would after cycling for eight hours) and I was not about to stop this woman from providing us with a delicious meal.

She didn't let us down, the dinner was amazing; carrot and coriander soup followed by chicken casserole with vegetables, homemade chocolate mousse, cheese and biscuits and coffee in the lounge. What's more, the meal was served round a huge dining table, with portraits of ancestors staring at us from the walls, and while we ate, we were comforted by the knowledge that our bikes sat in relative comfort, stored round the back of the house in the tack room.

After filling our bellies we retired to our bedrooms, scanned through the remaining maps in a bid to convince ourselves we'd now done the most challenging part. Unfortunately Drumochter Pass continued to stare back at us, but undaunted we took comfort from the fact we had more than a week to go before being challenged by that little mound.

As the light faded and the night set in, I lay alone in my bed thinking. It was funny how the darkness changed the way my mind worked. While out on my bike I could enjoy myself, despite the pain. In fact, maybe because of the pain. The pain gave me something to concentrate on. My brain was busy putting up with the ache in my legs, the pain in my backside and the glorious scenery surrounding me and had no time to consider my fate. I had no time to think about what lay install for me in just over ten months, but now, lying alone in bed, with darkness all around me, all I could think about was dying. All that filled my mind was the thought of never seeing another sunrise, never seeing the green fields, the mountains and hills, the running streams, and never hearing the birds in the trees. That thought made me cry. I lay in bed, a grown man, and cried. I cried so hard I was sobbing, and I wondered if Bike Buddy would hear me from the adjacent room. I wondered if he would come and check if I was okay, and despite the horrendous thought of seeing Bike Buddy in only a pair of pants, in some way I hoped he would. I longed to have someone I could talk to, someone who could absorb some of the worry, someone who would listen to me and tell me it would be okay, but I realised that person was at home with our children, and without her I was lost.

DAY 5: GRAVEL, GRASS AND A BRIDGE TOO LOW
– TIVERTON TO GLASTONBURY

Each night I went to bed thinking, 'I must stop eating so much crap', and each morning I woke up with a rumbling stomach and dreams of the full fry-up ahead of me. This morning was no exception, but I refrained from the full works by selecting just sausage, poached eggs and tomatoes. This was my healthy option, along with the cereal and toast, coffee and orange juice of course. Bike Buddy always had everything on the menu. I cringed a bit when he asked for fried egg, poached egg and scrambled egg all together!

My lycra shorts were dry, the t-shirt wasn't bad, so I was able to rejoice in the fact I could start the day dry.

The owner of the Bed and Breakfast kept going up and up and up in my estimations. When I went to pay she charged us only twelve pounds each for last night's meal, and then gave me twenty pounds towards our charities. See, the t-shirts did work! I noted down her generosity in the back of my diary. I even considered sending her a letter when we got back to tell her whether we'd made it or not, but I knew deep down that I would never write the letter.

After the normal morning routine, we collected our bikes from the tack room, gave them a quick rub down with the rag, sprayed them with the lube and were ready for the off.

My God it was cold in the mornings! Considering it was August I thought we might be able to get away with t-shirts all day, but oh no. Despite his better inbuilt insulation, Bike Buddy seemed to feel the cold more than me. It must have been his age. He always wore two t-shirts, a sweatshirt and his waterproof jacket. He always wore his long cycling trousers over the top of his shorts, and, as suspected, Bike Buddy was starting to complain about how I'd forced him to send back his other heavy-duty t-shirt. I pointed out that if he hadn't sent it back we might still have been in Cornwall, but he remained unconvinced.

I suddenly remembered the hill. Actually, that's a lie. I'd been thinking about it all night, a hilly nightmare coming at me from all sides, making me turn restlessly throughout the dark period, slowly driving me insane with its constant grind. A night of turning over, turning round, twisting in my sweat. They say there is no rest for the wicked one. Dear God, what had I done?

The drop back down to Tiverton was just as bad as I thought it would be. The road was still wet from the night, the surface was slippery, the incline deadly, and at the foot of the cliff was a main road. What a wonderful design!

Despite all the hills so far, I was grateful to discover my brake pads hadn't worn away, and the brakes were still working. We swerved across the road trying to make our descent flatter than it actually was, like a couple of skiers traversing across the slope, and eventually arrived at the foot. That was the first death drop completed for the day.

As we set off I knew today was going to be a long day in the saddle. Hopefully, not many hills, but plenty of canal towpaths. At the time canal towpaths seemed like a wonderful idea for using as a cycle track. Apart from the occasional lock, they had to be fairly flat – simple logic of water flattening itself out, and for that reason I was expecting a long day, but an enjoyable one.

We joined the towpath at Tiverton, only a few hundred yards from the bottom of the cliff we had just abseiled down. The towpath was nicely tarmaced so the surface was perfect for cycling on, although we had to be careful not to cycle too fast because of the many folk walking their dogs. I found the leads got stuck in my wheels if I ran them over.

The first mile was delightful. Pleasant, easy cycling on a baby-smooth surface, early in the morning with the local wildlife watching us as we watched it. The canal was picturesque, the clear, flat water glistening in the early morning sun. The air was fresh, and life was good.

A mile down the towpath the tarmac disappeared and the replacement surface was fine gravel. Oh joy! However, my initial reservations were soon forgotten and I realised this surface actually wasn't too bad for cycling on. A few more miles and I realised, that while it was okay for cycling on the surface was playing havoc with my buttocks. Mine were pretty tender by now anyway. Constant miniature divots aggravated the skin even more. Ouch!

The fine gravel soon turned to coarse gravel, and then to grass. The grass was still wet from the dew, and was rutted with tree roots. The countryside was still fabulous, but I spent quite a lot of time looking down at the path, trying to bunny hop the roots.

After the initial dog walkers we hardly saw anyone else on the entire towpath section. A heron flew just in front of us for about a mile and kept stopping on the towpath, but as we came closer he took off again. I'm sure he was thinking, 'Why are these buggers following me?'

The bikes were starting to show signs of wear and tear. Bike Buddy's front mudguard clipped out in the morning when he cycled over a stick in the road. Actually it was bigger than a stick, more like a large log, or tree trunk. How he didn't see it beats me. Somehow if a large tree branch was lying across the road in front of me I'd hope I would see it coming. It's not like it just jumped out of the tree and flipped his mudguard with one of its long spindly arms.

The towpath led us through some woodland and then back onto minor roads. At the same time Bike Buddy was being attacked by the tree branch from hell, I dropped my chain for the first time. This was not a calamity, but did give a sign that all was not quite right with my bicycle.

After a few miles on country lanes, we arrived in Taunton. Taunton is a shopper's paradise. The town streets were flowing with people spending money, but we needed to find the towpath again, and made our way through the crowded streets as best we could. Bike Buddy was still having problems with his mileometer, so we stopped in a cycle shop just at the start of the next towpath route. While there, in preparation for the cold winter days ahead (well Scotland anyway) I decided to increase my luggage, and purchased a thin long sleeved cycle top. It has a wicking layer, which I discovered meant it pulled the sweat from my body and stopped me getting sticky. The theory sounded good, but considering my ability to wash clothes only by bath water, I thought the garment may be a tad smelly by the end of the trip if it was holding all my sweat.

As we climbed back on our bikes a couple of pigeons landed nearby and started pecking away at an old cigarette butt. Why do they do that? For an animal that supposedly has good eyesight, surely it knows before it pecks that it's not food. Maybe pigeons like to smoke. Why do you never see baby pigeons? That question had been bugging me ever since Jasper Carrot asked it. At least I think it was Jasper Carrot who first asked it. Anyway, where do they go (the baby pigeons not Jasper Carrot)? Is there a pigeon crèche somewhere, with one or two adult pigeons looking after all the babies until they are old enough to crap on Nelson's column all by themselves? Maybe pigeons come out of their eggs fully grown. That would be a big egg! I bet that would smart a bit when it's being laid. I'll have to give that more thought.

Part way along the new towpath we were starting to get hungry. The sun was now high in the sky, and growing in strength all the time. The heat was making me drip with sweat, and when I glanced at my watch I realised it was nearly 1.30pm and definitely time for lunch. As directed by the chap in the cycle shop we tried to find Creech St Michael. This involved leaving the cycle towpath and searching the side streets for any sign of life. It wasn't difficult, especially now Bike Buddy had his mileometer working again.

In Creech St Michael we found a pub, locked our bikes outside and went in to order our fully deserved grub.

'Sorry we don't do food' was the response.

Bike Buddy looked at me in half-panic, so I grabbed his arm and marched him out the door and back to our bikes. Bike Buddy's face was ashen, but I calmed him down. The village was a decent size, and I was sure we'd find somewhere else to eat.

Back on the bikes, we drifted down the road until we found the Riverside Inn – success! Back on the cheese diet I ordered a cheese and pickle baguette with chips, which Bike Buddy copied (along with his beer). Bike Buddy and I had decided to compliment our new diets with large portions of chips at every opportunity. I was sure we'd end up fatter at the end of this journey than the beginning.

After washing sweat and flies off my face in the toilet, stuffing my face with food and downing a few cold drinks, I went back outside. Bloody hell it was hot! I sprayed myself with sun cream. (What a great invention - spray on sun cream. No more thick layers of cream on your hands and thin layers on your arms. Suddenly you can cover your whole body with the right consistency. Okay, apart from the bits covered by lycra shorts or t-shirts.) I decided not to cream my cyclist's tan on my hands. These marks would need as much sun as they could get.

Back on the towpath after lunch was very hard going in the baking heat. The sun was beating down and making me sweat profusely, particularly in my shorts. This in turn was making my bottom hurt even more than usual and resulted in me lifting my buttocks of the saddle, one by one, trying to give them some respite. It was certainly a welcome relief when the sun clouded over at about 3.30pm.

I spent most of the afternoon shifting my buttocks from side to side and backwards and forwards, trying desperately to make my seat more comfortable. I continued to lift myself out of the saddle to relieve the pressure, but it just hurt even more when I sat back down again. How could I carry on when I couldn't even sit down?

The National cycle route along the towpath was very pleasant, but the bridges were very low. And why was it the only time we met someone coming the other way was when we were bent double cycling under a low bridge? This meant they were doing the same thing, and neither of us could see each other coming. I worked out the best way to deal with the problem was to send Bike Buddy under the bridge first. Hopefully he would then warn anyone coming the other way of my imminent arrival.

The signs at these bridges told cyclists to dismount. We ignored them, mainly because we were making slow enough progress as it was without dismounting every hundred yards. Looking back, perhaps they were right, we should have dismounted. How we managed to avoid the water still defies me.

As the afternoon wore on I had two unusual meetings. First, just as the afternoon sun was fading away I was spotted by an assailant. He could see my bright yellow shirt and was, unbeknown to me, planning his attack. Slowly at first, he drifted up on the air-stream and waited for the right moment. Then - whoosh, down he came making full contact with my left ear, before lifting back up to survey the damage. I was lucky, I'd escaped with just a glancing blow, but my ear really stung. The dragonfly survived to attack another day.

A little further on, and down the quiet country lane, by the towpath we had made our home, came a monster truck. Thirty-eight tonnes of pulsating metal. It saw us, but didn't care. It saw the ten tonne limit on the rickety, rackety bridge, but didn't care. All it cared about was getting home for its dinner. With nowhere to go, and no way of turning round, we had to dismount quickly and make a rapid escape to the ditch. There still wasn't enough room so we were forced to walk our bikes back over the bridge and hope the truck would get across. If the bridge broke we would need to cycle another couple of miles to get to the other side. We stood waiting for the splash, but obviously the ten tonne limit was just scare mongering, the truck was across and away.

I made a mental note of the truck's number plate, just in case we met him again, but within five minutes of leaving the bridge the number plate had slipped surreptitiously out of my mind never to return.

The towpath remained pleasant, with decent gravel to cycle on, which was a vast improvement on the grass and tree roots. We passed a number of pillboxes, which Bike Buddy found highly exciting, and talked non-stop about for what seemed like hours. I tried to ignore him, but his constant drone finally drilled through and I now have a detailed knowledge of pillboxes myself, but I won't bore you with the details now.

Soon after we arrived in Bridgwater, which happened to be another bustling shopping town filled with happy shoppers. The outskirts of Bridgwater were very industrialised and we seemed to scoot around the sides, in amongst the most heavily polluted areas, for some time before finally descending on the centre.

As we worked our way through the bustling traffic, I considered whether I should have worn one of those facemasks so many cyclists in London seem to wear. I've tried to wear a facemask and cycle before, but never really got on with it. Mind you, it was a Scream mask on Halloween, and the idea was to scare as many people as possible on the way home. My problem was I couldn't breathe in the mask, let alone scream at passers-by. The other problem was seeing through the eye slots well enough to find the road.

A bridge and some peat fields were all that separated us from Glastonbury and the luxury of another Bed and Breakfast. Unfortunately the bridge involved a climb up steps, and our bikes were very heavy when fully loaded. Hoisting mine up onto my shoulder I suddenly forgot about the pain in my backside and concentrated on whether I would manage to get up the stairs without falling backwards and landing on my arse with my bike on top of me. It took all my strength, but I managed it; up the steps, across the bridge and then back down the steps on the other side. We then dropped down beneath a low arched bridge, and it turned out this arch was too low to walk under, let alone cycle under. So with our bikes by the side of us we pushed them through, heads bent.

Bike Buddy had difficulty moving in any way or form when not on his bike. I think his muscles had just become use to cycling and couldn't do anything else. After bending to get under the bridge, Bike Buddy stayed bent double on the other side. He couldn't straighten his back, so as I walked up behind him I helpfully shoved my bicycle pump up his bum. He stood up straight instantly.

'See, no problem,' I said.

From the bridge to Glastonbury was flat as a pancake. The minor roads were very quiet and led us through a series of peat fields, which I have to say, were amazing. Completely flat other than mountains of peat stacked up on either side and drainage systems criss-crossing the entire area. Easy cycling, and pleasant in the evening sun.

Just before we arrived at Glastonbury I realised I'd done it again. The Bed and Breakfast's address of 'Bove Town' was again, for the fourth night out of five, at the top of a hill. 'Bove Town', should have seen that one coming, it means above the town. Duh!

The climb wasn't too bad, and only a slight incline compared with the wall of death from the previous night. As the late afternoon sun shone down on our backs we found the Bed and Breakfast, and climbed the steps to the door.

The couple running our lodgings were very pleasant. The husband reminded me of a hunt master. He was very particular, ensuring we put our bikes against the correct wall in the garage, that we closed the garage door properly, that we wiped our feet on the way in, and shook hands with everyone else in the house. His wife seemed more relaxed and quickly showed us to our twin room, with en-suite bathroom. She reminded me of the little old lady who lived in a shoe.

Once in our room, it took us a while to work out the bedside lamps. There were no switches to turn them on or off. After searching under the beds we followed the cable to the socket only to discover they were already switched on. How strange! I decided the only option was to hit the light, and hey-presto it came on. I hit it again - the light grew stronger. I hit it again - the room was filled with brilliant white light. I hit it again, and we were once again plunged into darkness. Touch control lamps - what a stupid idea!

How many people do you know who can't work a light switch? What was it persuaded someone that what the world really needed to make it complete was a switch-less lamp? I couldn't get past the fact that I must be part of the electric circuit when I pressed the lamp. I wondered what would happen if I licked the lamp instead? However, since three people actually die in the United Kingdom each year from putting a nine-volt battery on their tongues, and since these lamps were plugged into the mains, I decided it wasn't a good idea to find out. I would ask Bike Buddy to do it later, after he'd had a few drinks.

We unpacked our meagre belongings and took turns in the shower, washing away the layer of peat that had covered our faces and bodies. My backside was really sore. I tried to inspect it using the bathroom mirror. (This was when being a contortionist would have been a major advantage.) Without this skill, I settled on a technique known as 'pull your buttocks to one side as far as you can.' It seemed to work, and I was soon able to examine the two red blood blisters on my bum. No wonder my backside hurt! I was slowly developing an allergic reaction to bike saddles.

After shining ourselves up and lathering my backside in Sudocrem (which I hasten to add, I did myself), Bike Buddy and I decided it was time to eat. Glastonbury was a strange place. King Arthur's bones are supposedly in the abbey, but we couldn't find them. Glastonbury Tor stood proudly above us. Bike Buddy suggested for a while that we should cycle up to it, but I persuaded him otherwise. I still wasn't confident we could do this cycle ride, and I wasn't about to do unnecessary miles just for the hell of it.

Glastonbury also claimed to home the Holy Grail, but again we couldn't find it anywhere. If they were keeping it, they weren't letting anybody else have a look that's for sure. The one thing that I will remember about Glastonbury is that everyone is a hippy! The Glastonbury festival has a lot to answer for. Flower-power rules and I had this overwhelming desire to put two fingers up to everyone (no not that sign – you know the one for peace man). Hippies had obviously descended on the town for the festivals and decided to stay. I couldn't blame them, it seemed a very pleasant place. After wandering through the town making more friends in twenty-seven minutes than I'd made in the rest of my twenty-seven years put together, we found a pub for dinner. Bike Buddy had his normal two pints, I stuck to the fruit juice.

Another early night. Cycling may be good for you, but it doesn't half tire you out. We were in our twin beds by 9pm desperately trying to keep our eyes open to watch the television. I felt happier tonight, mainly because Bike Buddy was with me. He might be an annoying git sometimes, but it was a comfort to have him in the room when darkness fell.

As normal, Bike Buddy's eyelids gave way first and within minutes he was snoring away. It was like sharing a room with a power drill stuck in hammer mode. Perhaps it was better to cry myself to sleep alone than share a room with a human power-drill. How on earth was I going to get any sleep with this noise going on? It was funny how it didn't matter how tired I felt, as soon as I heard snoring I was instantly wide-awake.

I decided to cough to wake Bike Buddy. It didn't work. I decided to slam the bedside drawer. It still didn't work. I switched off the television, then turned it back on. This did work, helped by the fact the television reset its volume level automatically when coming back on. A volume level much louder than I'd originally planned.

Why is it that sounds travel so much better at night? I wondered if this was actually true, or just a figment of my imagination. Going all scientific for a moment, perhaps without any other noise there are no sound waves to dampen the television waves down, hence loud TV. Or there again, perhaps I'm just talking bollocks.

Bike Buddy snorted again, shifted his body from side to side, lifted his head and kind of grunted, 'Uh – what.'

'Sorry,' I replied, 'didn't mean to wake you.'

What a liar I'm turning out to be. Bike Buddy turned over, shuffled, snorted again, and resumed his sleep. With him now facing away from me, his snoring didn't seem so bad. Perhaps the snore-wave was being absorbed by the far wall, rather than reflecting off it. I might have to scientifically test this over the next few nights. See what the prime television volume was for snoring efficiency.

I managed to keep awake until the ten o'clock news began, and was just starting to doze off when I heard something that woke me with a start. The news reporter was in St Columb Major, where a publican had been found dead in his bathroom.

'Holy shit, I'd killed the bastard!'

AM   PM

DAY 6: A GAME OF TWO HALVES –

GLASTONBURY TO TETBURY

Strangely, I didn't sleep very well last night. I watched the ten o'clock news, taking in the full horror of the pictures shown. They didn't show the publican, but with him being dead, I don't suppose they were going to. They did show the pub, and the Bed and Breakfast. The same Bed and Breakfast we had stayed in. They also showed the dog, found by its master's side. The newsreader spoke about the circumstances in which the body was found, but my mind was too busy staring at the scene in front of me. As soon as the pub was shown, my body went numb, and my hearing became impaired. I listened to the whole report, but didn't hear a word. The only thing going through my mind was that I'd killed the guy. He might have been an annoying arse, but did he really deserve to die? The answer to that was probably yes, but it didn't make me feel any better. I was a murderer!

The hunt master and little old lady who lived in a shoe showed us to the breakfast table and introduced us to the other guests who'd spent the night; an American couple who thought Glastonbury was, 'Very cute.' When they heard what we were doing it became obvious how 'Fantastic' it was. They might not have been so impressed if I'd told them I'd murdered my host from two nights ago!

The little old lady in the shoe served a continental breakfast of croissants with homemade jam and marmalade. We helped ourselves to strawberries. How healthy were we getting? Bike Buddy looked extremely pale when he realised he wouldn't get his normal helping of grease and fat, but I comforted him somewhat by informing him the day was still young, and he could soon make up for his fat shortfall.

The National Cycle Route took us from Glastonbury to Wells. The road was flat and the surface was tarmac, the traffic was light and for a moment I thought I was in heaven. Unfortunately my bottom soon informed me that I was not. It only lasted a few miles before the uncomfortable sensation returned; a constant aching in my nether regions, and whatever I tried to do I couldn't get comfortable - my butt cheeks were so sore. Please let me find a pillow. I thought about some guys I'd heard about who'd run out of talcum powder on a cycle journey across the desert. Unable to buy any more, they instead turned to corn flour to solve their problem and managed to have the most comfortable day's cycling ever. When they got undressed that evening they realised why. The corn flour had mixed with the sweat from their genitals to make a paste. The heat from the sun had made the paste rise into a nice soft dough that now had the imprints of their balls in it, but had acted as a soft, personally designed cushion. Looking back at our initial thoughts in Penzance I thought perhaps we shouldn't have discarded Bike Buddy's talcum powder quite so readily.

My bottom had been so sore first thing in the morning that I'd decided to wear both pairs of padded lycra cycle shorts. I thought the added padding would help numb the pain, but it seemed to make little difference and I continued to spend most of the journey moving from butt cheek to butt cheek trying to get comfortable. I moved forward and back, but there was nowhere to hide. My bottom would hurt forever more.

To take my mind of the pain, I started to think up poems in my head. My first attempt went something like this:

Lonely Cyclist
I cycle lonely as a cloud,
That struggles hard o'er vale and hill,
Then all at once I cry out loud,
My bottom hurts and it's raining still.

We arrived at Wells in good time. Wells was a delightful little town, actually I do believe it's England's smallest city. It must be a city because it has a cathedral. I know it has a cathedral because we followed the National Cycle route straight through the middle of it. This was fantastic. How had Sustrans managed to wangle this one? How on earth had they persuaded the vicar (or is it reverend or is it priest, bishop, monk, nun…?) to allow people to cycle through Wells Cathedral? The truth was soon thrust upon us. They hadn't!

We were just trying to manoeuvre our bikes down one of the aisles, when we were asked to leave. I looked at Bike Buddy, Bike Buddy looked at the map and then looked at me. I looked at the vicar-priest, and said I was sorry. I also told him it was my fault for letting my mentally retarded father-in-law map read that day, and I would ensure all his maps were taken off him before I returned him to the asylum.

The morning's cycle had been brilliant. My bum was still hurting but the weather was good and we were making reasonable progress. We had to go over the Mendip Hills later in the morning and planned to take our first break of the day when we reached the top.

Before reaching the start of our climb, we cycled through the picturesque villages of Priddy and on past Wookey Hole. Hey, I remember Wookey Hole! I came on a school trip here when I was about ten. Wookey Hole is a mass of underground tunnels and caverns, with the tale of a wee beastie lurking in the doom. If I'd had a little more confidence in our ability to knock-off the miles today, I would have been tempted to stop and take a guided tour. Unfortunately, I didn't, but instead comforted myself with a trip to the Post office who kindly stamped my book for me. I had a Wookey Hole post stamp. Did you hear me? I HAD A WOOKEY HOLE POST STAMP.

We could see the Mendip Hills in the distance, and then just as the incline started to bite we met a man strolling up the hill. He was full of the joys of spring; Mr Smiler.

'This is the gentle bit. It gets a lot steeper round the corner. Mind you the views are worth the climb,' he cheerfully cried.

I cycled past. 'I will make it! I will get to the top!'

Bike Buddy got part way up, but as the road lifted higher into the sky he accepted defeat and climbed off his bike to walk. A gentle stroll with Smiler.

The Mendip Hills were high. High when you're dragging your panniers up and you've been cycling for five days solid. It was a long, hard drag up to the top, but I wasn't going to be defeated and using my ever-ready granny gear I eventually dragged myself to the summit.

Looking over my shoulder I could see Bike Buddy slowly walking up the road below me. This was my chance for a quick urination. I glanced up the road, down the road and seeing the place empty I lobbed my little buddy (okay, less of the little) out of my cycle shorts and started to relieve myself in the hedgerow. No prizes for guessing what happened next. I have never seen so many cars appear from nowhere in such a short space of time. But a man in mid-flow is not a man to be stopped and I drained my lizard in front of their preying eyes.

Bike Buddy arrived a little later having left Smiler to walk across the fields. He looked knackered and after exchanging pleasantries we cycled along the summit to find a place to stop for a drink.

Bike Buddy appeared to be feeling a little down today. Perhaps it was the hill. Perhaps he was just tired. Perhaps he couldn't cope without his full English breakfast in the morning. Perhaps me continually turning the television on and off all night ruined his sleep. Shame!

We cruised along the top of the Mendips and came across a small café, with seating outside. It was a glorious day. The sun was out, the sky was blue, there was not a cloud to spoil the view, but it was raining, raining in Bike Buddy's heart.

I left him to man the bikes, and went for refreshment. A simple procedure, but one that would cause so much strife. Bike Buddy cannot be trusted to man the bikes. Bike Buddy cannot be left alone for more than a few seconds. He will go nutty, throw his toys from his pram. I returned to mayhem.

Whilst I was inside the café, a family had arrived ready to stay at the local campsite. This family consisted of two women and six young boys. The boys were out of control. The women were obviously immune to it. Bike Buddy was not! The boys climbed all over the bench Bike Buddy was sitting on. So Bike Buddy moved. The boys followed him. So he moved again. And so it went on, as they chased each other around the seats. By the time I arrived back, Bike Buddy had shouted at them many times, threatened to throw them off the wall and told the women that they were a good advert for sterilisation.

I do believe Bike Buddy gets more worked up than me. Perhaps I could tell him I'd murdered the St Columb Major arse, and he'd actually congratulate me. Maybe if Bike Buddy knew he was cycling with a murderer he might try to persuade me to murder again – starting with these kids.

I tried to calm the situation down for the veins on Bike Buddy's neck were pulsating and I thought he might pop at any time. The boys were immune to shouting, the women were not and insisted on fighting Bike Buddy's fire with some of their own. Oh the fun! Eventually the family left on their way to their allotted camp space, but within five minutes we saw them again - going home. Obviously Bike Buddy was not the only one to take offence from the children's behaviour. The camp officials were also unimpressed, and the family were asked to leave.

After our not so relaxing break, we were ready to set off once more. The sun was still shining, and I was trying my best to make light of the situation. Bike Buddy was still stressed, it would take at least a couple of months to calm him down.

Coming down the Mendips was a lot easier than going up them. Perhaps I should amend my earlier comment. I prefer going UP steep hills to going down them, but I definitely prefer going DOWN lesser gradients than going up them. Glad we got that sorted. We sailed down, and as we enjoyed the wind in our helmets, our spirits lifted. It wouldn't be long before we saw our wives, who were meeting us in Tetbury, could settle down in the Bed and Breakfast for a nice meal, enjoy some female company for once, and hopefully get a good night's sleep.

I took the lead, flying down the hill on the main road, swishing from left to right, right to left, I whizzed passed the Chew Valley Lakes and into the village of Chew Stoke. I'd eventually managed to shake off the shadow of Bike Buddy, confident that I could carry along a road without getting lost. I slowly drifted to a standstill at the bottom of the hill next to a garage and convenience store and waited patiently for him. Bike Buddy would arrive in a minute. He was always a bit of a wimp when it came to main roads.

Two minutes passed - no sign of Bike Buddy. Another two minutes, and still no sign. Where was he? Had he fallen off? Nobody could take this long to descend a road. Another two minutes passed, and now I was getting worried. I turned my bike around and started back up the hill. This was the end of our tour. Bike Buddy was lying dead in the road. I knew it! Up the hill a bit further, the gradient no longer mattered, I needed to get to Bike Buddy. It was amazing how the adrenaline kicked in at moments like this and pain was no longer an issue. He needed me! He was lying alone on the tarmac, his face squashed in the road, bits of grit indenting his skin, with blood oozing out. My poor Bike Buddy, what had I done to him?

Hang on a minute, there he was! Bike Buddy was standing by his bike, a little way round a corner on the right. He'd stopped at the turning and just left me to carry on alone. He wasn't dead. He wasn't even slightly grazed. He had just stopped. He was map-reading and he'd just stopped. Not worried about how far I was going on ahead, not concerned about me, just standing there.

'I knew you'd come back', was his greeting. 'We need to go this way'.

'You can go off people', I replied.

To make matters worse, before talking Bike Buddy's turning, we actually continued down the hill I'd just climbed up and visited the convenience store, stocking up on mars bars and tuna and sweet-corn sandwiches for lunch. The owner was interested in what we were doing, and quickly went behind her counter, re-appearing moments later with a postcard of Chew Stoke. What on earth was she going to do? She addressed it to herself, and stuck a stamp on the top. Then she handed the postcard to me, asking me to carry it to John O'Groats and post it back to her. I nodded and went on my way.

Outside I spoke quietly to Bike Buddy, 'After all that effort to reduce our load, she expects us to carry a bloody postcard all the way to Scotland for her, just so she can see it again? I've got a good mind to post it in the next post-box, or maybe this litter bin.'

This was a stupid thing to say. After all, how much did a postcard weigh? But it did show the frame of mind I was now in. Any additional weight, however small, could stop me from completing this journey. Bike Buddy sighed, took the postcard off me and stuffed it in his panniers.

After taking Bike Buddy's turning, we cycled on through quiet country lanes until we reached the village of Pensford. We'd been searching for somewhere nice to stop and eat our sandwiches, and ended up on a wooden seat by a bus stop. We propped our bikes up against an old stone monument and opened our feast.

'Hello,' a voice said. Bike Buddy and I looked around. We looked up the street, and down the street, and then, puzzled, we looked at each other.

'Who said that?' I asked.

'It was me,' came the not-particularly helpful reply.

'Who the hell is me?' I asked, slowly starting to believe I was talking to the ghost of Pensford.

'I'm up here,' came the reply, and as we looked up in the direction of her voice we saw the smiling face of a young lady leaning over the top of the monument.

'Hello,' we cheerfully replied.

'Saw you sitting there and wondered if you'd like a cup of tea,' she continued.

We gratefully accepted, and within a couple of minutes the kindly soul arrived from the side of the monument with two mugs of tea. We exchanged pleasantries, in which she asked us where we were going.

'John O'Groats,' I replied. This seemed to surprise her slightly. Perhaps it was the 'I'm completely knackered' look on my face, or the sight of an over-weight, huffing and puffing Bike Buddy.

'Just leave the mugs on the monument and I'll pick them up later,' she said as she turned and left us.

'Thank-you,' we replied.

A few minutes later, just as we were about to leave, the lady reappeared, this time clutching some money.

'For your charities,' she said.

I couldn't believe how kind this woman was. She didn't know who we were, but nonetheless she offered us a cup of tea and then gave us money for our charities. I could feel the need for another letter coming on, addressed to 'the kind lady who lived above the monument in Pensford.' I was sure it would get there.

After lunch we climbed back on our bikes and pushed off towards the Bristol and Bath railway. The old railway had been converted into a cycle track, thanks to Sustrans, and they'd done a bloody good job. The only problem was, where we joined it, the railway line had inconsiderately been built high above the ground and to get on it we had to walk up a couple of flights of stone steps.

I looked up the steps and couldn't help thinking how unusual it was to have steps on cycle paths. Not according to Sustrans, who like to make them a common feature. Looking closer I realised I'd misjudged them. They had provided a small wheel track by the side of the steps, to allow us to push our bikes up. This track was no more than an inch wide, and unfortunately was on the left side of the steps and I found I was completely incapable of pushing my bike on the left side of my body. Is that just me? I found it very similar to throwing a ball with my left arm, or using a computer mouse with my left hand. Though not one to complain, I did my best, and we eventually arrived at the summit.

The cycle track was very busy, obviously a favourite for taking children out cycling. 'If only we had something like this near us,' I thought.

The surface was very smooth tarmac, which meant we could zip along at a good speed, although it really wasn't designed for high-speed racing. There were too many children, making any kind of speed dangerous. If you thought a dog lead was bad when caught in your wheel, imagine the mess a small child can make.

Despite the good tarmac, the cycle track was a long way off the ground, and the wind was in our faces, which made cycling surprisingly hard work. Bike Buddy seemed to whiz along at a good pace, but I found it quite difficult and started to drag behind a little. Bike Buddy was great when he led, because he kept up a good pace. In fact he got gradually quicker and quicker, but never once looked over his shoulder to see if I was keeping up. He said this was because of a bad neck. I wasn't convinced! I thought it was because he just didn't give a damn.

Just as we left the cycle track to rejoin the minor roads, disaster struck. Bike Buddy said he was having difficulty peddling, and thought his tyre was going down. I told him not to be so silly and it would be alright, but eventually he persuaded me to stop to take a look, and he was right.

I'd always known he was right, but didn't want to accept the inevitable first flat tyre of our expedition. Unfortunately it wouldn't be our last.

Our first effort was to simply pump it back up. The tyre wasn't completely flat, so perhaps it had been deflating slowly over the last few days. We used the new super-duper pump I'd purchased specifically for the journey. The same pump I'd shoved up Bike Buddy's bottom the day before, to help him stand up straight. What a pump! This pump was going to earn its money over the next couple of weeks. I wiped the end clean, and handed it to Bike Buddy.

A few miles further on and Bike Buddy complained that the tyre was going flat again. We decided to stop and mend it properly rather than risk damage to the wheel rim. I took the opportunity to phone my dear wife, and tell her about our good progress. It was now three in the afternoon. I informed her that we would probably arrive in Tetbury within the next hour, despite the puncture. Some hope!

As Bike Buddy mended his inner tube, a couple of old ladies walked towards us in the lane. We were miles from anywhere, down very quiet country lanes, and two ladies who didn't look as if they could walk much more than a couple of hundred yards appeared, strolling round the corner. They stopped to say hello, and asked where we were going. When we told them, they asked if we had a bucket they could throw some money in.

A bucket? A bucket? How the hell are we expected to cycle holding a bucket? Do I look like a circus performer? Perhaps they expected me to have it strapped to the back of my bike. I have to be honest I think the constant chink-chink may have driven me slowly insane.

I told them it was difficult to cycle holding a bucket, but I would be glad to carry their donation in a plastic wallet I was using for the job. They very kindly made a donation.

Within minutes of seeing the kind old ladies, a man appeared from the opposite direction with a very mean looking dog. This dog was unleashed, and heading our way. I was a little wary of its small beady eyes, so took a step closer to Bike Buddy. I was safe in the knowledge that Bike Buddy was older and fatter than me, and I could easily out sprint him if need be.

The dog got to within a few yards of us, and stopped. I thought to start with it was deciding which one to eat first, but in fact it was scared. The dog couldn't muster enough courage to walk past us. It obviously hadn't seen two nutters in luminous yellow t-shirts before, and didn't know what to make of us. The owner arrived and, despite many attempts to pull the dog past, in the end he had to pick up this enormous whimpering beast and carry him. One of the funniest sights I have seen in my life, and one I will not forget for a while.

It didn't take Bike Buddy long to mend his inner tube and we were soon on our way again. We would be in Tetbury very soon!

What was that phrase about good ride in the morning? Here it comes again. Unfortunately, the afternoon's cycle was a nightmare. Not long after leaving the scaredy-dog behind we started a climb up a very steep and long hill near Doynton. At the top we joined the B road. Bike Buddy studied his map, and pointed off to the left. Off we went, throwing ourselves down the other side of the hill. The downhill stretch was lovely, six miles long, smooth, fairly steep decline, and we were cruising.

Mistake! Big mistake! It was at this point we spotted the motorway. The motorway that was going the wrong way!

'Hang-on a minute,' Bike Buddy said. 'It's not the motorway going the wrong way, it's us!'

Bugger! The only word to describe our feelings at this point. Now if you drive six miles in the wrong direction, you are slightly annoyed, but just turn round and go back. A little extra fuel cost, which most of us wouldn't even consider. On a bike it is a little different. Six miles the wrong way means a detour of twelve miles just to get back to where you started. Twelve miles is a hard hour's cycle. That hurts! What made this one worse than most was that we had come downhill for six miles, which meant we had to climb back up for six. Not a very nice thought, but we had no choice.

Now this is where we noticed something very strange. As soon as we realised we were going the wrong way, the heavens opened. Rain pummelled us, soaking us from head to foot, making the experience ten times worse than it would have been otherwise. Remember this moment, for over the next few weeks you will notice that every time we go the wrong way the heavens open. It was as if the Lord himself was giving us advice.

Now we were going to be late. Bike Buddy realised we still had a good twenty miles to do before reaching Tetbury, and it was already five in the afternoon. We were already later than I had said we'd be, and we had another two hours cycle to complete. We were going to be so late! My wife and Shrimp (that's Bike Buddy's wife, or should I say, my mother-in-law (don't tell her I called her shrimp)) were going to be so worried! We couldn't phone them anymore, unless we phoned the Bed and Breakfast, because neither of them had mobile phones. At least, the only mobile phones they did have were in our panniers. Besides, it was still raining, and we just wanted to get there and not stop to make numerous phone calls.

We put our heads down and pumped on the pedals as hard as we could. Once we reached the top of the hill, our original starting point twelve miles earlier, the road returned to a gradual decline in the right direction. The wind was now on our backs, and we quickly got up to a good twenty miles per hour. We were flying - long may it last.

The B road was pleasant apart from the rain, but we were getting tired, and we soon realised we had once again hit the wall and were feeling it badly in our drained legs. Then we came to the A46. Oh what a joyous thing to see!

We didn't need to actually join the A road, we just simply wanted to get across. Unfortunately this was easier said than done, because this wasn't a road, it was a wall of solid traffic - a wall stretching in both directions in a continual stream to the edges of the universe.

The wall was moving at a steady sixty miles per hour, and there were no holes in the wall. Each vehicle was just another car in the wall. Hey, that's a good line for a song:

Another Car in the Wall
We don't need no hesitation.
We don't need no car control
No politeness on the highway
Driver – leave those bikes alone!
Hey, driver – leave those bikes alone!
All in all it's just another car in the wall.
All in all you're just another car in the wall.

After what seemed like an eternity waiting and praying for a gap we suddenly realised nobody was going to let us across. The rain was pouring down, we were soaked through to the skin, our legs were tired, our arms were tired, our bodies were tired. We were physically and mentally drained, and nobody would let us across the road. We had to do something, if nobody was going to let us across, we would have to push our way through.

We heaved our bikes up onto the grass bank, and started walking against the traffic. After a few yards we stopped, turned the cycles round, and rested them on the road ready to cycle with the traffic. The cars still moved in a continual rush, so we just pushed off.

'I'll follow you,' I shouted, 'just wait for my signal.'

With the traffic flying past our right shoulders, I looked behind and very forcefully thrust out my right arm. Bike Buddy was ahead, waiting for instructions. The car behind forced his way past, the next one slammed on his brakes and pulled in behind me. Now I'd stopped one there was no way I was going to let him past. We had our gap.

'Okay, now move to the middle of the road,' I yelled.

Bike Buddy could only just hear me above the constant drone of traffic, but he nodded and obeyed.

There was a turning area in the middle of the A road, which we could use as our halfway mark. Bike Buddy wobbled, and nervously pulled out ahead of me. The first part of the plan was in operation. One of us might die, one of us might be so badly injured we'd wish we had died, but for now, we were part way across the A46.

We pulled into the central reservation and came to a standstill. Now all we needed was a kind driver to slow down and let us across the other half. Yeah like that was ever going to happen, and then what would we do? We were now stuck in the middle of the A46 with nowhere to go and no way of getting to either bank. While we waited, we dismounted our bikes in a desperate bid to look hopeless and play on the hearts of a kind motorist.

Bike Buddy doesn't like traffic. He has an in-built fear of being crushed by a metal fortress. Can't think why! Unfortunately Bike Buddy was getting more and more nervous. The traffic now flying past on both sides, and no escape from its constant whine. He was perspiring; I could see through the rain that he was actually sweating with fear. I had to do something otherwise Bike Buddy was going to throw himself in front of a car just to get across. The cars were constant, the rain was pouring and we felt very vulnerable standing in the middle of the A46 with cars whizzing past in both directions.

I lifted out my drink bottle, full of orange juice and water, and took a swig. I was going to offer Bike Buddy a drink, to calm him down, when he moved to a new level of panic and screamed at a driver, 'For God's sake let us cross.'

The driver stuck his fingers up, and kept going. The driver, who had his window down despite the rain, and who had passed Bike Buddy but was still to pass me. In what could only have been a fraction of a second, I instinctively aimed my orange and water mix at his open window and squirted. The juice flew out of the bottle and, as the car passed, made a line from his windscreen, across his open window and along to the rear of his car. The driver, with his mouth still open as he shouted abuse at us, took the juice full in the face. A direct hit!

Bike Buddy was completely oblivious to what I'd done, and so, it seemed was everyone else. Unfortunately the annoying driver was not. For he had orange juice in his eyes, which momentarily blinded him as he flew along the waterlogged road at sixty miles per hour.

Now, it is interesting to see how people react when driving a car blind. Some might touch the brake to slow down, others might continue in a straight line until their sight comes back. Mr Annoying Prick slammed his foot on the brake pedal, the car skidded on the wet road, left the carriageway and finally came to a rather abrupt stop thanks to a stone wall. Oops!

While this was happening, Bike Buddy had been given the all clear to cross the road by a kind driver who had spotted us in the road. He had slowed down enough for us to cross. Bike Buddy ran for it, I looked just in time to do the same, drink bottle still in my hand. No time to mount the bikes and pedal, just run and push. I have never run so fast in my life, and hopefully I will never have to again.

The driver who'd let us cross had only been two cars behind Mr Annoying Prick. Luckily for him, his kindness meant he was now going slowly enough to come to a standstill rather than pile into the back of the man who had just flung his car off the road. Even the car directly behind Mr Prick had somehow avoided him and the truck coming the other way. In fact, everyone was fine, continuing with their lives, other than Mr Prick who was lying in his car facing the stone wall.

Bike Buddy heard the crash as we crossed the road, and looked back in horror. I didn't say a word. The kind driver stopped to check on Mr Prick, and slowly so did a few other people. I told Bike Buddy we should just go because we hadn't witnessed the crash and it was pouring down with rain. He agreed, mainly because he didn't like cars and didn't like getting wet.

I checked Bike Buddy was alright. He said yes, but didn't look it. His face was ashen, sweat was dripping down his brow, and there were tears in his eyes. I had come very close to losing him there. This concerned me greatly. Partly because I was growing increasingly fond of Bike Buddy. Partly because he was my father-in-law and my wife would kill me if anything happened to him. Partly because I knew we had to cycle up between Manchester and Liverpool and that area would have even more traffic. But, I think, mainly because I knew if Bike Buddy died I would find it extremely difficult pulling his dead-lardy arse all the way to John O'Groats on my own.

We climbed back on our bikes and pushed off towards Tetbury. I might have just killed a second man, but it was an accident, like the first. I hadn't meant to kill him, just soak him in juice. Besides, cars have airbags especially for these kind of accidents, I was sure he would be okay.

From the A road to Tetbury we just got wetter and wetter, but the pouring rain just inspired us to go faster, and we made pretty good time.

At 6.30pm a door opened in our desolate world, and a small sign appeared with the word of our dreams written across it - Tetbury. We'd made it. We were soaked through, we'd cycled 71 miles, rather than the 53 expected, and we were shattered. But tonight we would party.

We cruised around the corner, with the rain still beating down on us and smiled. In hindsight, my earlier phone call, the one to say we only had eight miles to go and would arrive before 4pm was probably a little premature and a tad over-ambitious. I wouldn't make the same mistake again. Thankfully my wife and Shrimp had just arrived. They were very concerned we hadn't been there when they'd turned up, but hadn't had too long to worry.

Recalling the day, I realised we'd had our first puncture, but more concerning, I'd noticed earlier that the headset on my bike was coming loose. I'd asked my wife to bring the headset spanner with her, which she did, and I tightened it up, but really you need two headset spanners to do it properly and I realised I would have to go to a bike shop to get it sorted. Today had been hard going, 71 miles while carrying fully laden bikes up and over the Mendip Hills was a long way.

The Bed and Breakfast was very pleasant. We had two double rooms with private bathrooms upstairs above the restaurant, although our poor bikes had to spend the night in the back yard, with no shelter from the torrential rain that hit us that evening and night.

We ate in the restaurant below the Bed and Breakfast. The meal was delicious! Something the husband obviously took great delight in preparing. I started with fritters, followed by duck and then meringue, and a little sip of wine. I decided I deserved a sip, I would save a full glass until later. Bike Buddy downed a couple of pints and then drank wine until it came out of his ears. This pact was going really well!

After filling our stomachs it was time to retire for the evening and I decided to take the opportunity to get some sympathy from my wife. I explained how much my backside was hurting. I told the story of the horrible weather, the nasty car drivers and the hill we'd turned the wrong way at. I was particularly proud of my aching bottom. I showed her, much to her dismay, the two red blisters on my bum. Sympathy passed quickly and soon turned to laughter. Personally I couldn't see the funny side, however, she had brought my air-saddle with her. My trusty air-saddle which could be stretched over a normal bike seat, inflated with a bike-pump and made into an armchair type of construction. A day of comfort was on the cards tomorrow!

Even with my lover lying by my side, I still couldn't fall asleep. I thought about the arse in St Columb Major and Mr Annoying Prick in the car. Had I really killed them both? I'm not a vindictive man, but something was taking hold of my body and causing me to hurt other people. At this rate, I was going to be a mass murderer by the time I got to John O'Groats. Now there's a thought!

DAY 7: TIRED LEGS AND BALLOONS – TETBURY
TO WYRE PIDDLE

We woke up in the morning to a full English breakfast. I stretched my Airsaddle over the top of my normal saddle and pumped it up with the 'super-pump'. Now, that was what I called a comfy saddle. Today I would be mostly sitting in comfort.

I tightened my headset again. I'd been told for some time that I had a screw loose, and finally there was confirmation. At 8.30am, we said goodbye to my wife and started off on our way. For the day Bike Buddy would have his Domestique, and wife, Shrimp cycling with us.

For those who don't know, Domestique is the term used in the Tour de France for the lesser cyclists. That sounds a bit unfair, after all they'd all whip my arse in a bike race. What I mean is, they are the cyclists whose main aim is to help their man win. They cycle up the mountain in front of their leader, dragging him up the hill. They are the ones who chase down the opposition and sit on their back wheels, slowing them down. Something particularly useful for long journeys.

Today Bike Buddy had a Domestique. Bike Buddy's Domestique would help pull him up the hills, she would chase me down if I tried to make a break. She would sit on my back wheel and slow me down. Today would be a hard cycle for me. I had no Domestique. My Domestique had gone home in the car. I would have no mountain specialist to help me climb and no sprint specialist to help me sprint. I was alone!

Unfortunately Bike Buddy's Domestique had fresher legs than we did. She was built like a whippet and would be difficult to catch on the hills. She hadn't cycled over three hundred miles, a third of the way up the country, and she didn't have red blisters on her backside, which prevented her from sitting properly on the saddle for more than a few seconds at a time. I did! Bike Buddy did!

Despite the Airsaddle, today was hard going. It was only a short day, and we would arrive home in good time, but nonetheless it was hard. Perhaps it was the long day before, or just an accumulation of long days, or perhaps it was the way we had to watch Domestique sprint up every incline as if training for King of the Mountains. Bike Buddy and I found it demoralising. We found having a fresh cyclist with us like being kicked in the head by a steel capped boot. Tiredness seemed to ensnare us, pulling at us from all sides, dragging us backwards, weighing us down like the shell of a tortoise.

One thing we did have over our new companion was an ability to cope with traffic. Well that's probably not quite true because Bike Buddy hated cars, but that was nothing compared with Domestique. Domestique panicked whenever a car was in sight, and then this panic from Domestique seemed to spread to Bike Buddy, who became increasingly aware of his own mortality. This meant they bickered like little school children for most of the day. It went along the lines of:

'You're going too fast.'

'No I'm not, it's you, you're going too slow.'

'You're not indicating properly, turn your hand fully.'

'Why are you so slow down the hills?'

'Why do you have to cycle so quickly up the hills?' etc etc.

I'm sure if I'd cycled with them both for more than a day, I would have banged their heads together on more than one occasion. In fact, I might have even considered a little dog-crap coffee for them. As it was, I let it lie.

Domestique seemed to have read the script slightly wrong. Every climb we came to she sat on the tail of either myself or Bike Buddy. For those of you who don't cycle, this gives the leading bike the feel of dragging an extra body up the slope. It is extremely hard work. Whether this is because of breaking air streams or simply psychological I'm not certain. All I know is, it makes climbing much more difficult. It is always easier to follow someone when you cycle, particularly up a hill. Domestique was using this to her advantage, unfortunately Bike Buddy and I were in no fit state to pull her anywhere. Bike Buddy eventually broke the silence, in his normal subtle way.

'Will you stop cycling on my bloody arse,' he casually shouted.

'Here, here,' I replied (under my breath of course). You have to bear in mind that our companion may be Bike Buddy's Domestique but she's also my mother-in-law and she scares the crap out of me.

The climb out of Tetbury seemed to go on forever. One bonus for me was the comfort of my saddle. I could sit down at last. We climbed up and up, then dropped quickly back down, before climbing again. This continued for all of the morning as we made our way between major towns and cities and across the edge of the Cotswolds. Finally we dropped into Winchcombe for lunch. What a drop! It was like jumping out of an aeroplane without a parachute and just a bicycle to cling to. The road seemed to fall forever, going ever down into an abyss.

I tried to pump-brake as we descended, but was too afraid to let go of the brake and my hands started hurting from the effort. I realised I would have to release the brakes soon, and as soon as I did I would certainly plummet to my doom. Suddenly I could see the village ahead of me - Winchcombe. A very welcome break for my aching hands. I pump-braked like I'd never pump-braked before (well since the fall into Mousehole on the first day anyway), and arrived shaken but still in one piece. The drop into the village had been a white-knuckle ride, and made me all the more certain I needed to change my brake blocks as soon as I got home.

Winchcombe was a very peaceful and pretty little town. The descent was definitely worthwhile, just to potter down the relaxed roads, picking our way through the quiet hum of tourists. We found a lovely little pub for lunch, and stepped inside.

Continuing my cheese consumption world record attempt, my meal consisted of a very large ham, soft cheese and pineapple sandwich. For once Bike Buddy did not copy me. I think having Domestique with him confused his little mind. He just didn't know whether to copy me or his wife, in the end he let Domestique order for him.

After filling our bellies, we set off for the short trip home. The cycling was excellent. Flattish roads, warm sunny weather, and roads we knew. It made so much difference when we knew where we were going. No stopping at each turning, no doubling back on ourselves. Oh, the bliss!

With only about five miles left to cycle before getting home, I started to hear sniggers from Bike Buddy and Domestique behind me. At first I ignored them, assuming they were laughing at a joke together, but as the sniggering continued I started to get self-conscious. Were they laughing at me? Surely not! What could possibly be so funny? I slowed down, so they caught up.

'What 'ya laughing at?' I casually asked.

'Nothing,' came the reply. The kind of 'nothing' you get when you walk into a room at work, everyone goes quiet and you ask what they were talking about. The kind of 'nothing' you get when you ask a fourteen-year-old what they got for their birthday. The kind of 'nothing' you get when you ask your wife what she'd like for your anniversary. In other words, a bloody lie!

'I'll ask you just one more time,' I said putting on my most serious schoolteacher voice. 'What are you laughing at?'

'Your bum,' said Domestique.

The shock of this statement sent a shiver down my spine. Had my boil grown back already? Was it visible through my shorts? Besides, after all the cycling and swimming I did, I reckoned my bum was pretty pert.

'What about my bum?'

'I think you've sprung a leak,' came the not-too-pleasant reply.

I looked over my shoulder, and down at my bottom. Lo-and-behold a small section of my Airsaddle had started to balloon out. The balloon was pushing out between my butt-cheeks like an over-inflated, must hurry to hospital, do not stop whatever you do, case of haemorrhoids. There was obviously a weakness in the rubber, and the pressure from my bottom was forcing the air to push against the weak part of the wall. If I wasn't careful it was going to explode with my bum still on it. I started to cycle quicker.

We turned towards Pershore and I suddenly became very aware of my ever-growing ballooning backside. I knew people in Pershore. I had lived there for fifteen years, and now I'd moved back to within a couple of miles of the town. People would recognise me! People would see my bottom! People would laugh!

The balloon was made worse by the fact that I was wearing black lycra shorts. The Airsaddle was also black, so the balloon looked like it was actually coming from inside my pants. People would think I'd got a growth on my bum! Despite the fact I did, I didn't want them to know. I'd become a laughing stock. I'd be forced to wear a bell round my neck and ring it whenever I went out. I would be called 'leper' and 'freak'. I'd be known as the 'man with two bums.' I cycled quicker.

As we cycled through Pershore, I decided to stop for a Post Office stamp. Pershore was the nearest Post Office to home, I'd had thousands of letters stamped from Pershore, but I still wanted the stamp in my book.

Pershore is a working town famous for its fruit and vegetables. The abbey looks down over the local park and is a splendid sight when lit up at night. It is only moments like this when you notice all the things you normally take for granted. What's even better is that I live in a village called Wyre Piddle. Wyre Piddle not only has Pershore near by, but it's also got a great name. When I phone people up to order things, they always ask me to spell Wyre Piddle. I always reply, 'Wyre – W Y R E, and Piddle - as in, go for a piss.' It often takes a while, but it eventually gets through.

We arrived home at 2.30pm, my saddle and thankfully bottom still intact. A very welcome short day, and plenty of time to recover ready for the next.

As soon as we got home, and after greeting my children, who I hadn't seen for a week, I quickly whizzed my bike round to the local cycle shop to get the headset tightened properly. At the same time I purchased some new brake blocks and a gel saddle cover, which I hoped would bring relief for the days ahead since my Airsaddle was now defunct.

Once I got back home I spent a good hour cleaning the bike thoroughly, and changing the brake blocks. The bike hadn't had a good clean for a week and I'd survived up until now by wiping it with a cloth and spraying it with lube every morning. It deserved a good clean. The old brake blocks had worn away quite significantly, so it felt safer to start with new ones. However, in my attempt to install the new blocks, I realised I was having increasing difficulty pulling the lever to activate the back brakes. I hadn't fitted a new cable, and I didn't have one, but I did realise that in my hurry to clean and lube everything, I'd sprayed lube on a self-lubing cable - something that forces it to seize up.

What a stupid invention that is - self-lubing cables. It's all well and good inventing these things but you need to tell someone. It's all very well having self-lubing cables but not good that they seize up if you accidentally get lube on them. I now had only one set of brakes. My back ones were like car brakes after all the brake fluid had run out. Perhaps they would loosen up with use. Perhaps they wouldn't and I'd die trying to stop the bike.

Oh, how nice it was to be home again, even if it was for only one night. I'd missed my family so much. Eating out at pubs all the time was very pleasant, but after a while I started to crave some good, healthy, home-cooked meals. All the rich food I'd eaten, not to mention the mountain of cheese I'd consumed, was making me crave something plain, something ordinary, something I would normally eat, day-in, day-out. A nice jacket potato, that's what I needed, a nice jacket potato and salad. The food was one thing I was desperate for, but the other luxury was to be able to sleep in my own bed. Comfort, warmth, just the right size pillow and nobody snoring in the bed next to me. Perhaps by the end of these three weeks I'd be unable to sleep without Bike Buddy's pneumatic drill noises at night. I think not!

It had been a short day, with us clocking up only 50 miles, and cycling for just five and a half hours, but I was knackered. I settled into bed early, and switched on the television. Nobody was around, and I quickly turned to the news. I hadn't really seen any news for a week, apart from the brief glimpse of St Columb Major. I wanted to know if there were any more details. I wanted to know if they were searching for a mad-man on a bicycle, but nothing appeared. There was nothing about St Columb Major and nothing about a car driving off the road near Tetbury. I realised people in the country were too concerned about bigger things. Nobody cared if I was on an accidental killing spree. Perhaps I wasn't going to get caught after all. I was still a free man, with nothing to worry about apart from a few worms in my blood supply, and an ache in my bum.

DAY 8: ROUND THE WREKIN - WYRE PIDDLE TO
WELLINGTON

L ittle did I know when I woke up in the morning of the nightmare to come. In some ways this would be our worst day. Not our longest, not our wettest, but certainly the most emotional, and probably the most depressing.

We set off at eight o'clock. No cooked breakfast today, but a good healthy bowl of muesli, some toast, orange juice and a coffee. Certainly better for me than most breakfasts I'd scoffed in the last week.

Bike Buddy and I decided to rearrange our panniers a little. I added some long fingered gloves, Bike Buddy swapped over the maps. I changed the used disposable camera for a new one, Bike Buddy left behind his spare tyre (the one for his bike rather than the ones round his stomach). I put in a fresh pair of boxer shorts (the pair I'd had for a week were starting to smell a little less fresh) and two fresh pairs of socks. Bike Buddy added the heavy-duty shirt I'd persuaded him to lose in Penzance. We also sorted out a pile of fresh clothes to be sent to Callander for a week's time. The idea being we could then send back our smelly underwear and have some fresh for the final week. Finally, we were ready to go. My pile of clothes weighed little more than a teaspoon of sugar, Bike Buddy's weighed equivalent to four full bags, but he didn't seem to care.

A friend from the village who'd cycled John O'Groats to Lands End the previous year asked if he could join us today. This worried me slightly. He'd cycled the trip in just over a week, compared with our slow crawl for three weeks. However, he had ridden on a racing bike with a back-up vehicle, which I considered cheating slightly (my apologies to anyone else who has, or is planning to do the journey the same way).

Lance Armstrong turned up on his trusty racing bike and instantly my worry jumped to a new level. Bike Buddy and I were slow. We got where we wanted to, but we took a long time doing it. Carrying luggage made life difficult, and having a racer next to us would make the previous day's annoyances of a fresh rider pale into insignificance.

To make matters worse, Domestique came too. Double joy! Two fresh-legged cyclists carrying little or no luggage, ready to race alongside us while we pulled and tugged our tired bodies and heavily laden bikes along the tarmac. Luckily the early part of the day would be hill-less so Bike Buddy and I could tazz along at a reasonable pace. We also knew which way we were going, which made life easier.

For the first time since leaving Lands End we started out in the morning with the wind blowing in our faces. Lance told us it had been like that for him all the way down the country, and if he cycled it again he would go from south to north. We told him he was a jinx.

Feeling tired, and concerned for the hills ahead, I asked Lance what he felt was the worst part of the journey. I was confident his answer would be the hills of Devon and Cornwall, and when he replied with my expected answer I knew I'd feel enormous relief.

Alas! Lance answered, 'Definitely Cumbria.'

I was shocked. What could be so bad about Cumbria? Why was it the worst part of the journey?

He continued, 'The wind was blowing in my face as I came over the brow of the hill and I could hardly keep the pedals turning, even on the descents.'

Now I was depressed. Okay the wind probably made life more difficult than it would have been, but we still had to cycle through Cumbria, and I didn't want it to be the worst part of the journey. I wanted Devon and Cornwall to be the worst part of the journey because we'd already cycled them, and therefore could feel confident in our ability to succeed. Now I felt depressed! I felt like saying, 'Well if it's worse than Devon and Cornwall, we may as well pack up our bikes now, because I can tell you buddy-boy, there ain't no way I'm going to make it. And if I don't make it, old Bike Buddy here ain't got a hope in hell.'

I refrained, and kept my negative thoughts to myself. I couldn't depress Bike Buddy, he was suicidal enough at the best of times without me adding to his woes.

Lance said farewell at Flyford Flavell. It was probably just as well, because he was starting to really annoy me by then, and based on what happened to the last two people who'd really annoyed me, it was probably best we parted company. As a parting shot, and to prove how slowly we'd been going so far, he decided to cycle off into the distance and then wave us through.

God, I was feeling depressed. Everyone cycled quicker than me. Everyone on the planet was a better cyclist than me. I sucked at cycling. I was to cycling what a supermarket own-brand bean was to the baked bean family.

Lance waved us through and the remaining three cycled on to a small café at Jinny Ring. The plan was to stop at Jinny Ring for a drink before finally saying goodbye to Bike Buddy's Domestique. Unfortunately we arrived at Jinny Ring at 10am, and it was still shut. Not wanting to wait around for half an hour we said our farewells and watched Domestique turn and ride back home. I was fairly confident that would be the last time I saw my mother-in-law. Her sense of direction was about as good as a magnetic compass passing beneath a set of power lines. There was no way she would get home. She would probably cycle for thirty miles, turn the corner and be surprised to see Jinny Ring in front of her again. I half expected to meet her further up the country. Just as we pulled into John O'Groats there she'd be, 'Sorry I took a wrong turn.' But for now, we were alone again.

My rear brake cable was really starting to play up. I needed an increasing amount of pressure to force the brake blocks onto the wheel. Not a good sign! It wasn't too bad while the roads were flat, but the hills around Wellington were going to cause some problems. Perhaps it would loosen as I rode, either that, or I was going to end up in a ditch somewhere between Jinny Ring and Wellington. Please Lord, loosen my cables.

Despite the depression brought on by two fresh-legged cyclists, now they'd gone, Bike Buddy and I were in reasonably good moods. The jubilation from seeing our families had given us renewed hope.

It's amazing how you lose all perspective when you're alone in a strange place, but in a county we knew well and on the way to Bike Buddy's Aunt and Uncle, today was going to be a good day. Yeah, right!

As we continued through the country lanes, I persuaded Bike Buddy we should play a memory game. This would take our minds off the ache in our legs, and while away the time as we pedalled.

The game was 'If I ruled the world I would ban...' It was very similar to 'I went shopping and I bought...' In other words, the first person names one thing they would ban, the next person has to repeat what is said and then add another item to the list.

I started off. 'If I ruled the world I would ban motorcars.'

This was a particular favourite of both Bike Buddy's and mine. We didn't like cars. We both owned cars, we both used cars to get from A to B, but we didn't like them. We didn't like the way they were abused by people. We didn't like the fact that everyone had to have one, and because everyone had one the government felt they didn't need to bother with public transport. Cars are great toys, don't get me wrong, but they are slowly choking the country to death and nobody seems to give a damn.

Bike Buddy continued the game, 'If I ruled the world I would ban motorcars and drivers.'

You can see where this is going can't you? I suppose he had a point. He didn't like traffic, but it wasn't the cars that caused the problem, it was the drivers. Drivers in this country seem to be immune to the outside world. They drive too quickly in the ice, they drive to close behind each other in the wet, and they completely ignore cyclists. What is the first reaction of a driver when they see a cyclist? It's to push the foot down on the accelerator a little harder to get past before it's too late. Too late for what? If only people would just occasionally consider using the brake pedal. I know cyclists can be a pain in the butt. I for one cycle further from the pavement than I need to, but I do this for a reason. I do this because it forces drivers to slow down rather than squeeze past me and leave me in the gutter. Believe me, the gutter is not the nicest place in the world to cycle.

I continued, 'If I ruled the world I would ban motorcars, drivers and train delays.'

Yep, you got it, that journey down to Penzance was still playing on my mind. I also use the train to get to work occasionally, and half the time it's late or cancelled. If only we could sort ourselves out. If only we could sort out the transport system in this country. It needs someone to put their hands in the air and say, 'Enough, stop!' Then we could look at the country, put together a plan for the future and get on with our lives again, safe in the knowledge that there is a future for our children. Unfortunately if it was me who said, 'Stop!' I'd just get run over by a passing motorist.

Bike Buddy's turn, 'If I ruled the world I would ban motorcars, drivers, train delays and pot-holes'.

Good one, Bike Buddy! Not sure who invented pot-holes, but they were a stupid invention. Why is it that local councils feel they can mend a road by sticking a bit of tarmac in the holes? Are they mentally retarded? It's the same principle as throwing gravel over the road and calling it resurfacing. It doesn't work! If they'd ever been to France they would see what a properly surfaced road is like. IT'S SMOOTH. I get very annoyed with gravel throwers. On a bike it's bad enough anyway without having gravel flicked up in your face as you cycle. The gravel engulfs your tyres and is almost impossible to stop on. The road then goes bumpy because the cars and lorries have flattened the gravel unevenly and then we get more pot-holes. The money saved through this temporary resurfacing is soon lost because it has to be resurfaced again much quicker, and all the cars use up more petrol because the road isn't smooth. So councils, if you're listening, 'NO! YOU CAN'T SPEND OUR MONEY THROWING GRAVEL ON ROADS. IT DOESN'T WORK. IT AIN'T BIG AND IT AIN'T CLEVER – SO PACK IT IN'. I feel better for that!

Next, oh yes, it was my turn. 'If I ruled the world I would ban motorcars, drivers, train delays, pot-holes and St Columb Major.'

It had to be said. The pit of the world has to go. Nothing a good atomic bomb wouldn't sort out.

Bike Buddy, 'If I ruled the world I would ban motorcars, drivers, train delays, pot-holes, St Columb Major and blackberry bushes.'

'Controversial.' I said, 'I like blackberries, why ban them?'

Bike Buddy replied he didn't want to ban blackberries, just the bushes because they snagged his clothes. Wasn't quite sure how we were going to get blackberries without the bushes, but there may be a way. Perhaps test-tube blackberries?

Okay, let's be a little more sensible, my turn, 'If I ruled the world I would ban motorcars, drivers, train delays, pot-holes, St Columb Major, blackberry bushes and steep hills.'

Bit obvious that one wasn't it?

Bike Buddy, 'If I ruled the world I would ban motorcars, drivers, train delays, pot-holes, St Columb Major, blackberry bushes, steep hills and horse poo.'

This was at exactly the same time he cycled straight through a huge pile of horse manure on the road. Thank God he had mudguards otherwise he would have sprayed himself, his bike and me with crap.

Things were now starting to get a little tricky. Our concentration was broken occasionally by pot-holes, horse manure, and the odd car. We had to stop talking for a while whenever we got to a steep incline, and then had difficulty hearing each other as we sailed down the other side. My turn, 'If I ruled the world I would ban motorcars, drivers, train delays, pot-holes, St Columb Major, blackberry bushes, steep hills, horse poo, and cafés not opening early enough.'

Bike Buddy, between puffs of air as he climbed a hill, 'If I ruled the world I would ban motorcars, drivers, train delays, pot-holes, St Columb Major, blackberry bushes, steep hills, horse poo, cafés not opening early enough and bad manners.'

Why was I not surprised Bike Buddy gave this one. He hated people with bad manners. He hated children who couldn't behave. He hated adults who couldn't behave. In fact he hated most people whether they behaved or not, but at least bad manners gave him an excuse for hating them. Perhaps he should have said, 'Good manners', because without bad manners what would he have to moan about?

My turn, and one that ended up being the last in the game 'If I ruled the world I would ban motorcars, drivers, train delays, pot-holes, St Columb Major, blackberry bushes, steep hills, horse poo, cafés not opening early enough, bad manners and baked beans.'

I don't like baked beans, I think they taste like crap. I hate it when everyone has baked beans with a jacket potato and I have to go without. I don't know who it was decided that beans go with tomato ketchup. They don't, so stop eating them.

We turned the corner and saw a mammoth hill going up into the distance. It was time to end the game, because neither of us could remember what had been said before.

I have to admit to being a little annoyed that the game ended so abruptly. I was saving my trump card for later - supermarkets. If I ruled the world I would most definitely ban supermarkets.

'Why?' I hear you cry. Well if you're willing to listen I will tell you. They are annoying. They swap things round on the shelves just when you're getting used to where they are. They use their strength to squeeze the producer so much that the poor producer can barely afford to live. After all supermarkets are only there to make money. My view is that Mr and Mrs Supermarket are not very nice people. My view is they just like our money. Why do we trust them? Why should we believe anything they say? 'Oh yes it's one hundred percent pure British beef,' doesn't mean it's made only from beef farmed in Great Britain. It means there are traces of beef in it, and the animal spent a couple of hours visiting Britain before it was slaughtered.

While I'm on the supermarket front, what is it with supermarkets and fruit? Why do they insist on offering us all fruit all year? We've always survived before on eating apples in the apple season, strawberries in the strawberry season and blackberries in the blackberry season. Now we can buy them all the time, but there is a problem - supermarkets can't get the fruit all year round so they have to put them in huge oxygen-free stores to keep them looking good. At times of non-production, when the supermarkets decide, this fruit is then shipped from the oxygen-free warehouses to the shelves, and hey-presto, we have good-looking fruit all year round. It looks good, it even smells good, BUT IT TASTES LIKE CRAP. There is nothing worse than getting a nice juicy orange home, taking the trouble to peel it and then putting the first piece in your mouth only to discover it has about as much juice as a sun dried tomato. If it happens to you, take it back (half-eaten). In my view, unless we all start to take them back, Mr Supermarket will continue to sell us crap.

You might be starting to get the impression that I am easily pissed off. You're probably right!

After a good morning's cycle we stopped at Kinver in a pub for lunch. Kinver was a strange little village. Nearby were some rock houses, reportedly still lived in up until around 1970, but not anymore. Shame, given the housing shortage in the country.

The rain was just settling in, so we pushed our bikes up against the pub wall and covered them with Bike Buddy's rain cape. It was Saturday, but I had a craving for a full Sunday roast. This probably wasn't the best thing to eat in the middle of a cycle journey, so I settled for a pork baguette with roast potatoes and gravy. Delicious! Bike Buddy ordered the same, returning to his pre-Domestique rituals and then added his usual pint of beer.

We dined gracefully, enjoying the food and laughing about the cyclists we'd left behind. We didn't see Domestique cycling aimlessly past the pub window, which came as a bit of a shock because I was sure she'd have taken a wrong turn by now.

After lunch the cycling was hard going. Just near Halfpenny Green we found a new approach from the local council to road resurfacing. They'd used cobblestones rather than tarmac. At least I think they were cobblestones. The pummelling of the saddle through my new gel cover and onto my butt cheeks seemed to suggest they were cobblestones, but closer examination showed it was just the worst bout of road resurfacing ever seen.

The rain started to lash down as we climbed up and down the roads towards Ironbridge. The town itself was built on a steep hillside and the narrow lanes were jam packed with tourists, despite the poor weather. We stopped at the first iron bridge we saw, climbed off our bikes and took a photograph. The rain was lashing down, and we didn't want to wait any longer than necessary, so quickly got going again. A few metres further on and we came across another iron bridge. This one actually was the real Iron Bridge, so we stopped again, unpacked the camera and took another photograph. Did you know the real one was built by the Darbys and gave its name to the town, which beforehand was known as Coalbrookdale? No – well you do now.

Abraham Darby was the first man to use coke instead of charcoal for smelting, which made the mass-production of iron possible. How he managed to get coke to light I'll never know. It must have been really tricky, because whenever I've poured coke onto fire in the past it has always put it out. I sometimes wonder how people think of these things.

'I know let's use coke rather than charcoal, son.'

'Good idea our dad.'

I wonder if they used expensive coke, or that cheap supermarket own brand you can buy now.

To be honest I would have been happy with my photo of not-Iron Bridge. I could have gone through my life satisfied that I'd visited Iron Bridge, oblivious to my mistake. It wouldn't have bothered me! I would still be able to sleep at night, but apparently Bike Buddy would not. (Looking back, perhaps stopping Bike Buddy from sleeping wouldn't have been a bad thing – no more snoring.)

We passed a number of other iron bridges, until I realised all the bridges looked the same to me through the dark, damp weather. With the rain beginning to soak its way through to my skin, we didn't wait around long enough to take in any more views. My shorts were soaked, my socks could now be wrung out, and my feet squelched as I pushed down on the pedals, and we left Ironbridge behind and continued up towards a little hill called the Wrekin.

I had long heard the phrase, 'It's a long way round the Wrekin,' but never knew where the phrase came from. Now I knew, and I can confirm, it is a bloody long way round the Wrekin. So far, in fact, that I'm sure the road builders gave up in the end and sent the road straight over the top. What a climb! The Wrekin is no Mount Everest, not even a Ben Nevis, but everything else around it is so flat, that its 407 metres seem to go on forever. We were tired, wet and feeling lonely as we eventually reached the summit. The views were poor, mainly because it was chucking it down with rain and we quickly began our descent into Wellington.

The rain continued to fall as we arrived in Wellington, and a quick glance at my watch, showed me it was just after 4.30pm. It had been a hard day's cycling. An early start, and a fairly early finish, but the hills had been hard work and made worse by the weather. Wet panniers weighed more than dry ones, and carrying the extra clothes on our backs made us sweat more.

Tonight we were staying with Bike Buddy's uncle and aunt, but before I could relax I had one more cycle trip to complete. I'd told a friend from work I would pop over to the cricket pitch because, just by coincidence, his team were playing away at Wellington on the same day we were there. I unloaded my panniers and popped across the road to the cricket ground, which was only about a hundred yards away. To my amazement, and despite the rain, they were playing. Luckily, being captain allowed Pam to halt the game and come over for a chat. He said I looked tanned. I said I was just weather worn.

The other cricketers stopped and watched as we continued our brief conversation on the boundary. They must have wondered what on earth this smart cricket captain was doing talking to the luminous dross on his bike, but talking to a friend about the toughness of the journey helped me to gain renewed enthusiasm to complete it. How could I go back home if I failed?

Not only were we with family tonight, but they also knew how to spoil us. Mushroom soup, chicken, potatoes and salad, cream cakes and ice cream followed by cheese and biscuits. We had full bellies again, and thanks to Auntie's tumble drier we also had dry clothes for tomorrow morning. We dried and cleaned our bikes ready for the morning, and they spent a pleasant night in the garage, safe and dry.

Despite my cricket-gained renewed eagerness to continue, when I phoned my wife that night I lost all will to carry on. She sounded really depressed, just like I was feeling. She said she was lonely, and I said I was coming home. She objected and said the only thing keeping her going was that we would make it to John O'Groats. Bless her! Although my thoughts about giving up remained, my dear wife had made me more determined to complete the journey after all.

I decided to soothe away my worries with a nice long soak in the bath. I discovered when I entered the bathroom that Uncle and Aunt had a walk-in bath. One of those baths that is really just a great big tub, rather than an actual bath, and can be used as a shower or a bath.

Unperturbed, I filled the tub with water, checked the temperature very carefully with my elbow, just like they teach you for bathing children. I got my towel ready so I didn't have to splash water across the floor when I'd finished, I grabbed the shampoo, and I found some soap. I undressed, and carefully folded my clothes on the toilet seat. I was ready for my bath. With the water at a nice level, and full of bubbles (oh I do like a good old bubble bath to soothe my aching limbs), I carefully unfastened the door in the bath.

Now, is it me, or is this a stupid invention? Obviously when you open the door the water falls out. Unfortunately I didn't think about it until it was too late. With the door slightly ajar water started to trickle out of the broken seal. I tried to hold the door back, pushing it back towards the bath, but the weight of the water was too much. I couldn't hold it. It was like trying to hold back a river that had burst its banks - it wasn't going to happen. The bath water was going to go where it wanted to go. I screamed for help. I needed more muscle. Luckily Bike Buddy heard my cries. Luckily there was no lock on the door, and he was able to push his way in and help me force the door back into the gap. I closed the lock and sighed with relief.

I turned to thank Bike Buddy, who looked at me very strangely. Was it the idiotic thing I'd just done which made him look so confused? Was it the inch of water now covering the bathroom floor? Or was it the fact that I was completely naked, and his uncle and aunt were now standing in the doorway staring at the scene in front of them? Probably a combination of the three. I asked them to leave, and mopped up the water as best I could. I then climbed over the wall of the bathtub and settled into my lower-than-planned warm bubble bath.

DAY 9: THE DAY OF THE EXPLODING TUBE -
WELLINGTON TO MIDDLEWICH

Today was supposed to be an easy day. The mileage was low, only planning to do around 50 miles, and the terrain was going to be flat. Probably the flattest day of the entire tour. It was Sunday after all, a day of rest. We wouldn't exactly be resting, but hopefully recouping a little.

We set off at a good time again. It was difficult to steal ourselves away from Bike Buddy's relatives, but we had to get going. Thankfully the rain had stopped, so we set off in relative luxury, dry clothes, clean bikes and with full stomachs.

After saying our farewells we set off on our short cycle journey. Now there are a few things to remember about today. Firstly, it was a Sunday. You can bet your life that if you need to buy something it will always be a Sunday. Secondly, Bike Buddy is a big man, seven-foot-three and weighing in at just shy of twenty stone (okay that's probably a slight exaggeration, but he had been eating well on this trip). Thirdly, if you buy inner tubes you should buy thick ones. Thin ones are crap! Finally, it's probably a good time for me to remind you that the spare tyre Bike Buddy had carried all the way from Lands End to home, had remained at home two days ago.

A few miles down the road we arrived in Great Bolas. What a great name for a town!

'Where do you come from?' one could ask.

'I come from Great Bolas,' would be the reply. What a great reply! It's like saying, 'I've got massive testicles.' 'I'm from Great Bolas. Bloody Great Bolas.' Actually now I've said it a few times I'm starting to think of it more as something you would raise from your throat when you've got a bad cold. Perhaps it wasn't such a great name after all.

Anyway we'd arrived and Bike Buddy decided to have his first puncture of the day. We stopped by a bus stop, and Bike Buddy flipped his bike upside-down ready to carry out the repairs. He decided to use a new inner tube rather than mend the puncture. He could mend the puncture that evening (yeah right!)

The inner tube he was using was a Specialized lightweight one. Note the name - lightweight. He'd bought it from the cycle show a few weeks ago, and thought it a great weight saving device. After all, compared with a standard inner tube this weighed at least an ounce lighter. Whoopee, what a weight saver!

He took out the old tube, no problem. He fitted the new one, no problem. He started to pump up the tyre. At this stage a cat decided to come and see what was going on. It sat next to Bike Buddy and just started grooming itself. Bike Buddy pumped away. The cat groomed. Bike Buddy pumped harder. The cat groomed. Bike Buddy pushed with all his might. The cat groomed. Bike Buddy's tyre exploded in his face. The cat groomed. This cat must have been completely deaf. Bike Buddy jumped a good foot of the ground, which is quite a feat for a man weighing twenty-two stone. I jumped almost as high myself. I'm sure I would have jumped higher, but at the time I was having a wee by the side of the bus shelter. I jumped far enough to ensure both my legs and shoes got sprayed in urine. Never mind, I could wash them down when I got to the Bed and Breakfast that night.

With the inner tube now in tatters, Bike Buddy had no option but to repair the old one. This too was a Specialized lightweight. I suggested, in the most sarcastic voice I could muster, that he try not to trap this one between the wall of the wheel and the beading of the tyre.

After another few minutes the bike was ready to roll. We now had no spare inner tube for Bike Buddy, because the spare I was carrying didn't fit his bike.

The repaired inner tube lasted about three miles to Stoke Heath. We were now in trouble since it was Sunday and no cycle shops were open. We mended the already mended inner tube and got on our way.

Only another couple of miles and Bike Buddy was complaining of a flat tyre again. My God this man was a pain in the arse! Did he not know how to mend an inner tube?

After another repair we then managed to cycle for a number of miles. Suddenly we heard a clap of thunder behind us. I turned to see darkness behind us, but the clouds were moving quite slowly and I reckoned we could out-run the rain. We cycled as hard as we could. We could see the lightening brighten up the sky, we could hear the thunder - crack-crack boom, crack-crack boom. If we looked over our shoulders we could see the rain. It was so close we could smell it. There was no way we wanted to get caught in this thunderstorm, it looked a biggy. We pushed harder on the pedals, but could still hear the thunder behind us - crack-crack boom, crack-crack boom.

It was coming after us. As we got quicker, the rain got quicker. As we pushed harder, the thunder hit harder - crack-crack boom, crack-crack boom. It was coming, but we were flying.

Suddenly, Bike Buddy swerved across the road and came to a shuddering halt. I skidded in behind him. We were nearly at Longslow and the tube had punctured again. We couldn't escape now - there was nowhere to hide. We were in for a drenching.

Thinking about what not to do if you're caught in a thunderstorm, we climbed over the fence and hid under the biggest tree we could find. Sensible aren't we? Bike Buddy had turned his bike upside down, and left it in the middle of the road. His waterproofs were in the panniers and he was still holding his back wheel. I had pulled my bike over the gate with me, and was huddled with it under the tree. Thunder and lightening cracked around us. We were in hell!

Trees are great for sheltering from a quick shower. Unfortunately when the shower continues for more than a few minutes the tree becomes saturated and just lets the water straight through. In fact it helps join raindrops together and make them bigger. So you no longer get a little wet, you get soaked from each and every drop. We were getting soaked, but undeterred, Bike Buddy mended his inner tube for the twenty-eighth time. Very soon we would not only be out of spare inner tubes, but also out of puncture repair patches. Oh what a great day we were having.

I suggested to Bike Buddy that given his enormous bulk, which was now around twenty-four stone, he might want to swap the rear tyre and inner tube for the front ones. His rear wheel was the one continually puncturing, so it seemed a sensible suggestion to me, since the rear wheel was taking some seventy percent of his considerable weight. Bike Buddy agreed, and in the pouring rain we swapped the tyres over. I prayed this decision would gain us precious miles.

Once the rain stopped, we got back on our bikes and continued on our way. After all the punctures Bike Buddy had suffered, it was like cycling on a time bomb. We both spent more time looking at his tyres than at the road, but despite the trepidation we finally arrived in Nantwich and stopped for lunch. Bike Buddy's

Uncle and Aunt had very kindly made us cheese and ham sandwiches for the day. I felt happy to be back on the cheese diet, having insisted they buy some cheese to fill between my bread.

Nantwich was pedestrian-only in the centre, although we cycled in anyway. We were pedestrians, just pedestrians with transport. Part of the town had been destroyed by a firestorm in 1583 and rebuilt. The centre was very pretty, with black and white timbered houses, numerous window boxes ablaze with colourful flowers, and it was rather pleasant to sit in the centre eating our lunch.

Since we'd now arrived in a town, it seemed like a good idea to purchase some new inner-tubes for Bike Buddy. I made this suggestion to him, but he pointed out it was Sunday. I told him Halfords would be open – it was always open on a Sunday, and Bike Buddy told me he hated Halfords. I told him not to be so fussy, but he refused, so we ate our sandwiches, and held our faith in the repaired and swapped over tubes currently installed.

After lunch the cycle was straight down the main road to Middlewich. It wouldn't take us long, but the road was busy and Bike Buddy got scared. He was a bit of chicken if the truth be known. For a man his size, you'd have thought he would have been a bit braver.

Main roads were the only time Bike Buddy actually cycled in front. This was because I always volunteered to cycle behind, that way if a car was going to hit one of us, it would hit me first. This didn't bother me, because I was such a bastard when I cycled and hummed along at least three feet from the pavement. This tactic meant a car had to go on the other side of the road to overtake me and by forcing the car across the road I knew I had more chance of survival. They couldn't just whiz past, they normally had to slow first, take their time and only overtake when the way was clear.

Unfortunately this tactic only worked in thirty miles per hour zones. When the cars were going any quicker they didn't give a toss how far out I cycled, or what was coming the other way. If they closed their eyes they could get through any gap. Despite this problem, I still felt more comfortable following Bike Buddy. He always cycled faster when he was in front, and besides, being a superhero, my wings were like a shield of steel, so nothing could hurt me anyway.

By 3.30pm we'd arrived in Middlewich. Funny little town! To me, it seemed nothing more than a main road. A disappointment really, but with our record for punctures it was good to be at our destination and in a town that would hopefully contain a cycle shop that would open in the morning.

As we searched for our accommodation, the heavens decided to open again and give us one last deluge before we got to our rooms. Despite the punctures, it had actually been a fairly good day's cycling.

The Bed and Breakfast itself was rather pleasant, although the owners were very strange. They sounded German, and kept raising their right arms up to their heads when they spoke. I decided we needed to keep an eye on them.

I was relieved to know we would be sleeping in single rooms again, not wanting a repeat of Bike Buddy's snoring. The rooms themselves were on the ground floor and had their own front door. They reminded me of halls of residence at college, although there were only four rooms in total. The bikes were also in for a treat tonight, staying under the carport.

It was Sunday and I hadn't sent a postcard home. I'd become accustomed to sending a postcard home every day. I'd even started sending one to my old work colleagues every other day, plus a couple to my parents, one to my brother, one to my gran, one to my cat, one to my parent's cats, one to my gran's cat and one to my brother's dead cat. Okay this last one might have been a bit sick, but I was on a roll and nothing could stop me sending postcards. Nothing, that was, other than a wet Sunday in Middlewich. Nowhere sold postcards.

I decided to go in search of a shop that was open. I trundled off in the pouring rain in search of a piece of cardboard with a picture on it. After dodging the showers as best I could I managed to find a newsagent. I searched the shelves, but Middlewich just wasn't postcard country. Can you imagine being in Devon or Cornwall? Every shop sells postcards, we even saw postcards in the fish and chip shop in Penzance, but Middlewich just wasn't holiday material. Perhaps, Middlewich – the town on a road, couldn't think of anything to show on a postcard anyway.

Determined not to be outdone, I made do with a simple white postcard. It had no picture, it didn't even have the name Middlewich on it. It was just plain white, like a very expensive piece of cardboard cut to the right size. On the way back from the newsagents I tried the garden centre. Still no postcards! What is wrong with people in this part of the country? Do they not want anyone to know who they are?

Today's postcard would be very boring. I got back to the Bed and Breakfast, disappointed and soaked to the skin. Unperturbed, I sat down and wrote my postcard. 'It's raining, I can't find a postcard, so here's a blank piece of card. Missing you. Love Matthew.' Job done, now time for a shower.

The Germans' shower was actually very nice, although they wouldn't allow us to have hot water, so we had to make do with cold. There was no soap, obviously to avoid us grinding it up and trying to poison them with it, or attempting to use it to make our bodies slippery to slip out between the window bars.

Strangely, the Germans didn't give us a key for the front door, and told us to be in our rooms before ten o'clock. At ten o'clock all the electricity would go off, and we were to be in bed. No lights at night, no television past ten o'clock. If we wanted to read we would have to use torchlight. There was no electricity past ten o'clock. I was a little concerned by this. Bike Buddy took it in his stride (well his limp anyway).

Outside my bedroom the Germans had a big fishpond. To start with I thought they had exotic fish, but soon realised they actually kept piranhas in the pond. Perhaps that was where the previous guests ended up.

I asked mein gastgeberin where we might eat this evening. To start with she couldn't understand, so using my best German, I asked again, 'WHERE CAN WE EAT FOOD TONIGHT?' To ensure she understood I did little hand gestures as I spoke. 'Where can', I opened my arms wide and held my palms up, 'we', I pointed at Bike Buddy and myself, 'eat food', I did a little knife and fork movement with my hands and then lifted the pretend fork to my mouth, 'tonight', I gave up with this one. If she didn't get it by now we had no hope.

Mein gastgeberin looked at me very strangely, then speaking very slowly she replied, 'You can find ze pub at ze bottom of ze road.' I nodded thankfully, and lifted my outstretched arm up to the side of my head. She seemed to warm to my natural charms and quietly tutted before turning away.

Bike Buddy and I set off in search of food. I strode forcefully down the road, Bike Buddy limped behind. Actually it wasn't true that I strode down the road. I was starting to have a little problem. As I spent more and more time on the bike, my hamstrings were getting shorter and shorter. So much shorter, that occasionally when I stopped at junctions on my bike I started to topple sideways in an effort to reach the floor with my foot. At first I thought maybe I was shrinking, but then realised it was just I could no longer straighten either of my legs. I was getting a cyclist's walk. In other words, I walked like I'd been in an horrific accident and undergone months of physiotherapy on my badly mutilated legs. I walked like a bloke who'd drunk ten pints of lager and was in terrible need of a crap.

After a few hundred yards we came across a public house. This would be our feeding station for the night, and we settled down into the chairs. On the table next to us were the ugly family. The ugly family not only were incredibly ugly (you might have worked that out from their name, which was a little harsh, but fair), but also had Tourette's syndrome. This meant every other word needed to be a swear word. (Since I've been brought up with a strict Christian background there is no way I can use such bad language, so I shall just have to replace the f word used with another, perhaps 'ficken', and the s word with 'scheibe'. My apologies for my French - okay, I know it's German!)

Anyway their dinner conversation went something like this:

Ugly dad, 'This ficken fish tastes like ficken scheibe.'

Ugly mum, 'Aye ficken ugly dad, me ficken pasta tastes like ficken scheibe too.'

Ugly son, 'Aye ficken ugly dad and even ficken uglier mum, me ficken fish fingers even force fifty ficken four ficken fingers from ficken flies.'

At this statement, Bike Buddy and I looked at each other. What was it the ugly son had said? Could he make sense at all, or was he so encapsulated with his Tourette's syndrome that the other words just weren't important? We listened on. After a good ten minute conversation between them, we counted sixty-seven scheibes and more than five hundred and thirty fickens. Was this some kind of record? I decided to find out, so went over to ask them.

'Would you ficken excuse me for disturbing your ficken scheibe meal, but did you ficken know you'd broken the ficken record for saying ficken in a conversation more ficken times than any-ficken-one else?'

The ugly family just looked up and stared at me. Ugly dad finally broke the silence, 'Could you go elsewhere if you're going to use foul language?'

I gave up!

We continued with our ficken meal of chicken kiev and chips. Bike Buddy and I seemed to get drawn into the swearing rituals of the table next to us. We couldn't stop swearing at each other, until finally, just as we were finishing our main courses, the ugly family decided it was time to leave.

After stuffing ourselves again, Bike Buddy pushed himself up from the table, and we limped and hobbled back to the Bed and Breakfast. We had to get back before ten o'clock. No electricity after ten o'clock! Perhaps they needed it to electrocute the other guests?

As we walked I started up a conversation with Bike Buddy. The ugly family had really got to me, and I just wanted to know whether Bike Buddy felt the same way. I told him I thought people like them should be shot. I said I couldn't believe there were honest, hard-working people in this world who were suffering one way or another, and yet slobs like the ugly family seemed to get by with no concerns or worries in the world. Bike Buddy agreed. In fact he added to my venom with his own. He said he would like to teach them a lesson. He said he thought they deserved to suffer for ruining our quiet meal.

I was silent for a moment, trying to think what we could do. They'd left the pub before us, only a few minutes before, but there was no way we knew where they were, or where they lived. That is until we passed a house and heard the delicate tones of the ugly family inside. I looked at Bike Buddy and he looked at me. I asked if we should teach them a lesson, but Bike Buddy said he was too tired and we should go back to our room. After all, the door would be locked at ten o'clock. I shrugged, and we wandered on. Damn, for a moment, I thought I'd got him onboard.

Bike Buddy had suffered four punctures today. We'd only cycled 48 miles, so that worked out at 12 miles per puncture. Not very good was it? Bike Buddy also complained that his knee was giving him jip. This wasn't unusual. Bike Buddy liked to complain that his body was falling apart, mainly because it actually was falling apart, but I was sure by the morning he would be as right as rain.

We entered our little prisoner of war camp and settled into bed. I drifted off to sleep, much happier than last night. I had things to think about. I had Bike Buddy's knee to concern me, and plans to work out of how the ugly family could be made to suffer.

DAY 10: THE WICKED WITCH FROM THE WEST –
MIDDLEWICH TO CLAYTON-LE-DALE

Mein gastgeberin ordered us to breakfast before eight o'clock. The day had started with her shining a light into our eyes to wake us up, and ringing a bell in our ears. She was a very strict lady, but I wasn't going to argue.

It was strange to walk out of the building, round the house past the piranhas and back in through the kitchen for breakfast.

If you've ever seen piranhas they are very strange creatures. They seem to float in the water as if dead. Not a movement, no blinking, no breathing, nothing. I wanted to know what they would do if I put my arm in the water, but not wanting to risk injury I tripped Bike Buddy as he walked by the side of the pond. Quick as a flash I leapt on his body, and forced his arm into the water. I expected it to be ripped off, but to start with there was nothing. Then suddenly the piranha leader darted forward and took a chunk. It was at this stage Bike Buddy screamed, but I managed to hold him for a while. After the leader the next piranha darted in for a bite, then the next and so on. One by one they took a chunk, like queuing for a MacDonalds. Bike Buddy didn't enjoy the experience, but my view was he could do with losing a little flab from his arm.

When we re-entered the building, mein gastgeberin was waiting for us, looking at her watch. We sat down for breakfast and mein gastgeberin served up the full German breakfast - egg, bacon, wurst, sackgasse gast. It was very nice, and after filling our tummies, and then going through the normal morning rituals we made our way to the carport to find our bikes. Disaster struck. Bike Buddy had a flat tyre. Why was I not surprised? Obviously today was going to be very similar to yesterday. Luckily today was Monday and perhaps, just maybe, we'd be able to find a bike shop that was open. Bike Buddy set about mending his umpteenth puncture.

I told Bike Buddy I was going to pop down the road while he mended his tyre, just to post my postcard. I'd thought long and hard the night before about how I could get the ugly family, and now my wicked streak was taking over my body and forcing me to head towards their house. I had a plan, and was determined to make it work. I'd seen it done before, by Eddie Murphy, and thought it would teach them a lesson.

I crept up to their house, it was light, but there was no movement inside. The windows were still drawn, perhaps they were having a lie in. Okay, it was Monday, but the guy probably didn't have a proper job anyway, so had no reason to get up. I casually walked up to their car, an old Ford Escort, and slumped down next to the exhaust. In my pocket I had two bananas, which I slowly threaded into the end of the exhaust pipe. They were big bananas, and needed to be forced in. I pushed quietly and quickly then stood up as if I'd just tied my shoelaces. I walked to the end of the road, crossed over, and then walked back. If my plan worked, the car would now kangaroo down the road, and they'd have to go to the garage to get it fixed. I was sure nobody would think to look in the exhaust, and so it would probably be an expensive repair, and a complete waste of time. That would teach them!

After receiving a helping hand from the wind for most of the last nine days, today the wind decided to blow straight into our faces. This wouldn't have been so bad but following the chicken kievs last night, whoever was at the back kept getting wafts of garlic. Rather unpleasant!

Middlewich, despite being a town on a main road, did not have a cycle shop. Undeterred, and with Bike Buddy's tyre mended for the time being, we set off on our way. After a gentle jaunt along to Knutsford we decided it was probably a good idea to buy some proper inner tubes.

Knutsford was rather pleasant. Despite the traffic, with two roads slicing the town into a number of thin sections, it had an oldie-world feeling to it. We found the cycle shop, but, for some reason, the owner had decided against opening on Mondays. What kind of shop doesn't open on Mondays? Where the hell were we - the middle of the outback? For goodness sake man, open the bloody shop. After banging on the door for a number of minutes, the owner finally arrived. He was confused as to what we were doing, but not wanting to miss out on a sale he invited us in.

Typically the cycle shop had every size inner tube apart from the one to fit Bike Buddy's bike. I found this a little odd, since Bike Buddy had a standard racing bike with standard racing bike tyres. I mean, what kind of a cycle shop doesn't open on Mondays or sell racing bike inner tubes?

Finally the owner came up with a solution, and Bike Buddy bought some 'slightly too big' inner tubes.

Despite the new tubes, Bike Buddy refused to change the ones he'd installed that morning, and we continued on the old ones for as long as they would hold out. We cycled from Knutsford towards Tatton Park. The park was still locked, so I left Bike Buddy at the gate, and cycled back to Knutsford to get a Post Office stamp for my book. As I arrived back at the park entrance the gates were just being opened and we cycled in.

Tatton Park was wonderful, very few cars, and those that appeared were travelling slowly. The park was part of a large estate with a grand Georgian mansion at the centre. We didn't visit the mansion. We weren't even sure we could. Instead we trundled along by the lake, with people windsurfing across and aeroplanes flying overhead following their take off from Manchester airport.

I hate aeroplanes. I think it's the height thing. Aeroplanes scare the crap out of me. Before I lost my job, I'd occasionally flown to Glasgow on business. I would climb on the aeroplane at Birmingham airport and wait for the safety announcements. They scared me. Oxygen mask – no problem, emergency exits – no problem, seatbelt – no problem, but then the stewardess showed us how to put on our life jackets. It was at this point I always got confused. We were flying straight up the centre of the country after all, so I would stand up and shout, 'If we need a life jacket - we're going the wrong way.'

Tatton Park was home to a large herd of deer who seemed very interested in two bright yellow nutters on bikes. The deer watched as we cycled towards them, then all turned as one and darted off in another direction. Halfway across the park, Bike Buddy decided he needed a bladder stop. He found a tree and used the squirrel principle of urination. In other words, if he couldn't see the car drivers they couldn't see him. I took the opportunity to play with the deer. I cycled towards them, they stared at me. I cycled to the left, they all followed with their eyes. I cycled to the right, they all followed with their eyes. None of them thought about making a run for it, but they all wanted to know what I was doing, and why I was dressed in such a stupid outfit. I tried to explain, but to no avail. Have you ever tried to explain Lands End to John O'Groats to a herd of deer? I don't recommend it.

We left the park and not much further down the road, Bike Buddy decided it was time to refill his now empty bladder, so we stopped for a cup of tea. It was quite chilly, and warm food and drink were definitely in order. We found a small park in Glazebrook, and just for good measure opposite the park was a shop selling tea, coffee, hot pies and sandwiches. We bought some pies and drinks and sat in the park warming our insides. Simple but pleasant.

Just as we were about to mount our metal steeds once more, Bike Buddy noticed his front tyre was flat. What a shocker that was! It was so unusual for Bike Buddy to get a flat tyre I just couldn't believe it. Okay, it was going to happen, and it was going to happen sooner rather than later, so no big surprise. Bike Buddy flipped his bike over again and confidently unwrapped his brand new inner tube. This one would keep him going for a little longer, we were confident about that.

Bike Buddy had been whinging most of the morning about his knee. He said he'd hurt it the previous day sprinting to beat the traffic at a roundabout, and the pain was getting worse. To start with I assumed it was just another Bike Buddy ache and pain, but after two hours of complaining I started to think it might be more serious. Usually he only complained at set intervals throughout the day, but this new pain had caused him to complain randomly, and the random complaints were getting closer together and lasting longer. A bit like labour pains. To start with he was having labour complains every half hour, and each would last a minute, but now, not even halfway through the day and his labour complains were every ten minutes and lasting for a good five minutes. This did not bode well for the rest of the trip. Luckily the route today was fairly flat, but he would need to nurse it through the day and just hope for the best. Either it was going to get gradually better or it was going to get gradually worse (what a stupid statement). Only time would tell.

After the open countryside of Tatton Park we slowly made our way between the cities of Liverpool and Manchester. The traffic was horrendous, cars were flying past us at break-neck speeds, although to be fair, the drivers did seem more wary of cyclists than others we'd met who liked to use the country lanes as racetracks.

Leigh was huge, much bigger and busier than either of us had expected, and all the cities and towns seemed to blend together in this part of the country.

After Leigh we skirted around the side of Bolton, and continued through the next heaving metropolis. Oh how different from the open countryside we'd experience just days before.

Part way through the day and Bike Buddy's labour complains were now almost continuous. I did believe he was actually going to give birth out of his kneecap. Perhaps it would be a little kneecap. I wondered if it was going to be a boy or a girl? Still, I tried to ignore him.

We climbed up an unexpected long drag towards Blackburn and this just about finished Bike Buddy's knee off for the day. At the top of the climb we stopped in a picnic area and surveyed the damaged area. His knee was very swollen and red. I suggested we strap it up with something, and, as if by magic, pulled a triangular bandage from my first aid kit. Bike Buddy then pulled some duct tape from his panniers, and we had the makings of a great bandage. I strapped his leg up, first with the bandage and then with the tape, and off we went.

Surprisingly it actually seemed to work, and Bike Buddy momentarily stopped complaining and said it felt better. Perhaps his kneecap had come loose, and just needed to be strapped back on.

After a short break, and a quick refill from our chocolate supplies, we set off towards Blackburn. We had now covered more than five hundred miles on our journey, and were nearing the halfway mark. I was feeling confident that the second half of the trip would be easier than the first half, but was worried about how long our temporary fix of Bike Buddy's knee would last.

I had to complete this trip. This was the one aim in my rapidly vanishing life, and I didn't want to stop because of Bike Buddy's body. However, taking one tiny step at a time, I was confident we could finish the day because we were only a few miles from our destination, and most of that would be a leisurely descent into Blackburn city centre.

As we fell into Blackburn, I realised Bike Buddy had started grumbling again. The strapped knee was beginning to hurt again, and he was in considerable pain. Perhaps better than he had been at the top of the hill, but still in pain. (Before you are too sympathetic please bear in mind this is the same chap who is laid up in bed for three months every time he catches a cold.)

As we hit the outskirts of the city, we turned a corner and there in front of us was Ewood Park, the home of Blackburn Rovers Football Club. Quite how they'd managed to fit such a large building into such a small space was beyond me. There were houses surrounding it on all sides, and smack bang in the middle was a football stadium. We turned another corner and saw a sight I shall never forget - a small dog trying his best to reach high enough to give another, much larger, dog a good rogering. The poor wee fella was having great difficulty, up on his tippy-toes, trying to mount the bitch in front of him. This was the middle of Blackburn town centre. Where were the owners? Perhaps the owners were doing exactly the same thing round the next corner - a seven-foot prostitute and scruffy haired dwarf. We peddled on quickly, just in case.

Blackburn was surrounded by lovely countryside, but when we ventured a little further in I realised it had been taken over by the industrial revolution. The centre itself was actually rather pleasant. Lots of people, as expected from a large city, but some fine buildings amongst the bustling shopping centre.

Leaving the cycle route briefly we decided to take a detour straight through the middle of Blackburn shopping centre. Now I know cyclists are selfish bastards and have no respect for drivers or pedestrians, and they jump lights, cycle the wrong way down one-way streets, cycle on the pavement, run over little old ladies and such like, but we decided to walk and push our bikes through the shopping centre. Wouldn't do much for our street cred as lycra louts, but I didn't want to run over any little old ladies today, I was too worried about Bike Buddy's bionic knee.

We found a Superdrug containing a pharmacy and I waited outside with the bikes, while Bike Buddy hobbled in. He was gone quite some time and I was getting all the attention outside. People were stopping and staring, reading the 'Lands End to John O'Groats' written on the back of my t-shirt (which I have to admit I did push in their faces a little). Men were, 'Ooing', children were, 'Arring', and young women were swooning.

'Are you really cycling from Lands End to John O'Groats?' one asked.

'Oh yes,' I replied.

'Brilliant,' came the response.

There was something about being in the middle of the country that made Lands End to John O'Groats such an amazing feat. I suppose being so far from both ends made it seem a tremendously long way. When you're living only ten miles from one end, it somehow doesn't seem so far.

For a while I was hoping Bike Buddy wouldn't come out, because the way he looked and the way he was walking the onlookers would soon say we didn't have a hope in hell of making this journey. They would probably be right!

However, after a few minutes Bike Buddy did reappear. He had a proper bandage and some freeze spray. Apparently because he had high blood pressure and used beta-blockers, he wasn't allowed deep heat and had to rely on freeze spray instead. Not sure why freezing something was the same as warming it up, but I suppose the pharmacist knew best.

Having relinquished the route to find a drug store, we now had great difficulty finding it again. We cycled in what we thought was the right direction only to find ourselves at a motorway junction with nowhere else to go. If only we'd brought a compass. With no other choice, tutting and cursing, we turned around and headed back to Blackburn centre.

It was now rush-hour. Oh the fun of cycling in a major city during rush-hour. I loved it, it was like making love to a beautiful woman – not! After visiting the drug store again, and then seeing Ewood Park again, and then seeing the drug store, and then getting to the motorway again, we stopped. I looked at the map, Bike Buddy looked at the map. I tutted, Bike Buddy cursed and we turned around for a second time.

Eventually we found the road to Clayton-le-Dale. This was where we were staying tonight, Clayton-le-Dale. I then recalled speaking to one rather unpleasant woman when I'd booked up all the Bed and Breakfast's, and she was the one who owned the Bed and Breakfast at Clayton-le-Dale. As such, I wasn't really looking forward to tonight.

As we cruised into the village, I pulled up alongside Bike Buddy and commented on the Bed and Breakfast owner, 'I bet she tells us off for being late, or early or having mucky clothes or something.'

Bike Buddy was shocked by this comment, and said there was no way she would. I was confident I was right. After all, I'm a man, and therefore I'm always confident that I am right.

We arrived at the traffic lights in Clayton-le-Dale and met the main road. We didn't know which way to turn so flipped a coin and opted to go left. After a couple of miles we left the village and saw the sign for Clayton-le-Dale coming from the other direction. We stopped, looked at our maps, turned our bikes around and headed back in the other direction.

As the cars and trucks whizzed past our heads, our tyres popped in and out of the gutter, and our bodies swayed as each vehicle overtook, we made our way back into the heart of the village.

A while later we passed the junction we'd come out of, and a mile or so after that, we still hadn't found the Bed and Breakfast, so we assumed we'd gone wrong, and turned around.

When we found the same village sign again we stopped. Not wanting to risk our lives on this extremely busy main road more than necessary, I decided to phone the owner.

It is always difficult to hear someone on a mobile phone. It is more difficult when you are wearing a cycle helmet, and even more difficult when cars and lorries are flying past you at a rate of knots. I told her we were below the village sign. She told me we couldn't be. I assured her we were. She told me we couldn't be. I could hardly hear her, so I sighed deeply and hung up.

How the hell could she know where we were? How could she possibly know we weren't under the sign, which was right above our heads? Who gave her the Goddamn right to tell me I was wrong? Oh the fun we were going to have tonight! The jollity there would be, the laughter, the buzz of excitement. What a bitch!

Bike Buddy and I turned around for the second time and headed back to the village. We cycled up the main road until we came to the village sign at the other end. Now we had cycled through the entire village and not seen a sign for the Bed and Breakfast anywhere. Perhaps she didn't live in Clayton-le-Dale after all. Perhaps she was just having a laugh with us. Perhaps she really lived in Clayton-le-Dale, Pembrokeshire.

Frustrated and worried for our lives, we asked a chap who was sitting in his garden whether he knew of the Bed and Breakfast. Come to think of it, why was he sitting in his garden? It wasn't like he had a good view. I mean all he could see were cars and lorries trundling past. The noise was horrendous, the ground was shaking and there was smog everywhere.

He pointed up the road the way we had first gone. We set off again, and passed under the village sign that we hadn't been under when we first phoned her. Just one hundred yards further on and there was the Bed and Breakfast. What a bummer!

Not surprisingly the Bed and Breakfast was very noisy. After all it was situated in the middle of a main road so I suppose we should have expected it to be noisy. The building shook when lorries went past.

The owner came to the door and before we'd even stepped inside I won my bet with Bike Buddy. It was as much as she could do to draw breath before unleashing her verbal onslaught, 'Why had I phoned, surely I could see the signs, surely I knew where the Bed and Breakfast was, why did I phone, why, tell me, for God's sake, why?'

I tried to explain, but it was no good, the woman with the extremely long nose could not be tamed. I did not like this woman, she was a 'know-it-all' and extremely unpleasant. If Bike Buddy's knee hadn't been knackered I would have told her to shove her room where the sun didn't shine.

We climbed the stairs to our room, and I looked inside in disbelieve. The room was amazing. It was a twin room, but the whole space given to us was no bigger than a double bed. How she'd managed to fit in two single beds, a chair, a bedside table, a shower, a sink and a toilet, I really had no idea.

Obviously the beds were smaller than normal size beds, which I believe is a trick house building companies use in their show homes. Put in furniture just a little bit smaller than normal and everyone thinks the room is bigger than it actually is. Even with miniature furniture this room still looked small. What made it worse was the fact the shower and toilet were at the end of the room, with just a slither of opaque glass between them and the bedroom. Bike Buddy would be able to see me having a shower. Worse than that, I would be able to see Bike Buddy having a dump. Oh my God!

We took it in turns showering, while the other one turned his back on the shower and pretended to write his diary. I can tell you, it was very difficult to write anything in my diary, or fill in postcards, or do anything, when my mind kept telling me if I looked back I would surely turn to stone. I couldn't stop thinking about the naked Bike Buddy behind me. A large man with no clothes! I couldn't look, I would be tainted, I would be corrupted, contaminated, soiled for life if I ever looked.

It was one of those situations where you know you shouldn't look, you know it will be a hideous sight but your mind keeps asking 'how hideous?' Like when you pass the back of an open ambulance and you want to look inside. Like when you have terrible diarrhoea, but you want to look in the toilet afterwards. I fought the feeling, and refrained from peeking.

After keeping my eyes to myself, having my own shower and getting dressed, we set off for dinner. Tonight we would be dining in the only restaurant within walking distance, a splendid Indian cuisine on the opposite side of the road.

The restaurant called to us as we stood outside our accommodation desperately trying to cross the road. Cars flashed past us in both directions, and a couple of small gaps appeared and vanished before our eyes. We could have starved to death on that pavement. I considered myself fairly nimble on my feet, despite my leg muscles slowly tightening as I cycled up the country, but Bike Buddy was not. He was old and slow and his knee was hanging on by a thread. I could make a sudden burst of speed and zip between the cars to get to the restaurant, Bike Buddy could not. That was, until I pointed out to him that we might starve if we didn't take a risk. He looked at me, he felt his empty stomach, he looked across at the restaurant calling his name, and without a thought he fairly galloped across the road. So much for his bloody knee hurting! I followed.

The meal was absolutely fantastic. The best Indian meal I had ever eaten, and I'd eaten quite a few. The trouble was, Bike Buddy and I had done a deal on meals. We'd decided quite early on that we would alternate paying for food. The idea was one person would pay for all the food in a day, the other person doing the same the following day. Unfortunately this Indian meal was my shout, and it was the most expensive meal we'd consumed so far. I'm not a scrooge when it comes to spending money, but I do like to make sure I've got a good deal. As such, I would have to find another expensive establishment the following night as well.

As we rested our stomachs on our legs, I thought about what we'd just consumed. I wasn't sure cyclists in the Tour de France ate Indian meals when on tour. I didn't think curry was going to sit particularly well on my stomach the next day, I just hoped I hadn't eaten a dodgy one. I also worried that I was going to share a bedroom with Bike Buddy, and I didn't know how his body would react to the very hot curry he'd consumed. I could almost smell the exhaust fumes already. However, to be perfectly honest, I didn't give a damn, I'd eaten curry and I'd liked it.

Having safely returned to our room, I thought about the bitch who owned the Bed and Breakfast. I thought about teaching her a lesson, and bringing her down a peg or two, but unfortunately I was too full to have any useful thoughtful moments other than, 'how much my stomach could expand if it really put its mind to it.'

I lay in bed, the thought of curry running through my mind. I was so full, uncomfortably full, bloated like a really bloated, bloaty thing. I couldn't stop thinking about food. Food, food and more food. I was feeling ill, I was so stuffed, and to make matters worse I couldn't even go to the toilet without Bike Buddy watching me through the window. Tonight I would mostly be dreaming about how full I felt, but after 68 miles cycling, I think I deserved to eat well.

Bike Buddy drifted off to sleep while I considered my stomach, and then as my stomach muscles accepted the increased load, I was able to settle down and relax while listening to the monotone buzzing from Bike Buddy's nose. The noise didn't annoy me as much as it had on previous occasions. I think Bike Buddy was facing the wall for most of the night, and I was able to consider other, more urgent things, like what could I do to make that bitch suffer?

DAY 11: INTO THE COUNTRYSIDE – CLAYTON-LE-DALE TO SEDBERGH

Bike Buddy had a terrible habit of getting up at some unearthly hour in the morning. This morning was no exception. Maybe it was the smaller room that made me notice more, and the fact he was actually standing with his arse in my face while he prated around with the stuff on his bed, but today he was annoyingly early.

The first thing he liked to do was make himself a cup of tea. Now call me strange, but I hated a cup of tea first thing in the morning. It kind of puts a fluffy coating on my tongue before I've even had time to brush my teeth. I didn't drink much tea anyway, much preferring coffee, but to be honest I didn't like coffee first thing when I woke up either. What I really wanted when I woke up was to stretch my arms above my head, scratch my balls, rub my eyes (I know it wasn't very hygienic to do it in that order, but my view was I'd probably scratched my balls while I'd been asleep anyway, so what the hell?) and then slowly get out of bed. I wasn't into having an alarm clock wake me up. I didn't like alarm clocks, they always seemed to go off when I was in my deepest sleep or having my best dream of the night, and I was certainly not keen on being woken up by the arse of Bike Buddy hitting me in the face. This morning, I was pissed off.

After making himself a cup of tea, Bike Buddy decided to repack all his belongings in the noisiest plastic bags he could find. After rustling around for a few minutes while I tutted to myself under the blanket, he turned to me and said, 'Do you always have difficulty getting up in the morning?'

I looked at Bike Buddy, I looked at the clock, and casually replied, 'At ten past five in the morning? Yes I do!'

We sat and waited for our breakfast. Two and a half hours was quite a long time to spend in a single room no bigger than a shoebox.

'You were lucky, when I was a lad we used to dream of a shoebox,' said Bike Buddy.

Well I didn't!

At 7.30am we finally wandered down for breakfast. I gave the cooked breakfast a miss, with my stomach still bloated from the curry from the night before, besides there was only so much fried food I could take. Bike Buddy consumed as much as the witch could offer, and then asked for more.

I was interested to see so many other people in the Bed and Breakfast that morning. All resembled businessmen, who had probably spent days on end in this establishment with no one else for company other than the nasty witch. How could they stand it? How could they stand her? What about their families, and personal lives? Did people just forfeit them during the week to concentrate on work? How odd!

I wondered for a while whether the witch was providing some kind of additional service to her guests. I'm not saying she did, I'm just saying I wondered. It just seemed strange that all the guests were men – every single one of them. And most were on their own. In fact only Bike Buddy and I sat together, the remaining guests all dined in solitude and all had a good rapport with the witch. Maybe she'd cast some kind of spell on them, or maybe she was just a bloody good shag. Urgh!

After breakfast, we watched each other through the square window as we went about our normal morning rituals, and then Bike Buddy sprayed his knee with the ice-spray, and strapped it up with the bandage.

I'd been thinking about how to get the witch back all night and had come up with a little plan. It was something that would be so perfect, and was certain not to end in death. I couldn't kill another one of our hosts – it wasn't good manners.

As we left our room and wandered onto the landing, I suddenly blurted to Bike Buddy, 'You go and pay, I just need to pop back to the bathroom.'

I left him hobbling down the stairs and returned to our en-suite to carry out my plan. I opened the top of the toilet, and looked in at the cistern. First I blocked up the over-flow pipe with toilet tissue and then I unscrewed the float. With no float the toilet would over-flow. What a shame! I was becoming very vindictive, but I couldn't risk my little punishments killing anybody else, so had to stick with annoying things. This wouldn't hurt her, but make her bathroom flood. Instantly the water started to come through the inlet pipe, and the cistern began to overflow.

I put the lid back on, but with a little gap at the end, so the water could flow out, and then I pulled the chain. I needed a little delay to allow us to get away.

We set off on our bikes at 8.15am, and for most of the morning Bike Buddy's knee held up pretty well. He kept stopping and spraying it with the ice-spray, and after the ninth stop I asked him if I could see the can. Looking perplexed he handed it to me.

I read from the back, 'Do not use more than three times in any twenty-four hour period.'

'Oops,' said Bike Buddy.

To be honest, I've always been a little sceptical about warnings on the back of medicine, especially on children's cough medicine. Despite the fact the stuff is made specifically for children under the age of six, the manufacturers still feel the need to include a warning, such as, 'Do not use heavy machinery after taking.' How many five-year olds do you know that could climb up to the cabin of a crane safely after downing five to ten millilitres of cough syrup, let alone actually operate the crane? I mean, honestly!

Thankfully, the inner tube problems of the previous days appeared to have left us behind now that the rubbish Specialized inner tubes had been replaced. The other good thing was the traffic. Ever since we'd turned off the main A-road in Clayton-le-Dale the traffic had reduced considerably. It was amazing how quickly the roads became quiet and the countryside surrounded us once again.

Like so many other days, this section of the route was expected to be rather hilly, but the morning wasn't as bad as I'd expected. Unfortunately we managed to maintain our annoying habit of going the wrong way at almost every turn. The maps we were following for this part of the journey just didn't have enough detail for cycling. I cannot blame Sustrans this time though, because this was our route made up from scratch. The maps we used were just extracts from a standard road atlas really, and it was impossible to tell whether a country lane was marked or not. As a result, we turned up numerous farm roads by mistake because they seemed to be better maintained than the alternative minor lanes.

The sun came out, heating our backs perfectly, as we made our way through country lane after country lane. The birds were singing, the sky was blue and life was pleasant for the time being. Then the pleasant life suddenly turned into a pheasant life, as hundreds upon hundreds descended on us from the hedgerows. They ran back and forth across the road, desperately trying to avoid two strangers on metal machines. If I'd had a gun with me I could have bagged a tasty snack, although my eyesight is not great and I could have just as easily bagged a Bike Buddy with my shot.

One pheasant made a bid for glory by throwing itself at my front wheel. It nearly ended up as shredded pheasant, with the spokes slicing it neatly numerous times across the body. There was nothing I could do but watch in disbelief as it shot toward me, but luckily at the last minute, it changed its mind and turned back towards the hedge. I'm not sure that would have been a pleasant pheasant sight. Wouldn't have done my front wheel much good either!

The countryside was fantastic, but there was just one problem - I needed the toilet. This wasn't an ordinary 'just pop behind a bush for a pee', no this was a full blown 'I must find a toilet and now.' I didn't tell Bike Buddy about the pressure building up in my bowels. What could he do about it? What could I do about it? There were no public toilets anywhere. No public toilets for miles around. We passed the occasional farmhouse and I was very tempted to knock on the door. 'Excuse me. You don't know me from Adam, but would it be okay if I dumped a tonne of pungent waste down your toilet?' Perhaps not! I tried to hold on. I tried to think about something else, but the more I tried to think of something else, the more I needed to go.

It was like the feeling you get on a cold winter's night as you lie in bed. You casually think, just in passing, that you might need a wee. Then suddenly, nothing else matters, you must wee, and you must wee now, but it's cold and you don't want to get out of bed. Then slowly the small wee feeling soon overwhelms your whole body until you ache in your bladder. The ache grows until it is an excruciating biting pain running through your urinal tract, until, eventually, you give in to the pain, climb out of bed, step into the toilet and release the smallest, weaniest trickle of wee ever recorded. Why does that happen?

Anyway, I needed to go and I needed to go quickly. I pulled up alongside Bike Buddy and told him half the story.

'I need a wee, so I'll scoot off ahead and find a tree. You can keep going. If you pass me, I'll just catch you up.'

Bike Buddy nodded in agreement and I pushed down harder on my pedals to give myself some shitting space. I knew I needed to find a bloody big tree so I could squat behind it and Bike Buddy would then be none the wiser about my predicament as he grumpily cycled past.

Just up ahead was a small wall surrounding a wooded area. I looked further up the road and then back over my shoulder. I looked through the wooded area and realised I couldn't penetrate its depths from the road. This was perfect.

I pulled up and leant my bike against the wall. I jumped the wall, leapt over a number of logs and legged it into the wood, no longer able to hold back the urge. Things were coming, and they were coming quickly.

Luckily I'd been carrying some tissues with me, just in case of emergencies. Not toilet emergencies, but to wipe off excess oil if we had to change tyres or replace chains. I suddenly remembered them as I dashed between the trees, and realised I had to go back to my panniers. I turned, looked down the road and saw Bike Buddy in the distance still behind me. I leapt over the wall for the second time and searched furiously through my panniers for the delicate pieces of paper.

Success, the tissues were in my hand, but time was running out. By now my stomach was so bloated and starting to push the waste through. I had to move fast. I turned back and jumped the wall again. Unfortunately, this time my lead leg clipped the top stone and I plunged over the wall headfirst, landing amongst the leaves, with my toe throbbing and my arms grazed. The fall had done little for my dignity, but I knew the urge was still growing, so I picked myself up onto my knees and crawled through the undergrowth.

Finally, I arrived far enough away from the road not to be able to see Bike Buddy. Using Bike Buddy's squirrel technique of 'if I can't see him, he can't see me,' I pulled down my lycra shorts and squatted behind a tree. Relief! Oh, the relief!

I used my tissues, buried my treasure, and turned back round the tree only to come face to face with the farmer.

'What ya doin?' he asked.

'Nothing,' I tried to casually reply.

'You crappin on my land, ya dirty bugger?'

What could I say? I looked him straight in the eye, and told him what any respectable human being would say in such a situation.

'Don't be silly. I just thought I'd dropped something.'

Then I legged it.

Despite the difficulty in making decisions about which road to take, the countryside was spectacular. The wildlife seemed to follow us, with pheasants (many, many pheasants), rabbits, and deer to name but a few. I felt like Noah bringing the animals to the ark, with the numerous wild beasts following us on our way. Like Doctor Doolittle, with his merry gang of furry friends.

After we'd completed about twenty miles it was time for our mid-morning break. Along one of the lanes we were surprised to come across a wooden bench. The bench faced away from the minor lane we were cycling along, and looked out toward the sea. A breathtaking view looking down from the countryside towards the open water. I'm not sure who decided to place this bench in this position, but whoever it was, I must thank you. This is a fantastic place to put a bench. Probably not one used by too many people, but certainly a most welcome resting point for those who find it.

As we rested our weary limbs and stared out toward the countryside and sea before us, Bike Buddy pointed out the motorway below. It was so far away we couldn't hear the normal drone of traffic, but appeared as a tiny line in the distance. Fantastic! This was what cycle touring was all about. This was why we had taken up the challenge of Lands End to John O'Groats. It was times like this we felt a real sense of peace. Silence, just the wind in the trees and the birds singing. Nothing else. No traffic noise, no children shouting, no car stereos. Just peace and quiet.

Bike Buddy and I could have stayed on that bench all day. We recharged our batteries while taking in the view. It was the kind of view we wanted to photograph in our minds and replay over and over again in times of strife, but we knew it couldn't last, and eventually we dragged ourselves away from our haven.

We still had some serious cycling to do, and had only just passed the halfway mark on our journey, but with refreshed hope for the future, we set off towards Caton.

Caton was a small town, or may even have been a village, with just a couple of shops and a sprinkling of houses. We had put 35 miles behind us in the morning and were feeling good. I thought I'd better re-clog my arteries, which must have been disappointed not to have had a full fried breakfast this morning, so we found a quaint little pub and ordered a triple-decker breakfast sandwich with chips. When the food arrived it was delicious.

After lunch I popped across the road to the Post Office to get a postcard and to get my book stamped. The Postmistress talked to me about our adventures, stamped my book, and gave me a chocolate bar for the journey. She said I looked like I could do with feeding up. Not sure I really deserved it, after all it wasn't like I'd been skimping on my meals, now was it? I didn't tell Bike Buddy about the chocolate, after all he would only have wanted to share it, and it was my find, not his. I'd made the effort to cross the road. I'd spoken nicely with the pleasant Postmistress, and besides I was only really saving him from himself.

Unfortunately the lunchtime break not only filled our stomachs and rested our weary bodies, but it also was long enough to help Bike Buddy's knee seize up again. When he tried to cycle off from the pub his left knee just refused. He tried again and again, but each time his knee just would not bend. However, Bike Buddy was a big chap and managed to persuade his leg to bend by pushing down on his thigh with his hand. I wasn't sure this was a particularly good way to cycle. After all, not only was this going to be doing unknown damage to his knee, but he also kind of needed his left arm to steer and brake.

Despite the unorthodox method of cycling, we made our way over bridges, beside trickling streams and through beautiful open countryside until we found Kirkby Lonsdale and decided to stop for a coffee and to give Bike Buddy's knee a rest. Kirkby Lonsdale was a quiet little town. There were some very interesting old buildings and nice country shops, and most of the cafés appeared to have a lovely oldie world feel to them. Unfortunately we picked the one that didn't. We chose a café that offered coffee in plastic cups, on tables covered with plastic sheets. I suppose the plastic was just in case one of the customers got caught short and needed to piss all over the table.

Caton to Kirkby Lonsdale had probably been the hardest part of the journey so far for Bike Buddy. His knee was really hurting, and it was obvious he was feeling very low. I wasn't sure we would be able to continue after today. I had a sneaking feeling Bike Buddy was going to wake up tomorrow morning completely unable to move because he was forcing his leg to do things that his leg was trying to tell him it didn't want to do. Still he was determined to carry on even if it meant ending up in a wheelchair for the rest of his life, and since I wouldn't be around to see his future suffering, I allowed him to destroy his body now.

It was at this point I remembered a skiing trip we'd been on a few years earlier. Bike Buddy, who at the time was called Ski Buddy, took us down a rather nasty little slope. I believe he did this because he knew I was the worst skier in the bunch, and he thought it would be funny to see me suffer. Anyway, Ski Buddy fell over near the top, mainly because, at the time, his left knee was completely knackered (is this starting to sound familiar?) His knee was so knackered that he couldn't turn to the right. Unfortunately the slope required both left and right turns, and Ski Buddy just couldn't do it, so he ended up in a heap on the floor.

The rest of the group (including me) skied to the bottom and called out ski rescue who arrived with a stretcher. They went up the ski lift and met Ski Buddy halfway down the slope. The rescuer took one look at Ski Buddy and said, 'no more ski for you – ever.' However, Ski Buddy refused to get in the stretcher and winced and whined his way down the slope under his own steam until he finally reached us at the bottom. For some reason, his current approach to cycling reminded me of how stubborn he had been on the slopes. Bike Buddy would not give in – ever.

While cycling today, I'd tried to think up a limerick of our cycling situation. Something that would lighten our lives, and I finally settled on the following:

Limerick
Matthew and Bike Buddy went to Lands End,
With three weeks of cycling to fend,
After a week and a half,
Matthew gave out a laugh,
'cos Bike Buddy's knee would no longer bend.

After much moaning and groaning throughout the afternoon, we continued to make steady progress towards our nightly destination. Bike Buddy whinged constantly, but I cycled ahead and ignored him. When his moaning got louder, I simply cycled quicker for a few moments to get a bigger lead. After all, despite Bike Buddy leading the way and map reading, we were pretty much staying on the same road for most of the afternoon, and I could cycle ahead confidently.

The green grass continued to surround us, as did the overhanging trees, and the chirruping birds. The countryside was relaxing and encouraging, and only Bike Buddy's sobs destroyed the peace.

We finally crept into our Bed and Breakfast at 4pm. Oddly enough the Bed and Breakfast was right next door to the original Quaker meeting room, and was itself a converted cattle shed. Extremely pleasant, one of the nicest Bed and Breakfast's we'd seen on our journey.

The couple who ran it had moved up from London a few years earlier because there had been too much stress in their lives. Their biggest concern now was whether one of their fish would survive the night. This was the kind of life I now wanted for myself, even if it wouldn't last for very long. Nice and relaxing, looking after people on their holidays. No more rushing to work, no more stressing over contracts, no more selling rounds, no more customers and no more arrogant bastard for a boss. A life of bliss!

The Bed and Breakfast was in the middle of nowhere, which would have made getting an evening meal difficult, if the owner hadn't very kindly offered to cook us a meal. We sat with the owner and his wife, enjoying their company, discussing their fish, and consuming their food. Bike Buddy was happy again, his aches and pains washed away with gallons of beer and good wine. I thought I might just leave him in this place while I continued my journey. He'd be happy and safe.

After eating we set off down the drive to visit the Quaker meetinghouse. What a strange little place it was. Appearing much like a small church from the outside. I walked up to the door and tried the handle. It was open, so we wandered in.

No light had penetrated the inside, and for a moment we were left in absolute darkness, but slowly our eyes became more accustomed to the dark, and we realised there was a small amount of light coming through the minuscule windows. Bike Buddy started up the wooden stairs - creak, creak, creak. As he reached the wooden landing, the floorboards started to groan under the strain of holding up his considerable weight. I thought, perhaps, the creaking wasn't the floorboards, but Bike Buddy's knee as he continued his tour of the meetinghouse.

I searched down below, certain that if I added my weight to Bike Buddy's the upstairs would once again become the downstairs. I entered a side room, which by the look of it, was still in use. I was fascinated by the artefacts littered throughout the building, but stopped when I noticed the sacrificial stone at the front of the room.

'That must be where they slaughter young virgins.' I said, not really talking to anyone in particular.

At that moment I was glad I'd already produced two children, so my virgin status was already destroyed. They weren't going to adorn me in a white dress, stick a dagger in my chest and drink the blood from my still-pumping heart.

I could hear voices outside. I suddenly wondered whether we should have been snooping round this building. Was it sacred to some hardened religious cult? Perhaps the Quakers were coming back, maybe they had heard us in their meetinghouse. Maybe they were going to kill us anyway, despite us not being virgins. I realised we had to find somewhere to hide, and quick. At the back of the room the pews were in almost complete darkness. That would be our hiding place. I ran for the back of the room, Bike Buddy hopped as quickly as he could down the stairs and followed me behind the pew.

Just as the door started to creak open, Bike Buddy and I hit the deck. Under the pew we could see feet appear at the doorway. They weren't ordinary feet, they were the dirty shoes of a huge man. He snuffled and grunted as he entered the house, his nose up in the air like a divining stick searching out water.

'Fe fi fo fum, I smell the blisters on a cyclist's bum. Be him poor or be him grand, I'll pop his blisters to make him stand.'

I didn't like the sound of that. Bike Buddy looked at me, and I looked at him. We were in deep scheibe. Up the creak without a paddle. In crapper's ditch. Whatever phrase you could think of, we were in it.

Bike Buddy started to shake like a nervous baby. I tried to remain calm, certain it would be Bike Buddy they sacrificed rather than me. The giant walked slowly towards the back of the room, heading for exactly where we were lying. Bike Buddy was whining quietly, and I was sure the giant would hear him, but just as his feet were poking under the bottom of our pew, another pair of shoes appeared in the doorway. These shoes were smaller than the giants and the voice that accompanied them was sweeter, 'What are you doing darling? Come, come we have a virgin to find. I hear there's a bunch of Morris Dancers staying down the road, they must be virgins!'

With that, the giant stopped, turned back, had one last sniff in the air, and walked towards the small shoes. We were saved! We just had to wait for a while until they'd both disappeared and could then make our exit.

Slowly the giant and little shoes walked out of the meetinghouse and closed the door behind them. Bike Buddy sucked in a huge lung full of air. He'd been holding his breath, and so had I. We climbed out from beneath the pew and tiptoed to the doorway. No sign of them outside, so we slowly opened the door and crept back along the drive to our Bed and Breakfast.

Even now, Bike Buddy and I never talk about that moment together. It was something best left alone, left back in the meetinghouse where it deserved to reside forever.

I recalled the day. We'd finally managed to get through a day without any punctures and had no other breakdowns apart from Bike Buddy's knee, which was starting to threaten the continuation of our tour. We had cycled 59 miles in the day, in just under eight hours, and were doing okay. Bike Buddy's knee was a major concern, but we'd done 598 miles by now, and as far as I was concerned that wasn't bad. Not bad at all!

After eating and escaping the Quaker giant, Bike Buddy retired to bed, but I wanted to stay up a bit later. There was a television in the guest's lounge, so I settled down to watch the news. I was alone. One thing I liked to do when I was alone with the television was play around with the text. I clicked the text button on the remote and waited for the information to load. Now usually I look at sport, but today I wanted to look at the local news. I was intrigued to know whether there was a big-nosed bitch from Clayton-le-Dale trying to find two cyclists who'd flooded her upstairs toilet. I wasn't sure which region of the country Clayton-le-Dale counted as, so looked at a wide variety, scanning the information in front of me. I was a little shocked at what I read.

There were two stories that caught my eye. One of them was about a Bed and Breakfast owner near Blackburn who had been electrocuted in her own home. Apparently, she'd switched on a light downstairs, without noticing the water dripping down the wall over the switch. Guests called the ambulance, but she'd died instantly. Police reported some strange circumstances, and mentioned something about an erotic collection of unusual items in her cellar, but there were no more details on the short two-page summary.

The second story was about a family of three who had been involved in a horrendous car explosion in their own driveway. The father had managed to escape with bad burns, but his wife and son had died in the car.

I stared at the screen. Could that possibly have been the ugly family? Surely not! Surely I couldn't blow a car up with a couple of bananas. But what if I had? What if I'd killed two of the ugly family, the bitch from Clayton-le-Dale, the publican from St Column Major and the driver near Tetbury. That would make me the murderer of five people. That would make me a mass murderer. Holy crap!

DAY 12: WHY DON'T YOU JUST PISS OFF? –
SEDBERGH TO CASTLE CARROCH

I woke in the middle of the night, my left arm completely numb. I'd obviously been sleeping on it, and had stopped the blood supply. Being only half-awake I was unable to make sense of what was happening. I instantly thought someone had crept into my bedroom and sliced off my arm with a big machete. Perhaps it was the giant, come back to find us. I groped around with my right arm, and eventually found my lifeless limb. It was still there, halleluiah!

I hated it when my arm went to sleep. It made me panic that the worms were taking control. I hated it when I couldn't feel my fingers, or my wrist or my elbow, but I hated it even more when the feeling started to come back. On this occasion I jumped out of bed swinging my lifeless limb from side to side from the shoulder, and waggling it around with my right hand trying desperately to fill it once more with pumping, oxygenated blood.

I've often thought it would be great if I could detach one of my arms before I went to bed? Even when I slept alone, I would lie with one arm beneath my body just getting in the way, but now I was married it was even worse. What are you supposed to do with the bottom arm when you're cuddled up to your wife at night? It can't go over your partner's head - too high. It can't go under their body - lack of blood circulation. It can't go behind you - too awkward. Eventually I always give up and turn around. So what are you supposed to do? Answer me that. Well, my answer is to detach it before going to bed. That way you would never wake up with a dead arm. You could cuddle up to your partner with your still attached arm, getting close in the spoons position without your bottom arm getting in the way.

Having said it would be good to detach an arm, I suppose you'd need to be a little careful. Imagine someone coming up to you in the street and detaching them both. Like this new craze of happy slapping; call it happy detaching. What would you do then? You might even have the same problem at home. If you took them both off at night, your wife could grab them in the morning, dance round the bed, swinging them round her head, and you would have to rely on her being kind hearted enough to reattach them. Even detaching one could cause problems. What if you got up in the night for a wee, you went to hold your manhood and, oh my God - no arm. You would have to pee using the other arm. How awkward would that be? I'm not sure I can pee using my left arm as the guide. Knowing how stupid people are, there would probably be a number who would forget to put their arm back on in the morning, until they got in the car and realised they couldn't release the handbrake.

Having got my arm back to life, I settled back into bed. Unfortunately, now I was awake. I thought about waking Bike Buddy, in a bid to get revenge for him waking me so early the morning before. I glanced at the clock – 1.40am. It seemed a little early, and besides he might decide it was time to get up, start packing and make himself a cup of tea. Not worth taking the risk.

I couldn't get back to sleep, so I decided to sing myself a lullaby, as I often did when sleeping was getting difficult.

'Mamma. Just killed a man.

Put a gun against his head, pulled my trigger now he's dead.

Mamma, life had just begun, and now I've gone and thrown it all away.

Mamma oo-oo-oo zzzzzzzzzz'

When I woke in the morning I was still stuffed from the night before. Which was starting to become a bit of a habit. For the second morning running I declined a full English breakfast and limited myself to just cornflakes and toast. By eight o'clock we had completed our morning rituals and were ready to set off. The owners wished us well, and gave us a donation towards the charities. We asked them if the fish had survived, and luckily it had. Everyone was happy! Bike Buddy could move his left knee, so without further ado we got on our way.

As we pottered down the drive, we both took one last glance at the Quaker meetinghouse and thumped harder on the pedals. There was no way we wanted to be around that place any longer than necessary.

Again the morning was good. Bike Buddy's knee seemed to be okay first thing in the morning, so we decided to get as many miles in as possible before lunch. We passed through Sedbergh, which was a small town at the foot of the Howgill Fells.

There had been uproar in Sedbergh only a few years earlier when the town council decided to replace the nicely cobbled streets with tarmac. From my point of view I much preferred the tarmac. I wasn't sure my bottom could take cobblestones.

We arrived in the village of Orton and visited the Post Office so they could stamp my book. We purchased some cheese and ham sandwiches, and took the opportunity to refill our water bottles. At the same time, I bought an insect bite relief stick, just in case we got attacked by midges in Scotland. In fact, it was pretty much a certainty midges would attack us in Scotland (and that was a very painful place to be attacked!)

From Orton the road went vertically upwards. To start with the climb was quite gradual, but then we saw the real climb stretching out in front. The map had shown it with a number of black arrows, and we had been looking forward to the climb all morning – not! Here it was, like a tarmac stairway to heaven. I can assure you, if you take this route, there are certainly more than three steps to heaven.

I was more concerned about Bike Buddy's knee than my own fitness. Bike Buddy had more weight to drag up a hill, and with a broken left knee that put a lot of pressure on the right one. Surprisingly though, I needn't have worried as he managed to haul himself to the top slowly, eventually joining me at the summit.

From the top of the climb the views were breathtaking. I took the opportunity to unload some of the excess urine I was carrying, and we then tucked into some muffins we'd purchased at the Post Office. I wasn't sure it was particularly hygienic to pee then eat muffins, especially without a sink to wash my hands in, but I didn't care. Besides I was sure I'd read somewhere that urine was sterile when it left your body, so provided I stuffed the muffin into my mouth quickly I couldn't be in any trouble. Could I?

It took a while for us to get our breath back from the climb, but within a couple of hours we were ready to cycle on. Down the other side of the hill we whizzed, finally coming to rest in a small village just past Gulgate. This seemed a good spot to eat our sandwiches so we unfastened our panniers and set to work finishing off our grub.

Eerily, the whole of Cumbria was covered in disinfectant mats. Following the Foot and Mouth epidemic, which was prevalent in this part of the country, Cumbria council had laid down disinfectant mats at every road junction. This was obviously a good idea, but I was a little concerned about how our bikes and tyres would cope with continually being soaked in acid. I was particularly concerned about Bike Buddy's tyres, which had already proved to be a little unreliable. But then, what could we do about it? I didn't want to be known for spreading the epidemic further around the country on the wheels of my bike so we merrily cycled over every mat laid in our way.

After lunch we set off in search of more disinfectant mats, and weren't disappointed. The lanes zigzagged across the countryside, with few cars in sight, but cattle grids becoming a common occurrence and laid in the most annoying places. The trouble with cattle grids was they weren't particularly cycle friendly. Cycle tyres tended to fall between the grids, in the same way a cows foot would. This was not brilliant when we had just zipped down the side of a hill and hit the cattle grid at twenty-five miles per hour. Still we shouldn't complain, after all they were keeping the sheep and cattle apart. I mean some of those sheep can be really mean, they can rip a cow to shreds in seconds.

Most cattle grids were put down with the bars running at right angles to the road. This is the encouraged way of fitting such a grid. It is the way described in the 'Cattle grid fitter's guide' and as such is the safest for most forms of transport. This way we could rattle over them with little problem. Unfortunately in Cumbria we occasionally came across cattle grids that had the bars the other way round, parallel to the road. Whether this had been done deliberately or by accident, I'm not sure, but I do know they are not good for cyclists.

I discovered, after the first parallel cattle grid, that there was no way I could cycle along a single bar. Unfortunately, I discovered this inability by wedging my front tyre in between the bars, and since I had my feet still clicked into the pedals I had nowhere to go other than sideways. I slowly collapsed onto the grid, landing with a thump on my left shoulder my hands still attached to the handlebars, my feet still attached to the peddles. Bike Buddy came over and hoisted me back up. It was good to be vertical again.

What made matters worse, was it was impossible to determine which way the bars of the cattle grid had been laid until we were upon them. I tried to sit behind Bike Buddy so that he could take the pain and make the decision of what to do, but it didn't work very well. Bike Buddy decided to career towards the grids, make a last minute decision, and either slam on his brakes or keep going. Unfortunately, I didn't know which until I'd ploughed into the back of him. In the end we decided to slow down and come to almost a complete standstill at every single one.

Despite the grids, the views were spectacular, and worth avoiding the main roads for. The green rolling hills and virtual silence surrounded us, with the smell of fresh air filling our lungs, mixed with a very mild hint of citric acid.

Having started in good time and cycled well in the morning, the afternoon was short and we arrived at Castle Carroch at little after 3.15pm. This was our destination for the day, and arriving so early when we were making such good progress was disappointing, because it meant we could have gone further if only we'd avoided booking all our accommodation before leaving.

When reviewing the route, I realised one of the reasons we'd arrived early was because the accommodation wasn't where I'd expected it to be. I'd calculated the mileage based on a destination of Brampton, but Brampton was another four or five miles further on. We would have to do those extra miles the following day, which was a shame with so much time to spare today.

The Bed and Breakfast was a working dairy farm. In all the time we spent there, we didn't see the husband, but the wife worked extremely hard. She was cleaning the milking parlour when we arrived. There were more disinfectant mats at the entrance to the farm, which we dutifully walked through and pushed our bikes across, the smell of citric acid once more filling the air.

The wife came out from the milking parlour in a pair of baggy shorts and Wellington boots. There was nothing strange about this, until she showed us into the farmhouse took off her boots and revealed her brightly painted pink toenails underneath.

I groaned a little when she showed us to our twin room. I could still remember the bad nights' sleep from previous twin room experiences. The owner heard my groan and asked what was wrong with the accommodation, so I quickly explained it wasn't the room but Bike Buddy's constant drilling at night. She smiled and promised me a separate room if no other guests arrived. Then she walked back out to the yard, put on her wellies and started sending the cows in to be milked. I watched in awe as the black and white beasts slowly plodded into the building, disappearing for a few minutes before reappearing through another door. I tried to identify them from their individual splodgy patterns, and wondered if the farmer had names for his animals.

I have to say my bottom still hurt. It had continued to hurt for over a week now, but for some reason I think the gel saddle was helping. Not only that, but as we moved up the country the weather was getting gradually cooler, and the lack of a hot sweaty bum crack meant the main reason for pain was being avoided. Oh for a cold snap!

As we'd arrived quite early we had showers, got dressed and wandered down the road to see if we could get a pre-dinner drink. The cow-loving owner had pointed us down the road in the direction of the local pub that could offer us some liquid refreshments prior to our meal.

I had become a man of habit. Apart from my numerous postcards home, I also phoned home every evening as soon as we reached our destination. Unfortunately I was doing this on my mobile phone, and had decided not to bring the charger, because in my mind it was unnecessary extra weight. My phone was now getting past its charging best. To make matters worse, nobody I'd met so far had a charger to fit my phone. Now, in Castle Carroch not only was my battery dying, but I couldn't get a signal anyway.

What would I do? How could I survive with no mobile signal? Panic started to set in. I started to run around in a circle, shouting, 'Don't panic, don't panic.'

Bike Buddy looked at me and tutted. He'd started this annoying habit of tutting at me. At some stage I would have to get my own back and tutt at him, but for now I had more important things to worry about. How could I make contact with my family? I was lost! How would I survive the night? We were cut off from civilisation and would surely die in this never-ending wasteland. Bike Buddy then suggested I might like to try the phone box down the road. Brilliant! Why didn't I think of that? New technology, who needs it? I walked down the road and phoned from the landline.

There was only one pub in the village and after the phone call home we headed straight for it. It was early, probably about 6.30pm, and the pub was still closed. There were no signs on the door to tell us when it would open, and with nothing better to do, we sat down on one of the benches outside enjoying the last of the day's sunshine. This was a big mistake! After a few minutes the landlord poked his head out of an upstairs window and shouted down at us, 'What the hell do you think you're doing there. I'm not open yet!'

We calmly replied that we were just waiting for him to open.

The friendly landlord then suggested we, 'Piss off and come back later.'

Not wanting to argue we did just that. Well at least our intention was to do half what he had asked, namely, piss off and not come back later.

As we walked down the road we met a young lady coming the other way. We asked if there was anywhere else in the village to get an evening meal. She shook her head and sighed, 'Unfortunately not. Which is a shame because nobody likes the landlord in the pub we've got.'

This didn't come as a surprise, so we fought our instincts telling us to go without, and after half an hour we set off back to see Grumpy.

This time the pub was open. Just as well, we couldn't have walked much further, Bike Buddy's knee was starting to seize up again. Walking into the pub Grumpy looked at us and tutted. What a friendly chap! The bloke needed a good slap.

Despite Grumpy, the menu had an excellent choice of food. So much choice that I was having difficulty deciding. The waitress arrived after what seemed like only microseconds and asked if we were ready to order. I said I needed a little more time. With that the waitress walked away, until she was just out of sight, counted to three, and then strolled back. 'Are you ready to order now?' she asked joyfully.

'A little more time, please' I replied.

This time she walked a bit further, probably counted to at least ten and then came back. During the whole of these shenanigans I'd stared at the menu but not read a single word. I was too preoccupied with how long it would be before the waitress reappeared.

'Ready now?' she asked.

'No!' I replied.

'Bit slow are we dear?' she continued to pester me.

'Yes, I am.' I replied, 'I've just got out of prison. I was serving twenty years for strangling a waitress to death after she kept rushing me.' This time she got the message and left us for a couple of minutes. In fact she didn't come back until I called her over.

When we eventually ordered our meal it was very nice; lasagne and chips followed by apple and raspberry pie. Surprisingly, the waitress actually became quite chatty, probably in an attempt to calm me down so I wouldn't slaughter her on her way home from work. I felt sorry for her, with Grumpy as her boss. I then realised he'd been joined by Mrs Grumpy behind the bar, who'd arrived in a final bid to drain the dying embers of life from the pub. She was aggressive looking, with a bright red, fat face, and she spat as she spoke. I watched her and Mr Grumpy as they worked, and felt increasingly sorry for those nearby.

If there was one person we'd met on this cycle who really deserved to suffer, it was the owner of this pub. Unfortunately I was a little concerned. Everyone else I'd tried to teach a lesson to was now dead. I didn't want to become a mass murderer. On the whole, mass murderers are not nice people. Actually, that's a little unfair, since I haven't actually met any mass murderers personally. They might be jolly nice people, but for some reason you kind of get the impression you wouldn't get on too well with them. Did I really want to become famous for slaughtering a whole load of people? If I carried on killing, maybe I would meet some mass murderers, as I spent the last few weeks of my life with them in a prison cell.

When we left I gave the waitress a tip. I told her, 'Don't harass people into making life or death decisions about their food intake. That way you might get a real tip.' She seemed pleased with her new-found knowledge. Simple girl, but pleasant enough!

As we walked back up the street, I started doing some calculations in my head. I mentioned them to Bike Buddy, 'Do you know we've now covered a distance of 648 miles?' Bike Buddy was obviously impressed, until I added, 'But unfortunately it was only supposed to have been 601.'

648 miles. 47 miles further than planned. 84 hours on a bike saddle. No wonder my arse was hurting so much!

We wandered back to the Bed and Breakfast, and into our shared bedroom. I wasn't looking forward to listening to Bike Buddy snore all night, and when he dropped off to sleep at 9pm I thought I would have to slay him in the night. The noise was drilling through my head and making my brain shudder. I could feel my blood pressure rising. This was no way to relax! After a few more minutes I could take it no longer, and at six minutes past nine I started back down the stairs to see the farmer's wife.

Earlier that evening she had offered me another room if nobody else arrived. I was hopefully the offer was still open. When eventually I found her, she agreed, and I gratefully took residence in the room next door to power-drill buddy. Finally, I could have a good night's sleep!

DAY 13: PEACE AND QUIET (AND LOGGER LORRIES) – CASTLE CARROCH TO ETTRICK VALLEY

Bike Buddy told me he'd got a bit of a shock when he'd woken up in the morning. He'd looked across at my bed and noticed I wasn't there anymore. He wondered if I'd woken up before him, but quickly dismissed such a stupid idea. He then wondered whether I'd been abducted in the night. Perhaps aliens had come down and taken me off to examine the strange red blisters that had appeared on my rear end. Luckily he didn't panic, but just sat on the side of his bed waiting. Waiting for some kind of sign to tell him what to do next. Eventually the sign came to him - I walked in the room.

Unsurprisingly, the farmer's wife was up before we were in the morning. Awake even before Bike Buddy. She'd mended the gate, refreshed the citric acid at the entrance to her farm, been out to see the milk tanker driver, assisted in the collection of her milk, washed the milk vat ready for the next influx of white stuff, fed the cows, rounded them up and taken them in for a good milking. She'd set out the breakfast table for us, cooked our food, and was busy feeding the calves when we arrived downstairs.

I had a full English breakfast. I couldn't resist, besides, I didn't really have much choice since our host had gone to so much trouble of cooking it for me. I couldn't really just snub her efforts now could I? The food was excellent, and the coffee was topped with fresh, unpasteurised, green milk. I didn't realise this as I downed my third cup, but when Bike Buddy pointed it out, I felt a little concerned. I didn't have the stomach of a farmer. I didn't even have the stomach of Bike Buddy, and yet I'd drank a considerable quantity of unpasteurised milk which could contain a multitude of bugs just waiting to attack me. For the next few hours I would definitely feel I was going to be ill.

By quarter to eight we were fed, watered, packed, dumped, and ready for the off. A good early start, which meant we could take it easy on Bike Buddy's knee. I left a cheque for the farmer's wife, who by now, was outside cleaning the yard. We collected our bikes from the shed, and walked across the disinfectant mats once more, the fresh scent of lemons filling the air.

Today's cycling was going to be even better than yesterday's. We would come to another milestone in our journey, by leaving England for the colder climate of Scotland.

Only a few miles into the day and we arrived in Brampton, a lovely town with some very picturesque buildings and even a Norman priory built with stones recycled from Hadrian's Wall. Now that was a sensible thing to do with an unwanted wall. Not like the German debacle when it was just pulled down and turned to rubble. However, as we cycled I realised this recycling may have caused a problem, because we couldn't find Hadrian's Wall anywhere. We'd been searching since we'd left the Bed and Breakfast, and decided the locals must have taken a few stones too many.

After leaving Brampton we made our way through the last morsels of civilisation and towards the Scottish border. We kept searching for the sign, desperate to have a photograph at such a milestone. Suddenly as we descended a steep hill we could see the Scotland signpost on the other side of the bridge. What a silly place to put a signpost! We had to slam our brakes on, jump off our bikes to have our photos taken by the sign, but having lost all momentum we then trudged up the other side at snail's pace. Bike Buddy walked for a little way, I was determined to cycle. The only problem was I'd forgotten to change gear before I'd stopped and now I needed to start up in one of my highest gears. I jumped down on the pedals, but they hardly moved. I jumped again, and the bike crept forward. This was useless, there was no way I could get the bike going, so I decide on a new plan. I turned around and started back into England. There was a small downhill section first, so I managed to get the bike going, quickly changed gear, and swung back round in the middle of the road with the wheels rotating. Finally I was moving, and back into Scotland. I climbed the hill, puffing and panting as I went, slowly dragging myself to the top.

As soon as we crossed the border, I could feel the cold air ensnaring me. Scotland was so much colder than England. We were going to freeze in this icy, barren land.

In this new cold world the climbs became much longer with some stretching for mile upon mile in the distance, however, these climbs were then followed by long gradual descents making the journey extremely pleasant.

Suddenly enthused by the foreign land, excited by leaving England for an obviously much smaller country, I started to sing. To start with Bike Buddy ignored me, but soon he was joining in as well. We sang strong and loud, our voices echoing through the valleys. There was no one to hear us, no one to tell us to be quiet. Like a male voice choir our joyous song filled the air. The song started slowly, as we climbed up the hill, then increased with speed as we reached the brow and started our ever-faster descent down the other side:

Ring-Ring-Ring

While riding on my bicycle, what to my surprise,
A big Bike Buddy was following me, about three times my size,
The guy must have wanted to pass me out as he kept on ringing his bell,
I'll show him that my bicycle is not a bike to quell.
Ring-ring. Ring-ring. His bell went ring-ring-ring.

I pushed my foot down on the pedal to give the guy the shake,
But the big Bike Buddy stayed right behind, he still had on his brake,
He must have thought his legs had more pace as he kept on ringing his bell,
I'll show him that my bicycle is not a bike to quell.
Ring-ring. Ring-ring. His bell went ring-ring-ring.

My bike went into racing gear and I took off with gust,
Soon we were doin' nineteen, must have left him in the dust,
When I peeked o'er the shoulder on my bike, I couldn't believe my eyes,
The big Bike Buddy was right behind, you'd think that guy could fly.
Ring-ring. Ring-ring. His bell went ring-ring-ring.

Now we're doing around twenty-three, this certainly was a race,
For big Bike Buddy passing me would be a big disgrace,
The guy must have wanted to pass me out as he kept on ringing his bell,
I'll show him that my bicycle is not a bike to quell.
Ring-ring. Ring-ring. His bell went ring-ring-ring.

Now we're doing more than twenty-five, as fast as I could go,
Bike Buddy pulled 'long side of me as if we're going slow,
The guy pulled down his glasses and yelled for me to hear,
'Hey, buddy, how can I get this bike out of granny gear?'
(This was when we rang our bells with gusto.)

With a couple of young children of my own, I had over the past few years amassed an amazing and detailed knowledge of children's songs.

Despite the singing, there was a problem today - the temperature. As I climbed up I got warmer and warmer. By the time I reached the summit I was sweating profusely and decided to take off my jacket. This was a big mistake. Never take your jacket off at the top of a climb. As I descended my arms started to freeze up, and the speed I reached meant the air dried out my sweat and gave me a terrible wind-chill. I shivered all the way to the bottom, not wanting to lose the momentum. As the road started to ascend again, I rolled to a halt. With my shivering fingers I withdrew my jacket from my panniers and put it back on my cold back. Unfortunately, you should never put on a jacket at the bottom of a climb. The extra effort and slower speed up the hill meant I started to get hot again. All I ended up doing all day was taking my jacket off and putting it back on again. You would have thought I'd have sussed what to do by mid-morning, but no.

Our route followed streams up the hills, and then joined other streams and followed them back down. The scenery was spectacular, the views breathtaking, and the peace and quiet unbelievable. We only saw about half a dozen cars all day, plus a handful of logger lorries.

These logger lorries turned out to be a bit scary when cycling on a single-track road. Just as I was starting to daydream of a better life, I would hear a rumble of thunder behind me. Before long the rumble became almost deafening, and I could feel the ground shake beneath my tyres. Suddenly a logger lorry would fly past, brushing my shoulder and making me wobble from the wind-suck. Most drivers were fairly courteous, but we did get the occasional bugger who thought it funny to sound his air-horn just as he was approaching. To show my frustration I dinked my bell back at him, although I wasn't convinced he heard. In fact I could barely hear it myself above the rumble of his tyres.

I did have an air-horn of my own, back home; a proper air-horn just for a bike. I bought it (much against my wife's better judgement) when my work moved office and I had to start cycling through a city centre to get there in the morning. The idea was to inform drivers of my presence. Okay, the idea was to let them know when they'd pissed me off. It worked very well, but after I received my third black eye I decided to swap back to a tinkling bell. Much safer! It was all very well letting people know how annoyed I was, but I needed to make sure I could escape afterwards and a bike isn't the best getaway vehicle.

After a splendid morning's cycle we came across the town of Langholm. It was quite strange to cycle on country lanes for so long and then suddenly come across a large town. The place was buzzing with local people shopping, all busy going about their daily chores. This was obviously the place to come to get one's groceries, and looked like a good place to purchase some lunch. We stopped in a small supermarket and, for a change, bought turkey and coleslaw sandwiches (there wasn't any cheese). After buying postcards and getting my book stamped we left civilisation and set off in search of a nice place to eat our newly purchased supplies.

Ten miles further on and we still hadn't found a bench or anything to sit on to rest our weary legs. Finally we cycled over a small bridge and decided to rest against a stone wall. A bit disappointing that we had to resort to such an uncomfortable lunchtime experience, but there were no benches this far up the country. Perhaps such luxuries hadn't been invented in Scotland yet, or maybe all Scots are so hardy they could sit on cold stone walls without fear of haemorrhoids. Bike Buddy, with his excess padding, had no problem making himself comfortable, but unfortunately I did. Not the best seat ever, but better than nothing.

After eating our sandwiches I decided I'd better relieve myself before getting back on the bike. By the side of the bridge was a farm track, so I started wandering down it to find a sheltered area for urine release. The track had a disinfectant mat, so I walked slowly across ensuring I didn't infect anything, especially given my departure from a dairy farm only that morning and the unpasteurised milk held in my stomach. I hoped I couldn't carry Foot and Mouth in my urine, otherwise I was about to really bugger things up. I hoped the unpasteurised milk wouldn't be a source when I released it back out of my body, but I really had little choice.

I pulled my friend out the top of my lycra shorts and started to wee. I was just in mid-flow when a bloody great dog bound over the hedge just a hundred yards further on down the lane and started toward me. My God, I was about to have my manhood bitten off by a rabid dog. I tried to increase the flow, but it just started to hurt. I tried to stop, but once in mid-flow I couldn't prevent the torrent continuing. Surely I would finish soon, but no, the wee just kept coming. I hadn't drunk that much in the day, surely it would stop soon.

The dog was now only a few yards away, and gaining quickly. I shrieked, and started to run, my penis still out the top of my shorts, and the wee still trickling down to the floor. I tried to run holding my dick away from my leg, so as not to splash urine all over my legs, but that was very difficult with a mad dog on my tail. I shrieked again, as the dog snarled at me and jumped up in a bid to bite my padded bottom.

Bike Buddy heard my screams and saw me running down the track. He grabbed his bike and was off down the road before I'd even jumped the disinfectant mat. My brief hopes that the dog would stop now I was off his land soon vanished as I watched the dog jump the mat as well. He was now so close I could feel his breath on my bare legs and I knew this dog was going home with a big chunk of my arse in its teeth.

I ran faster, I tried to run faster than I'd ever run before. The dog was still with me, snarling away, but I was a panicking man and a panicking man can be pretty damn quick. I sprinted with all my strength, got to my bike and grabbed it from the wall, still in mid-run. The dog barked, and made a bid for my back wheel. I pulled the bike forward, straddled the saddle and started peddling. The dog was still right behind me, but now I had a vehicle, and a weapon. I grabbed my water bottle, turned and squirted the dog between the eyes. He blinked, stopped running, blinked again, and stood still. I cheered as I looked behind, took a sip of water and ploughed straight into the ditch.

Bike Buddy woke me by shaking me vigorously, 'Matthew, are you alright?' he asked.

I was alive. I'd survived the dog attack, and I was alive, my penis still hanging over the top of my shorts.

After brushing the grass, twigs and leaves off my bike and body, I climbed back on my trusty steed. We headed back to the bridge, cleared up the remains of our lunch, and made sure there were no traces of cyclists. Then we turned again and headed north once more.

The cycling continued to be excellent in the afternoon, although the cuts and bruises on my legs were hurting a little, and my energy level was quite depleted following my over use of adrenalin to outrun the dog.

After another ten miles or so, we saw a tree overhanging the road on my side. I dodged it, pushing Bike Buddy onto the opposite side of the road, but luckily nothing was coming. Round the corner we came across a small village called Eskdalemuir. What a strange little place this was! A mountain village built in the valleys; it was like entering the twilight zone. There was only one road into the village, no side streets, no back lanes, just one road. As we cycled down the road, people looked at us through the corner of their eyes, and turned their backs as we approached. Nobody spoke, nobody dared open his or her mouth. Nobody entered the village, and nobody left, ever.

There was a large cemetery with beautifully presented graves and headstones. Surrounding the graveyard was a fence, and just within the confines of the fence was a small wooden bench looking out over the graveyard.

Bike Buddy and I decided to stop for a drink and a rest. This was the first bench we'd seen in Scotland, and thought it could be or last, so we pushed our bikes up against the fence and walked inside the graveyard towards the bench. We sat down, we opened up our food and drink parcels and started to tuck in.

I liked to play a game with Bike Buddy whenever we saw a graveyard. I liked to go along the graves, describing them as 'older' or 'younger.' That was older than Bike Buddy or younger than Bike Buddy. I'm not sure he appreciated it much, but I found it good fun. In this graveyard, I started to wander down between the graves.

'Older,' I said.

Bike Buddy just tutted.

'Younger. Younger. Younger. Younger. Younger. Oh hell!'

Bike Buddy looked up at me, 'What's wrong?' He asked.

'There's something very strange about these graves,' I replied. 'There appears to be just one death in every year. Just one, always one, and that death always happens on the same day each year. And that day is today!'

Bike Buddy went ashen. Colour drained from him, like he'd been told he could no longer drink beer. I admit I was a little freaked myself. Bike Buddy suddenly took the lead and legged it out of the graveyard. I followed, certain that we had to get out of this village quickly.

The road through the village seemed to stretch on for eternity. We cycled off, still heading north as rapidly as we could, but then came to a tree overhanging the road. This was a familiar sight. A chill ran down my spine. I remembered this tree, but then thought surely not, it had to be a different tree. Cycling round the corner my fears were compounded as we saw a sign for the village of Eskdalemuir. Holly shit!

We couldn't turn around, we needed to get past this village, and we needed to head north. There was no other road to take; it had to be this one, so we peddled harder, pushing down, thumping the pedals into the ground. Just ahead of us we could see the graveyard. Folk were coming out of their houses to see the strangers and to watch us go past. They were all grey, with grey faces and grey clothes. Not wanting to provoke the locals, I kept my eyes on the road ahead and pushed in closer to Bike Buddy. There was only one death per year, perhaps I could persuade them to take Bike Buddy instead of me.

We flew past the graveyard for the second time, and sighed with relief as the village became a distant mark behind us. Just a little further on and suddenly my heart sank once more. There in front of us was an overhanging tree. Oh Lord, save us please! This time, as we entered the village, the street was full of villagers. They had all come out in their greyness to block our path. They were going to slaughter us, here and now, and I knew there was no escape, so I simply closed my eyes and prayed.

Suddenly I felt my body being shaken. I was sure this was it, my ultimate doom, but then opened my eyes to see Bike Buddy standing over me looking concerned. I thought about panicking, desperately searching around his bulbous body looking for the villagers until I realised there were none. Nobody except Bike Buddy, and me lying in a ditch. The same ditch I'd dropped in after my run in with the dog. It had all been a dream. Hadn't it?

We set off properly down the road towards Ettrick. Just a little further and we turned the corner to see a tree overhanging the road. My heart suddenly jumped out of my chest and landed with a bang in my mouth. There it was – Eskdalemuir.

Bike Buddy suggested we find somewhere nice to stop and have a drink. I suggested we carried on cycling as fast as we could, and didn't stop until the village was a distant memory far behind. I must have looked a little concerned, all colour had left my face and I was in a cold sweat. Bike Buddy looked at me, and agreed to continue. I didn't want to stop in this village, ever.

Only a few miles further on and we came across a very strange sight - a Tibetan Buddhist temple and monastery. Bike Buddy continued to cycle, but I decided to take a photograph so stopped my bike. I propped it up against the wall, and pulled out my disposable camera. The temple was hidden slightly from view by a large tree, but I wanted a photo, so started to creep down the path towards it. I was now on Tibetan Buddhist territory. Was this a sin? Would I be struck down for standing on holy ground, and made to come back as a daddy-long-legs with two legs missing?

As I placed the camera to my eye I saw a vision through the lens. It was pale, but definitely a monk or Buddhist or something similar. I dropped the camera away, but there was nobody around. I picked up the camera once more and looked through, and sure enough there was the monk. My God! I pressed the button, turned and ran. I really had to show Bike Buddy that photo when it was developed.

As I ran back to my bike, I could see Bike Buddy disappearing into the distance, still oblivious to the fact I was no longer behind him. He was a selfish bugger sometimes!

The journey through Ettrick Valley was stunning. The sun was beating down on us, the temperature was just perfect for cycling, and we were having a brilliant day. Having done most of the miles by lunchtime we took it gently in the afternoon, eventually stopping at a caravan site just before Ettrick village. A sign on the door said they sold ice cream so we stopped to buy one. Unfortunately they weren't open, but the owner let us in anyway and made us a cup of tea. She offered us seats on her patio, and then gave us postcards to fill in. We sat overlooking the valley eating ice cream, drinking tea and listening to the silence. This was beautiful countryside, high mountains, green fields, and flowing streams. Silence, apart from the sound of water trickling down the mountains and the occasional call from the buzzards.

After resting our legs and chatting with the caravan site owner, we said our farewells and set off on our way. The Bed and Breakfast was only a couple of miles further on, and having started so early this morning we'd arrived by four o'clock.

This Bed and Breakfast was an old coaching inn. There was nothing else around the area, so I was glad I'd booked rather than leaving it to chance, despite the fact we could have cycled further if we'd had the opportunity. It would have been nice to actually get ahead of schedule, just in case something bad happened in a few day's time.

The Bed and Breakfast owner was extremely friendly, but didn't expect us so early and really wasn't ready. He had to get the bar prepared for the evening, so we sat in the lounge area and talked non-stop, trying our best to put him off. After setting up the bar he prepared us some tea and cakes, and then we walked the bikes round the inn to the shed.

This was some experience. Given the location of the pub, high above the river, the back garden sloped dramatically towards the riverbank. As such, the owner had built a shed in the back garden that could only be accessed by walking along a rickety wooden walkway. Now, I'm not a fan of heights, and this walkway gave a decent drop on either side and nothing to hold onto. I looked over the edge a few times as I tried to make my way along it. Unfortunately the wooden walkway wasn't quite wide enough to walk by the side of a bike. I tried to stand next to the bike, but the wheels kept slipping off the side of the walkway. I tried to climb aboard, but got scared I might fall off. Eventually I settled on an unusual approach that saw me walk backwards pulling my bike behind me by its handlebars.

After putting our bikes to bed for the night we retired to our twin room, which was splendid with a fantastic view over the valley, although by now I was starting to dread twin rooms. I wished I'd been more selective, I wished I'd chosen only single rooms, or at least twin rooms with soundproofing between the beds. Bike Buddy was driving me insane. I'd escaped the previous night thanks to the good nature of my host, but I knew I couldn't cope much longer. If he snored tonight I would surely kill him.

I showered and tried to view my bottom blisters again. Putting Sudocrem on my bottom was not the easiest thing in the world, but however difficult it was getting I vowed never to ask Bike Buddy to cream it for me.

After the shower, and filling in my diary, we set off for the long walk to get something to eat. Okay, the walk meant going down the stairs and settling in the bar.

As expected from such a fine establishment, the meal was excellent. For once I waited for Bike Buddy to order, so I could avoid him copying me. For some reason he had no difficulty and quickly ordered an Ayrshire steak. Not sure what the difference in taste was between an Ayrshire steak and any other steak, but he seemed to enjoy it. I decided to eat healthily, and ordered garlic bread followed by haddock and chips followed by fruit dumpling with custard. My stomach was bulging by the time I dragged myself back up the stairs, but I was happy. Happy that was until the pneumatic drill started up in my bedroom.

At 3.45am I was still awake, with Bike Buddy still snoring. I was sure everyone in the Bed and Breakfast could hear him. In fact I believed everyone in the valley could probably hear him. He was so loud! He was louder than so loud, in fact he was mega-loud.

It was no good, I needed to get some sleep! I contemplated the best way to slaughter Bike Buddy. Perhaps I could hold a pillow over his mouth and suffocate him. Perhaps I could beat him to death with my bicycle pump. Now where did I leave my pump? Was it still on the bike? Perhaps I could pull the wire out the back of the television and shove it up his arse. Perhaps I could bludgeon him to death with something else nice and heavy like the television itself.

I needed to take my mind off the noise. I needed a distraction. What's the best distraction for a man? I know, sex! I tried to think about naked women, I tried to think about lots of naked women. I tried to think about lots of naked women dancing in front of me, but all I could see were ugly naked women with drills, pumping holes in walls. The drills were loud, deafeningly loud, and getting louder, and the women were getting uglier. It wasn't working! I could still hear the drills!

I tried to think of something else - why were buildings called buildings when they'd already been built? Now that was an interesting thought. Why were litterbins called litterbins when the very fact that the rubbish was in them meant it wasn't litter? They should be called anti-litter bins. Why was a dolphin a mammal, but a shark a fish? What would a chair look like if my knees bent the other way? Why do ugly women have drills? Oh my God, will you shut the fuck up?

If the universe is everything, and the universe is expanding, what is it expanding into? Whoa, that's a big question. It must be expanding into nothingness. Nothingness - what is that like? Perhaps nothingness is what death is like. Completely blank, no noise, no smell, no vision, nothing, zip, zero. Have you ever tried to think of nothing? It's impossible. Whenever I try I always think of pink elephants. Not sure why! I tried to think of nothing. Nope, it was no good, I could still hear drills!

I reached across the bedside cabinet and picked up the remote control. I pressed the small red button on the top. Nothing happened. I pressed harder, still nothing happened. Why is it we press harder on a remote control when we know the batteries are dead? I suddenly had a thought, and pressed one of the numbered buttons. The television flashed on, at double its normal volume. Oops! (hee-hee) Bike Buddy snorted, grunted, turned over and went back to sleep.

At first I was disappointed, but then I realised the wall was actually absorbing the noise. It was amazing, like he was in another room, or another country. I was free from the drill. He was now drilling the wall. From now on, I just needed to ensure I got the bed on the left-hand side. Bike Buddy always slept facing the right, so if I got the left-hand bed he would always face away from me. Now, I could sleep!

DAY 14: NEVER JUDGE A BOOK – ETTRICK
VALLEY TO WILSONTOWN

Today I had some difficult decisions to make. Should I wear my yellow cycle top and black lycra shorts, or my orange cycle top and black lycra shorts? Should I wear my red cycle helmet, or my red cycle helmet? Should I wear my black socks, or my black socks? Should I wear my black cycle mitts, or my black cycle mitts? Should I shut up before I went completely insane?

After a good three hours sleep, I woke this morning as fresh as my lycra shorts. I could barely raise the energy to step from beneath my duvet. Bike Buddy was wide-awake, making himself a cup of tea and rustling his plastic bags. If only I'd thought of the plastic bags last night - easy way to suffocate someone.

In my exhaustion I decided to use a different technique to get out of bed. I pulled back my duvet and just flung myself onto the floor. Bike Buddy looked up and tutted. I crawled across the bedroom on all fours, slowly making my way to the bathroom. I needed to pee!

After a pee, splashing water on my face to wake myself up, and making the difficult clothes decisions for the day, we went downstairs for breakfast. This morning's breakfast consisted of a boiled egg and toast. No fry up for me, not after fish and chips last night. Bike Buddy had the full Scottish breakfast. Which I think was exactly the same as the full English breakfast, but just a lot colder.

At half past eight we were ready to go. This was a late start for us. We were normally up and away well before half past eight, but despite the late start when I opened the door I suddenly realised how cold it was. The air misted up when I breathed, and there was a heavy dew on the ground. I closed the door, and crept back inside. Bike Buddy followed me up the stairs and as soon as I climbed in beneath my duvet, he grabbed me by the legs and pulled me out of the bed.

'We have to go,' he demanded.

He could be so bossy sometimes.

I pulled on some more layers so that I now wore two pairs of cycle shorts, two pairs of socks, cycle trousers, a long-sleeved top (as purchased earlier in the trip), a luminous orange T-shirt, a luminous yellow T-shirt and a luminous yellow waterproof jacket. I also put on my full-length gloves. These were full-length as in 'they reached the ends of my fingers', not as in 'they went right up to my elbows.' I now had nothing in my panniers.

We went back outside, attached the panniers to our metal steeds and hauled our bikes out of the shed along the wooden walkway. The dew made the manoeuvring more difficult than the previous night, but I continued with my 'pull you bike behind you' technique and soon arrived back on solid ground.

The morning was cold, even wrapped up I was still cold. The owner of the Bed and Breakfast wished us good luck, and then for some unknown reason, decided to warn us of the long climbs up ahead.

'Ack eye, they go on forever ya nah.'

Now why would anyone want to say something like that? How, I wished he'd kept his mouth shut.

We pushed off, and after only a few yards my eyes were starting to water. I had my sunglasses on, mainly because they were prescription glasses and without them I was almost completely blind. The glasses did protect my eyes from the cold wind, but not enough to stop my eyes watering.

As we continued to cycle my vision got blurred and I couldn't see through the tears flooding from my sockets. I wasn't sad, I just couldn't stop my eyes watering. I tried to wipe away the downpour, but that was easier said than done with glasses on. Finally I pulled to a stop, took off my glasses and wiped my eyes properly, then set off again. Within a few hundred yards I needed to stop again. And so it went on most of the morning, me stopping so I could see, and Bike Buddy completely oblivious to the goings-on behind him. Sometimes he was just so self-centred!

Apart from being very cold, the countryside around us continued to be amazing. I cycled for a number of miles with a kestrel flying just above my head. To start with I thought this was remarkable, and started dreaming of being the kestrel looking down on me, but I quickly banished this thought from my mind when I remembered I didn't like heights. Soaring in the sky was not good for someone who didn't like heights.

After overcoming my fear of falling, I suddenly wondered what it was the kestrel was thinking. Perhaps he was just as intrigued by me, as I was with him. Perhaps he wondered what a brightly coloured idiot was doing on a bicycle following an equally brightly coloured blob along the road. Perhaps he was going to dive-bomb me, tearing out my dripping eyes.

The climb first thing in the morning was long and steady. I realised the owner had been right, but that still didn't give him the right to tell us. I didn't mind long, steady climbs. I could just keep spinning my legs and keep the wheels turning. I soon warmed up and very nearly took off my jacket as I reached the top. Suddenly I remembered the climbs from the previous day and came back to my senses. I wasn't going to make the same mistake again, and decided to keep the jacket on until I got to the bottom of the next descent. How glad I was I'd made that decision! The wind whipped around me as I descended, and a cold breeze blew in my face making my eyes water even more than they had already that morning. Where did all these tears come from? I must have been in tear-production overload.

Through the countryside we cycled, seeing more green valleys and more streams running through them. Some we followed up to their source, some we followed down to the rivers. The sun came out and warmed the air, the birds were singing, the trees were gently swaying and life couldn't get any better than this.

After a few hours cycling we skirted round the side of Innerleithen and then came across the town of Peebles; an attractive, small, country town set alongside the river Tweed. Peebles had attracted a number of visitors, but continued to have a tranquil feel, set in a valley and surrounded by green hills. It would be one of only a few towns we would see today, so we took the opportunity to stop for a bite to eat. Bike Buddy had been panicking all day in case he was unable to find food. It was only around 10.30am, but Bike Buddy was already hungry. His extremely large full Scottish breakfast obviously wasn't large enough.

We crossed the bridge into the town and rolled our bikes up against the window of a café. Time for coffee and scones. We ate and drank, and then searched for somewhere to buy sandwiches for lunch. Today was going to be a fish day, another fish day, following my haddock last night, and I decided upon some tuna sandwiches. I then needed to get my book stamped, and find some postcards. I was spending as much time getting my book stamped and buying postcards as I was actually spending on my bike during this trip. Never mind, I'd started now, so I was going to finish.

The only problem with buying sandwiches to take along was finding some space for them in our panniers. The day had warmed up, and I had removed many layers of clothes and piled them back in my panniers. My panniers were packed, so a bit of reorganisation was required. I finally managed to squeeze the sandwiches in amongst my sweaty clothes, lovely! Now all we needed to do was find somewhere nice to eat them.

The cycle out of Peebles was quite hard, but I suppose being in a valley it would be. We climbed back up to the road we'd left earlier and then sauntered along by the river, watching the wildlife beneath us. Two herons flew side by side along the riverbank, and then darted into a tree. The whole tree shook under their weight, and the branches continued to wobble long after they had landed. We watched the herons and they watched us, staring with their little beady eyes as we passed them by. The river was busy with fish jumping out of the water, and birds trying to catch them. There were no cars on our road, and we spent more time looking at the river and trees around us than the road in front.

After taking a turning off the road, we climbed up above the town and then had a fantastic view of the whole area. This was beautiful countryside! The lane suddenly dropped back down to the river, crossed a small wooden bridge and then rose back up to the main road.

Away from the quiet lanes, we realised life did exist this far up the country and the main road was busy, but luckily we were only staying on it for a couple of miles, so pushed our legs hard on the pedals and shot along. The busy stretch only seemed to last a few seconds before Bike Buddy yelled at me to turn left onto another country lane. From that moment we didn't see another car until we were only about ten miles from the Bed and Breakfast. The lanes were so quiet, and below us was another river to follow.

At one o'clock we decided to transfer some of the load from our panniers into our stomachs, and stopped for lunch. There were no wooden benches, no stone walls, nothing to sit on, except the grass verge. We took a seat, resting gently against the grass bank, outstretched, watching the world go by below us. This was the life. This was why we'd ridden halfway up the country. There was no better feeling of complete freedom than that day, just sitting, watching the countryside, without a care in the world.

As we ate our food, and watched the countryside in silence we suddenly became aware of the road shaking. Something was coming along the lane, and it was big. Bike Buddy and I moved our legs off the road, and tucked our bikes in against the grass verge a little further. Shortly afterwards a large tractor turned the corner and came straight towards us. The farmer waved, slowed his mighty beast, and gently passed us with a smile.

It was very difficult to raise the effort to leave this peaceful spot. I could have stayed there forever, but my wife probably wouldn't have been too impressed. She might have thought me a little selfish if I'd spent my last few days sitting on a grass verge in Scotland, rather than with her and the children. I pushed myself up from the ground, wiped the grass off my bum and then offered my hand to Bike Buddy to help him up. Time to go!

Cycling was hard work in the afternoon. Post-lunch leaden leg syndrome kicked in, and although the roads remained quiet to begin with, they were hillier. Shorter, steeper climbs and rapid descents. They reminded me a little of Devon and Cornwall, and then with only ten miles to complete before getting to our destination, we suddenly arrived back in civilisation. The roads were getting busier, and louder. The countryside left us behind and was replaced by built up areas, covered in litter, broken bottles and burnt out cars.

I'd cycled in front for most of the afternoon, and Bike Buddy was by now getting very tired. He'd been dropping further and further behind, and as I slowed down to let him catch up, he slowed even more. I was sure at one stage he actually came to a complete standstill, and once again I felt like I was slowly dragging his sorry arse up the country. I knew at that moment, that if I'd cycled any slower I would certainly have fallen off, and from an outsiders viewpoint we must have resembled the slow-bike race.

We joined the main road at snail's pace. I was in the lead, but not sure which way to turn, so I waited for Bike Buddy, but he was travelling so slowly it was starting to be painful. Perhaps now was a good time to stop for another drink. When Bike Buddy arrived I suggested we stop, and he agreed, puffing and panting, and looking extremely pissed off.

Just round the corner was a little town called Biggar. Not sure what it was Bigger than, but it was certainly Biggar. The town was situated on a busy main road, which seemed to stretch sideways through the whole area ripping the town in two. The road had become the town, with people just stopping their cars and getting out rather than actually bothering to park them. We pulled up against a café and ordered orange juice. Bike Buddy looked dead. I went over and checked for a pulse. He had one, but it was slow.

'Bike Buddy might die today!' I thought, but kept it to myself. For some reason it didn't seem sensible to make it so obvious to him.

In conversation the owner of the café thought what we were attempting was inspiring, and gave us a donation to our charities. It was amazing how many people had donated money to us, even though we hadn't actually asked them.

Bike Buddy continued to struggle after our juice stop. The road was remarkably hilly, but I think this was just our tired legs trying to tell us it was hard work. Leaden-leg Syndrome, when you feel like your veins have been stripped out and replaced with lead.

As the minutes slowly ebbed away, we got more and more exhausted. We had to fight for every mile, every tenth of a mile. When I got really tired I started to watch the mileometer, just begging the numbers to change, but they just wouldn't respond. I felt like I could cycle forever and never put another mile on the clock. I thought time and time again that my mileometer had broken, but just as I started to slow down so I could stop and take a look, the next tenth of a mile would click by.

Bike Buddy started to drag behind again, and was getting increasingly annoyed with me. I couldn't do anything about it. I was exhausted too, but I wanted to get to our Bed and Breakfast. I wanted to rest, but I couldn't cycle as slowly as he could. I was losing the slow bike race.

Soon after Biggar we came to the village of Carnwath. Carnwath appeared to be famous for very little other than the fact Robert Burns passed through it on his way to Edinburgh, and might have glanced at the market cross in the middle of Carnwath to determine the mileage he still had to cover. I'm not saying he did look, I'm just saying he might have.

Just a couple of miles from Wilsontown, our destination for the day, we cycled past a large field with cows in it.

'Nothing strange about that,' you might say.

However, one of the cows in this field was dead. We could tell it was dead because it looked like a dead cow from a comedy film. It was lying on its back with all four feet stuck straight up in the air. I thought it was quite amusing, but there again, I have a very sick sense of humour. Surely the farmer had noticed this cow! How could he go round his farm without seeing a cow lying dead in the field with its feet stuck up in the air? Maybe the farmer was blind, but if he was blind how did he milk the cows? If he had bulls as well, some of them might get a surprise when they followed the cows in for milking!

We arrived in Wilsontown eventually, and just needed to find our Bed and Breakfast for the night. We didn't really know where it was, but took a route on the back road. I set off in front, as I had done all afternoon, but after a few yards, turned and glanced back. Bike Buddy had vanished. Disappeared off the face of the earth. No Bike Buddy. Poor Bike Buddy - gone!

What could I do? I stopped my bike, turned around and headed back the way I'd come. I was furious. Bike Buddy might have been tired, but he'd been a pain in the arse all day. I was tired as well. I was tired and dying, but I'd kept going. I hadn't whinged and whined through the day and dragged myself slower and slower to prove how tired I was.

I couldn't believe he'd just stopped and hadn't followed me. Perhaps he'd turned the other way down the back road. I tried that way just in case. I came across a lady in a car, and asked her if she'd seen an overweight man in luminous yellow on a bike. She said she hadn't. I asked if she knew where the Bed and Breakfast was. She pointed me in, what I knew was, completely the wrong direction, so I just thanked her and ignored her.

I had to find the Bed and Breakfast. Bike Buddy could make his own way there and then we would meet again. Besides, he was the one with the bloody map. I turned north and headed back up the road the way I'd originally been going. At the top of the hill, the back road met the main road once more. I glanced up the road, and down the road. No sign of Bike Buddy! I turned left and went back down the main road towards where we'd started only a few minutes earlier. Perhaps he was down there!

After a few hundred yards the road bent round to the right and there in front of me was the Bed and Breakfast, and standing in the drive was Bike Buddy. What a pain in the arse he'd been today!

I didn't bother to ask him where he'd been, I was too angry. Bike Buddy just smiled and said 'Hi.'

A few hours after this incident Bike Buddy admitted to me that he'd done it on purpose because I'd left him behind going up the hills. This came as a relief because I was starting to think he was just really stupid. The problem I had was I couldn't cycle up hills as slowly as Bike Buddy could. I preferred to cycle to the top and wait there, but this was obviously annoying him, and when Bike Buddy was annoyed he liked to annoy me. It was an ever-decreasing circle, and I had to do something to break the trend. I would try to stay behind him tomorrow.

The B & B was a bit of a dump. The town was an old coalmining town and when we walked into the bar it was full of gentlemen watching the racing results on the television, and speaking in a foreign language. This foreign language later turned out to be Scottish, but to be honest it could have been Zulu for as much as we could understand. What amazed me was some areas of Scotland had really strong accents, whereas other areas appeared to have hardly any accents at all. I suppose England and Wales must be exactly the same, but perhaps I just hadn't noticed.

Inside the Bed and Breakfast the rooms were quite pleasant - single rooms with en-suite. There was a large restaurant, which looked very nice, and the bar was full. Perhaps it wouldn't be too bad. Bike Buddy looked concerned, but in my mind I had a single room and that was all that mattered.

After locking the bikes up round the back of the hotel, showering, writing our diaries and postcards, we went downstairs for some food. The restaurant itself was decorated in red velvet, and looked like a posh Indian, or something out of The Moulin Rouge. There was a miniature working mine along one wall, which intrigued me. The owner had built it all himself, and as the wheels turned, I couldn't take my eyes of it.

Bike Buddy again decided to order what I ordered, but this time I decided to tell him I didn't like it when people did that. I told him I like to make my own decision, let others do the same and then see what we both get. I don't like people ordering the same as me, because it makes it look like the menu's crap. We may as well say, 'Well there's shite on this menu, and this one is the only one that appears edible.' Maybe I'm overly sensitive, but that's my view.

Our evening meal of beef stroganoff, followed by apple pie and ice cream was excellent. I really did love this part of the day. This was our reward for all our hard work, the payback for all our physical exhaustion and almost worth having Bike Buddy whinge for. Our little indulgence, so richly deserved.

When I went to pay, the owner told me to settle up in the morning, so Bike Buddy and I set off back to our rooms for yet another early night.

I came across all romantic in the evening after my meal. I decided I should order my wife some flowers, to let her know how much I was missing her. I told Bike Buddy my plan, and suggested he do the same for his wife. He looked at me as if I was completely bonkers.

'If I buy her flowers I'll get told off,' he said.

'Why?' I enquired.

'Because she'll say I'm wasting money and think I've been with another woman.'

This shocked me! Not only because the thought of Bike Buddy with another woman was repulsive, but also because my wife might think the same of me. How could I have been with another woman? Firstly, I had two red blisters on my bum, and the constant pressure on my delicate area meant I hadn't managed to get an erection for two weeks. Secondly, I was with my father-in-law - her dad. Who in their right mind tries to get off with someone when their father-in-law is around? I may have been a stud, but I wasn't stupid.

Bike Buddy's concerns slapped the romance out of my tired body, and I returned to my room without placing the flower order. How dare my wife doubt my sexual behaviour? She didn't deserve any special treats, and certainly not any flowers. She could blooming well go without.

I settled down into my bed, looked at my watch and realised it was only nine o'clock. What had Bike Buddy done to me? He'd turned me into a spinster lady, and old before my time. I'd been contaminated with his early to bed exploits, which were now eating away at my tired body along with the worms. If this boil didn't kill me, I felt life probably wouldn't be worth living soon anyway, because I was slowly becoming Bike Buddy.

It had been a day of contrasts. The morning's cycle had been through gorgeous, beautiful countryside and quiet roads. During that morning my health concerns had floated away, and I'd been able to enjoy the ride through our beautiful land. I'd forgotten about my worms, I'd forgotten about Bike Buddy snoring, and I'd forgotten about the people I'd unfortunately caused mishaps to on my way up the country. But, now something was starting to eat away at me. Somehow, when the land got busier, I started to have an overwhelming feeling to cull some of the lesser mortals. For the last ten miles I'd got more and more worked up. Perhaps it was Bike Buddy doing this to me, or just tiredness. Maybe Bike Buddy was not only contaminating my body with early-to-bed syndrome, but was slipping his intolerance to me too. I was becoming Bike Buddy. I was going to explode into a mass of heaving fat over this final week, until my knee wouldn't bend and my blood pressure exploded. Actually, I think it was just the over-population.

DAY 15: ELEPHANTS, GUNS AND RACING BIKES –
WILSONTOWN TO CALLANDER

When we went to pay in the morning the owner decided to give us the evening meal for free.

'To go towards the charity,' he said.

This came as a real shock to me. He must have been struggling in a town rocked by mine closures, but even through this difficult time he had enough warmth to offer us a free meal. For our own conscience, we noted down the real price of the meals so we could donate the equivalent when we returned home. Bike Buddy and I didn't believe in getting the charity to pay for our crazy ideas, and needed to ensure all donations were correctly handed to the charities.

The breakfast was as good as last night's meal, and my barely-emptying stomach was soon refilled with poached eggs on toast. The fear of slowly becoming Bike Buddy meant I avoided the full fry-up, but of course the real Bike Buddy could not resist and had the works again. By 8.30am we were ready to leave.

What amazed me most about Britain was how quickly the countryside changed. The previous day we had set off in green land with running streams and blue skies. Today, the start of our journey was through a landfill site. Actually, I think it was a housing estate, but it looked more like a landfill site, apart from the fact nobody had remembered to actually bury the rubbish.

A few miles from the Bed and Breakfast and we were in trouble. All around us were burnt out cars, discarded beds, settees, fridges and dead animals. Just ahead of us, from the side of the road suddenly appeared two men, climbing through a fence. The men were dressed from head to toe in black, and wore balaclavas on their heads. They looked a little suspicious. It might have been the balaclavas, or the sawn off shotgun one of them held in his hand, or maybe the other man's sack with 'swag' written across the side. Anyway, Bike Buddy and I saw them, and this did not bode well for us. I didn't think such men really wanted anybody to see them, and knew we needed to get away, and get away fast.

Bike Buddy knew what he had to do, and so did I. We headed straight for them at top speed. The men were still getting off their knees having crawled through the fence, when two luminous men on bikes crashed into them from the side. Bike Buddy took out swag-man, and I ploughed into gun-man. No time to think, just straight up to him and smacked him in the face with the end of my bicycle pump. The gun-man hit the deck. At the same time Bike Buddy whacked swag-man with his bionic leg, and swag-man also hit the deck. This attack gave us vital seconds to escape, vital seconds to get far enough away from them to be out of range of their gun. We peddled like crazy.

I didn't dare look over my shoulder for the first few metres, and after that I didn't have the energy to look over my shoulder. Every ounce of power and every muscle in my body was being used to propel my bike forward. Bike Buddy had strong legs, and his recent attempt to look feeble soon disappeared as he flew off into the distance. Bike Buddy could out sprint me! Could you believe it, this man-tank could out sprint me? Now I was gutted, but I was also determined to catch him up. I put my head down and raced after him.

We had now put at least a mile between us and the villains, and there was no sign of them. Perhaps they would lie by the side of the road until arrested by a passing policeman. Perhaps not, and we didn't want to find out.

Another mile down the road and Bike Buddy was starting to tire. We'd taken a number of turnings by now and were confident the villains would be unable to find us. Bike Buddy slowed up, his energy levels completely diminished. I rolled up beside him and pretended to be cruising. It was important to make other cyclists believe I was finding it easy, particularly when it was Bike Buddy.

'We've escaped,' I said. 'We've made it.'

Bike Buddy just nodded, he had no energy left to speak.

Another five or six miles down the road and the area wasn't improving. I expected the gunman to run out at any time and shoot us down, but he didn't Then we came upon a village with a very worrying sign. Right underneath the village name, 'Welcome to Black Ridge,' was another sign reading, 'A Handgun Free Village.'

What kind of village needs to tell you that when you arrive? How many handguns had there been in this village? I was worried entering this place, not only because of the possible gunman on our tail but also the numerous other outlaws that obviously roamed these parts.

Black Ridge had been developed in association with mining and quarrying industries and, when we arrived, more than three quarters of the population lived in council houses. The village was deserted, as if folk knew it was safer to stay indoors rather than venture down the street for the daily newspaper. Dog crap was building up on the pavements, and wild dogs could be heard howling in the distance. Dried bushes rolled along the deserted roads, jumping over the remains of burnt out vehicles and the corpses contained within them. I looked at Bike Buddy, and he looked at me, but we didn't say a word. We knew bringing unnecessary attention to ourselves was not sensible in the village, so we cycled silently, just the gentle hum of over-used pedals and the occasional click from Bike Buddy's knee.

As we cycled silently through the village, we became aware of shadows in the windows, watching from behind the curtains, almost expectant of some terrible outcome for the strangers before them. We kept quiet, until we reached the opposite end of the village and departed Black Ridge, leaving the handgun free zone empty once more. It was at that moment I realised if it really was handgun free then we were safer in the village than outside it. I didn't want to do this anymore. I wanted my mummy!

A few miles away from the handgun free village, and we were actually moving back into the countryside. The Bad Lands disappeared behind us and we gained a fresh spring in our pedals. Unfortunately this newfound knowledge meant Bike Buddy and I started to relax, and when we relaxed we forgot to look at the map. Coming to a right hand turn, Bike Buddy and I glanced up the road and decided it was just a farm track. Carrying on our way for another four miles before coming upon a town that wasn't on the map. Oh dear, a wrong turn again! Bike Buddy looked at all the maps he had, and decided our only choice was to turn round and head back the way we'd come. Oh the fun! Nothing for it except more cycling, and the most demoralising cycle imaginable. For the return four miles, the heavens opened and God taught us about going wrong. 'Thou shall cycleth unintended miles in the rain, for thou art sinners.'

After getting back on the right track, we headed towards civilisation once more and skirted round the side of Falkirk without daring to enter the centre. Following the previous solitude, the traffic was suddenly horrendous, with cars whizzing past our shoulders, shaking the ground and blowing us from side to side. I'm sure half of the drivers didn't even see us because they certainly didn't appear to make any effort to give us space.

A few miles on from Falkirk, at Carron Bridge, we were suddenly confronted by an elephant standing in the middle of the road. This was a little concerning, but not quite as bad as it would have been if it had been a real elephant. This elephant was holding a lollipop stick, and was stopping passing traffic. We slowed down and chatted with the grey beast.

It turns out the elephant was collecting money for the Children's Hospice, and to raise further money the pub in Carron Bridge was having a bit of party. We decided to join in. After all, if elephant lollipop ladies were welcome, I was sure two strangers dressed in luminous yellow tops and lycra shorts would be grabbed with open arms. The party had games, drinks, skittles, and a barbecue. Just what the doctor ordered, a drink for Bike Buddy and a couple of burnt burgers for lunch. Splendid!

As we entered the pub, it became obvious what a strange place Carron Bridge was, really nothing more than a bridge on the river Carron. Built in 1695 to replace the ford that had previously existed as the only means to cross the river. The pub was packed with partygoers, yet there were only a few cars in the car-park, and no houses within sight. Where had all these people come from? Who cared, they were enjoying themselves and they made us feel very welcome. We were hugged and patted like a couple of well-behaved dogs, our glasses were filled and our stomachs were satisfied. We tried our luck at skittles, where Bike Buddy managed to score an impressive eight, and I hit two bales of hay and the young lad taking the money. We tried our luck at 'hit the rat', but managed to hit nothing except the table underneath. I asked Bike Buddy to put his hand at the end of the pipe (where the pretend rat would scurry through) so I had more chance of hitting it. Being a bit stupid he did as I asked, and then I missed the rat and hit Bike Buddy on the knuckles. Made me laugh, and it made a number of onlookers laugh too, but Bike Buddy didn't look too happy.

We moved from stall to stall trying our luck and emptying our wallets. The food kept burning, we kept buying it and Bike Buddy kept eating. After two hours of merriment we looked at the road and decided it was time to go. The tarmac was calling us back, so we hugged the ladies and shook hands with the men, before striding out of the pub gardens and back to our elephant-watched bikes.

The afternoon's cycle was much more pleasant. Maybe the burgers were better for us than I'd thought, or maybe having met some friendly people we suddenly felt warm inside once more. The route itself took us alongside Carron Reservoir, which was not a loch, but a large man-made reservoir (you might have guessed that from its name.)

I cycled slightly ahead of Bike Buddy, ensuring he kept close to my back wheel, and enjoyed the views over the water, which stretched onwards into the distance. Birds hung in the air above the surface, occasional ripples could be seen in the water as fish tried their luck at fly-catching, and ducks paddled their way across in search of better things. The wind was still, the air was fresh and clean, and the silence was perfect.

Just a couple of miles alongside the water, and we heard the hum of cycle tyres behind us. I glanced over my shoulder, just as two men on racing bikes whizzed past - one dressed in white the other dressed in blue. They were sailing (cycling fast), but that wasn't going to stop us giving chase.

Bike Buddy was always keen to chase down racing cyclists, and I must admit I enjoyed it myself, although you must bear in mind Bike Buddy and I were carrying our houses on our bikes whereas these racers were carrying nothing more than a puncture repair kit. A slight disadvantage for us, but we did have one thing on our side - we were chasing them and they didn't know it yet.

Bike Buddy showed a fantastic turn of speed, and was soon clocking twenty-three miles per hour. I matched him, using his ample slipstream to save energy. We were in a race - the end-to-enders versus the professional racers.

We tracked the racers for a few miles, just long enough to see blue racer look nervously over his shoulder. He could obviously sense the sheer power coming up behind him, and we could smell his fear. There is an art to tracking a cyclist. You can cycle as hard as you like, but when they look over their shoulder you have to look relaxed. We did it perfectly, the blue racer glanced backwards just as I took a swig from my water bottle and coasted along without pedalling. Blue racer spoke to white racer, who turned and looked at us too. At this stage both Bike Buddy and I were freewheeling, we had our feet up on the handlebars, and our hands behind our heads. We looked relaxed. We looked very relaxed, and the racers looked scared. They glanced at each other again, and then looked down at their front tyres and pushed harder on the pedals.

Not wanting to rub it in, and confident we'd proved our point, Bike Buddy and I slowed slightly, and laughed together. End-to-enders rule!

It was good to see Bike Buddy laugh again. He hadn't laughed for fifteen days.

Jollity filled the air for the next few miles as we replayed the moment over and over, the hilarity of the situation funny only to those who were there. But what happened a few miles further down the road, was even better. Just as we were coming to the end of the reservoir, I suddenly caught sight of the racers in the distance. Blue racer was looking nervously down the road towards us while white racer had his bike upside down and his back wheel in his hands. He had a puncture!

I looked at Bike Buddy, Bike Buddy looked at me, and we nodded. A little more pressure applied to the pedals, we upped our speed and headed straight past the distraught racers. When we went past we were back up to twenty-four miles per hour, and flying. Just as we got within hearing distance of the racers, I leant across to Bike Buddy and said, quite loudly, 'No staying power.' End-to-enders rule, again!

After leaving the loch and the racers behind, we ventured into Kippen. To start with I thought this was the home of a cartoon dog, whose voice sounded very similar to Martin Clunes. I got quite excited, but was sorely disappointed to find Kippen was nothing to do with a dog. Actually Kippen was a delightful little village, beneath the Fintry Hills and overlooking the valley of the river Forth. We considered stopping, but decided to get on with the final miles of the day and give ourselves another early finish.

After our racing exploits, just past Kippen, Bike Buddy started to tire. We only had ten miles to go, but they seemed to drag on forever. Perhaps because they were ten miles we shouldn't have been cycling. If we hadn't gone the wrong way earlier in the day we would by now have been sitting comfortably in our Bed and Breakfast. This was always a depressing thought, but one we were kind of getting used to.

The cycling in this area was still relatively flat, and the roads stretched ahead into the distance, with just the occasional turn required. It made map reading exceptionally easy, and gave us the opportunity to chat aimlessly or drift into a semi-conscious dream world.

While drifting in this daydream along a quite country lane, just a few miles before we joined the main road to Callander, I was woken by the roar of a jet engine behind me. I expected to see the plane streak overhead, but the engine noise grew louder and louder, and I was starting to get a little concerned the plane was about to land on my head. Suddenly two bullets shot past us; two motorbikes travelling so fast they made both Bike Buddy and I jump. We jumped, our bikes jumped, and our hearts pounded against our chests. The idiots were obviously having a race, and were going at least 130 miles per hour, possibly even more.

I had never seen anything travel so fast on a normal road before, and I hoped I would never see it again. My only consolation was that every corner they turned could be their last. If I'd ever seen someone deserve to die - these two bikers did. Not a very Christian attitude, but I preferred to use the, 'An eye for an eye' approach rather than 'turn your other cheek.'

As I saw the bikers disappear in the distance and listened to the roar of their engines, it suddenly dawned on me that these motorcyclists were doing a circuit and we were cycling in the middle of their makeshift racetrack. I could hear the motorbikes as they zoomed back past us a few miles to the east, and I knew at that stage they would come past again, and this time I would be ready.

Bike Buddy was oblivious to it. I told him I needed a pee, and would cycle off ahead, have a wee and then wait for him. Looking at his map, he told me we were turning off the road in a couple of miles, just before a sharp bend in the road. I nodded, and pounded my legs on the pedals. Time to lay a trap.

I quickly put a hundred yards between Bike Buddy and myself. I needed to get to the bend in the road, and was soon so far ahead of Bike Buddy he was just a dot in the distance behind me. I could see the bend ahead, and headed straight for it. I passed the road we needed to turn down, but kept going straight. Round the bend, I stopped and pushed my bike up against a gate. By the side of the road was a ditch, and I searched the ditch for something heavy. Just a few yards further up was a log. It looked hollow, and when I lifted it out of the water, it proved to be hollow, and much lighter than I'd expected. This log was as long as my outstretched arms, and as thick as my thigh. I pulled hard. Despite being hollow, this log was still only just within my strength capabilities. I hauled it up to the roadside and laid it across the road. Just perfectly positioned so the motorcyclists couldn't see it until the last minute, giving them only a fraction of a second to make a hasty avoidance manoeuvre. I turned my bike around, jumped back on, and headed to the turning, just as Bike Buddy was approaching from the other side. I nodded to him, and he nodded back as we turned off the road up a side track.

Listening intently I could hear the motorcyclists coming again; the roar of their engines in the distance as they approached. We knew they wouldn't turn up the track, but Bike Buddy and I looked at each other anyway in a disapproving way. The thing was, I knew they would soon have a major panic, but Bike Buddy didn't.

Perhaps my log scare would be enough to slow them down. That would teach them a lesson. Stupid buggers!

We'd only travelled about two hundred yards up the track when the motorbikes were almost upon us. The engines screamed as they flew passed the turning, and towards the bend. The next noise scared me, and sent a shiver down my spine. We heard the sound of tyres screeching as the rubber burnt to the tarmac, and then the air was filled with an enormous crash as metal bike hit metal gate. There were definitely two crashes, but so close together, they sounded almost as one. I knew the bikes had been travelling side by side, all I could imagine was one of them had seen the log, tried to avoid it, and in doing so sent himself and his buddy in a straight line off the road and into the metal gate.

'What the hell was that?' blurted Bike Buddy.

I looked at his worried face, and just casually answered, 'It sounds like those nutters have got their comeuppance.'

'Should we go back and see if we can help?' he asked.

I just shrugged my shoulders, 'I don't see why we should waste any energy on them, they deserve everything they get. Besides I'm sure someone will find them.'

To my amazement Bike Buddy agreed, and we just carried on our way.

At a little after 5pm we found the town of Callander. The place was heaving. There were tourists everywhere; most had visited the vintage car rally down the road, which we'd passed only moments earlier. Apparently Callander is a Victorian spa town, and starred in the television series, 'Dr Finlay's Casebook' under the fictional name of Tannochbrae, although I wasn't sure this was the reason it was so busy.

Now all we had to do was find our Bed and Breakfast, which happened to be at the top of the steepest hill in the town. I thought I'd got out of this habit, but it seemed to be coming back with a vengeance.

We found the turn, looked up the drive and started cycling. Granny gear was back in use, and I heaved the weighty contents of my panniers up the drive at little more than snail's pace.

Surprisingly, despite its severity, and the tiredness in our bodies, we both managed to cycle up the track. Even Bike Buddy. Perhaps he wasn't as useless as I thought.

We wanted to get to this Bed and Breakfast more than any other. This was our favourite Bed and Breakfast. Not because it was especially beautiful, or particularly comfortable, but because this was where we'd sent our clothes parcels when we'd left home. It was like waking on Christmas day morning in expectation of the presents ahead, but in our case we knew what were contained within them.

The parcels were waiting on our beds - fresh clothes at last, and the opportunity to lose the rather nasty sticky, sweaty, smell for at least an evening. After undoing our Christmas presents, we set about returning the smelly clothes we'd been wearing for the last week to our homes. We put them in carrier bags and strapped them up with the last of our duct tape. Secure, and ready to go home. I'm not sure my wife would look forward to receiving her parcel as much as I'd looked forward to receiving mine.

While we changed into fresh clothes, our bikes were taken down to the garage by the owner and securely locked away. The rooms were splendid, comfortable and separate - two single rooms – hurray! Comfort, warmth and somewhere to rest our weary limbs, and a good night's sleep. I can assure you by now my limbs were very weary, and I dread to think what Bike Buddy's were like.

We went to Poppies Restaurant for dinner, one of the nicest meals I'd had on the trip. After fifteen days and fifteen nights, I finally broke my alcohol free pledge and shared a bottle of wine with Bike Buddy. For some reason I felt like we were actually going to make it now. Not sure why, but something told me the worst was over. I hoped I was right. Of course we still had Drumochter Pass to look forward to, but that was just one hill.

I ate potato and leek soup, followed by chicken with vegetables, followed by apple pie. I stuffed my face, and drank wine by the bucket load and then suddenly realised why Bike Buddy had been so keen come to such a posh restaurant and order a bottle of wine; it was my shout again. How did this work? Why did I always get the expensive meals? Perhaps Bike Buddy was doing it on purpose. Last night's meal should have been paid for by Bike Buddy, but he'd somehow managed to get it free. Jammy bugger!

As we went to leave the restaurant, the waitress tucked a note into my hand and winked. To start with I thought I'd pulled and was going to have a very lucky night. I winked back at her, brushed the hair back from her face and smiled ready to plant a kiss on her left cheek. Something made me stop. I don't know what. Perhaps it was having Bike Buddy staring from his seat, or the fear in the waitress's eyes, but whatever it was, I stopped. I looked down in my hand and realised the note she'd given me wasn't a telephone number or address for us to rendezvous later, but a donation towards the charities. I nodded and walked away, after all it was the least she could do considering the amount of money I'd just spent there.

That evening I sat on my bed and decided to write another poem. Despite going the wrong way, Bike Buddy had led me through some of the worst areas of the country I'd ever seen, and having his lardy butt next to me gave me comfort where there was no other. He was my shepherd, and deserved to have this Psalm dedicated to him:

Psalm 23

Bike Buddy's my shepherd, I shall not want,

He maketh me cycle in green pastures,

He leadeth me beside still waters,

He restores my soul.

He guides me in paths for bicycles, for his own sake.

Even though I cycle through the valley of the shadow of death,

I fear no evil,

For Bike Buddy's with me.

My gel saddle and mars bar comfort me.

The Bed and Breakfast prepares a table for me,

At the top of a hill – my enemy.

I anoint my bottom with Sudocrem,

My bottle overflows.

Surely my bottom will hurt all the days of my life,

And I will have to stand in my house forever.

We'd survived another day, we were more than two-thirds of the way to John O'Groats and I was starting to think we could actually make it. We'd cycled 827 miles, 66 of them today. Okay, it should have been just 758, which meant we could have got to Callander a day earlier if we'd gone in a straight line (although the Bed and Breakfast owner would have got a shock). We'd been sitting on our bike saddles for more than one hundred hours, and were very tired, but we were going to make it. We had to make it!

I lay in bed and switched on the television. I was intrigued to know if the motorcyclists had made the news, and how badly injured they were.

Not only had they made the local news, but they were one of the lead stories. The motorcyclists had been airlifted to hospital, but were both dead. They were both dead. Okay, they probably deserved it, but I'd done it again. I'd killed two more! Then another story started about two men found by the roadside. One man was in intensive care having been hit full in the face with a blunt instrument. The other man had suffered a broken leg. The broken leg man explained how he and his brother had just come off their farm, after feeding the chickens, when two guys on bikes had attacked them for no reason. Oops!

DAY 16: FOOD, GLORIOUS FOOD – CALLANDER
TO ABERFELDY

This morning I decided it would be better not to tell Bike Buddy that the two supposed burglars we'd stopped the previous day were in fact good, hard-working farmers. I thought it better not tell him that one of them was currently in intensive care after being hit full in the face with a cycle pump by a guy cycling past at twenty miles per hour. I also thought it better not to tell him that the police were now looking for two men in luminous yellow cycle tops, and instead simply opted to wear my luminous orange cycle top instead. That would throw them off the scent.

I also decided to start treating my body as a temple again. Instead of the full fried breakfast Bike Buddy ordered, I simply had fruit salad and a couple of boiled eggs. This made me feel remarkably good. Perhaps it was the fruit, or the protein from the eggs. I always thought about Mr Strong when I ate boiled eggs, because Mr Strong used to eat hundreds for breakfast, and if it was right for Mr Strong then it was right for me.

After breakfast the owner gave me some scones for the journey. Funnily enough he didn't give any to Bike Buddy. Perhaps he thought fruit and eggs weren't enough to see me through to lunch, or maybe he just thought Bike Buddy had obviously eaten enough food in his life already.

As it was Sunday, the plan was to get as far as we could in the morning, and then risk the possibility of a Sunday lunch. This would only work if we had minimal miles to do in the afternoon. We didn't think it wise to stuff our faces, have a couple of glasses of wine and then try to cycle a long distance. Besides, after Sunday lunch Bike Buddy always fell asleep. I didn't want him doing that on his bike, he might cause a nasty accident.

When we stepped out of the Bed and Breakfast our bikes had miraculously rolled up from the garage and were parked outside the front door. How clever! We dropped down the drive and instantly met the Sustran's route number seven. The route ran along the road out of Callander, skipped over a bridge and then ran beside the loch on a purpose built cycle track.

The rain had stopped, the scenery was stunning and it was a glorious fresh morning, but there was one small problem - Sustrans had insisted on covering the track in gravel. Most of this was fine, but some parts of the track, including steep climbs and descents, were covered in a much thicker layer making it very treacherous. It was like being back at Lands End again. I spent most of the journey looking down trying to avoid large stones or rocks protruding out of the ground. This was particularly annoying given the fabulous view I would have seen, if only I could have risked looking up.

We followed the track for a few miles, and the gravel soon turned to rough stones and flints. These were not good for bike tyres, but luck must have been with us, because even Bike Buddy's tyres survived unscathed. One part of the track was particularly unpleasant when there were large rocks sticking out of the ground on a steep descent. No problem on a mountain bike, but not good on a touring bike (or in my case, on a bike pretending to be a touring bike). Why did Sustrans do that?

After a number of bumpy miles we rejoined the A road, and climbed up Glen Ogle Pass on the main road. This was hard going, and very dangerous. Cars and lorries got very close and didn't seem to worry about knocking us down the side of the mountain. The climb was at least four miles long, and steep enough to make me sweat a little (okay, a lot). I followed Bike Buddy. Bearing in mind his attitude to cars, I thought it was safer to be behind him, offering him some protection, but our progress was slow and wobbly, and made even worse by the death drop on one side and multiple vehicles passing on the other.

At the top of the climb, we pulled into a parking area and stopped outside a mobile café. This was obviously a favourite amongst motorcyclists, and we felt quite at home, despite the fact that I had inadvertently murdered two of their kind the day before. The café itself was quite rundown, but had a lovely picnic area, looking out over the pass, and the fear in our bodies from the slow ascent rapidly left us. At last we could enjoy the views, while sipping our coffee and eating our scones.

After the mini-break (that sounds like something Andy Murray might get in a tie-break), we climbed back on our bikes and were pleased to see the route down the other side of the pass was away from the main road. We headed off-road, through the forest.

To begin with this off-road route was fabulous. The path was almost brand new, with black, newly laid, smooth tarmac. Fantastic! On smooth tarmac our bikes ran beautifully, like the well-oiled machines they were; just the faint whistle of rubber on the ground as we descended at speed. The track departed the main road entirely, winding its way through the forest, and as the sound of the vehicles disappeared we could imagine ourselves miles from civilisation once more.

After a couple of miles of peace and beauty, the tarmac funds had obviously run out and the path turned to gravel. I was beginning to hate gravel! Bike Buddy just smiled, he knew I hated gravel. I hated gravel about as much as he hated cars. On gravel Bike Buddy became the stronger, Bike Buddy became the number one, the premier rider, and I became the Domestique. I didn't like being the Domestique, and that was probably why I hated gravel.

After another mile on the bum crushing gravel I suddenly became aware of how much I actually liked gravel, compared with grass. Grass wasn't nice to cycle on, unless you had mountain bike tyres. I didn't! I hated grass! I hated grass even more than I hated gravel.

Another few hundred yards and the grass became mud. I hated mud! I hated mud more than I hated grass, and I hated grass more than I hated gravel. I had started to become the man who hated everything. I had started to become Bike Buddy!

Eventually we slipped and slid our way to the bottom of the muddy pass and I started to think I actually preferred the main road. At the bottom of the muddy bank was a gate. What a stupid thing to put at the bottom of a cycle track.

This gate was seven feet tall, eight or nine feet wide, and it was locked. Within the gate was another gate, a much smaller one, only five feet high and eighteen inches across. (Tell me, why am I quoting things in feet and inches, and earlier in yards? I'm only young for goodness sake. I was brought up on metres. Having said that I would have sounded stupid saying the gate was one hundred and fifty centimetres high and forty-five centimetres wide. You'd probably picture me using a tape measure. Well I didn't. I measured it with my foot.)

Anyway, we had to fit through the mini-gate. The mini-gate which was too short for a grown man to walk through, and too narrow for a pannier-laden bike to slide through. We had no option but to dismantle our bikes, taking off the panniers, pedals and seat-posts, and turning in the handlebars, until we could finally squeeze through. Well, actually I got through, my bike got through, Bike Buddy's bike got through, but Bike Buddy himself did not. He couldn't get his belly between the posts, and eventually I had to push him back the way he'd come and join him back on the wrong side. This time I let Bike Buddy go first, and as he squeezed his bulbous body through the tiny gap, I took a few steps back and ran full-pelt into his flabby arse.

Despite my running start, Bike Buddy was stuck. I dug my feet into the mud, forcing my legs forward, desperately trying to budge him. Bike Buddy pulled on the sides of the outer gate, heaving his body forward inch by inch, until eventually he arrived on the far side with a pop, like a Champagne cork exploding out of a bottle.

Unfortunately my running start meant I was lodged quite securely between Bike Buddy's arse cheeks, and I arrived on the other side with him. Somehow (and I'm still not sure how this happened) I ended up in the mud, with Bike Buddy sitting upon me, my arm still swallowed by his anus.

Bike Buddy pulled himself up, and I released my arm. We rebuilt our bikes, wiped down my arm, and set off once more on our way. On the other side of the gate we found Killin, a village set at the start of Loch Tay. What a strange name for a village - Killin. What were they killin'? We didn't want to hang around too long in case it was English cyclists.

After the torture of gravel, grass and mud, we finally found a road to cycle along. I was happier on roads. Bike Buddy wasn't. This road was the supposedly quiet route along the southern edge of Loch Tay. Quiet, my arse! I'm sorry, but this was the worst road I had ever cycled on. It probably didn't help that it was Sunday of a Bank Holiday. It probably didn't help that this was one of the greatest tourist attractions in the area and that all the locals, and a number of people not-so-local, had decided this was the day to visit Loch Tay.

Even with all these excuses, this was still a crap route. The road was only just wide enough for one car and had occasional passing places. Everyone else in Scotland seemed to want to use this road as a racetrack. It was also difficult to see the loch for much of the journey, with a screen of trees between the road and the water. To make matters worse the road undulated. Call me stupid, but I'd assumed if we picked a road running alongside a loch it would be fairly flat. Nope! This road was not just a little undulating; it was an endless path of short sharp climbs and falls. Mix these with the constant need to brake to avoid cars and you have the perfect road for cyclists to avoid. Unfortunately we were on it, and had to continue.

At the end of the road of torture was a settlement called Kenmore. Kenmore was an attractive little village. The place was heaving with tourists, like the road we had just cycled along, but we decided this would be a good place to stop for Sunday lunch. We had cycled forty miles. It was 1.30pm and we were in desperate need of something to eat.

We cycled up to the hotel in Kenmore, which was reportedly the oldest hotel in Scotland, and luckily they had space for two lycra clad gentlemen. I was amazed they let us in. The restaurant seemed awfully posh, with all the other guests dressed in their best Sunday attire - posh frocks, suits and tartan. But they let us in. We were in lycra and luminous tops, covered in flies, and they still let us in. My backside, legs and back were caked in mud, my arm had been swallowed by Bike Buddy's buttocks, but they still let us in. Were they mad?

The food was good, in fact probably too good, considering we still had about ten miles to cycle in the afternoon. We stuffed our faces with soup, roast beef and lemon meringue pie, and then slumped back in our chairs and let out, in unison, one enormous belch.

Thankfully, the cycle from our belly-filling Sunday lunch was nice and flat. After six miles we arrived in Aberfeldy, a small, quiet, pleasant shopping town with an eighteenth century stone bridge leading to the town.

The Bed and Breakfast owner had informed me when I'd booked that there was nowhere to get a meal within walking distance of our accommodation. This was another reason why we'd decided to have a big lunch, and now we'd found a town it seemed like a sensible idea to get some food ready for the night.

I always found it difficult choosing something to eat when I was already completely stuffed. Luckily for us, Bike Buddy never seemed stuffed, and was quite capable of looking forward to more food. He chose bread and cheese for our tea, plus anything else he could find that didn't need warming up. With his arms full of food, and this food transferred to plastic bags, we left the shop and recovered our bikes. I looked at Bike Buddy and his handfuls of bags, and wondered how we were going to carry them while cycling. Our panniers were relatively full, with the weather being rather pleasant, so there was no room for such extravagance. Instead we chose to carry a couple of bags each with our right hands as we cycled. That is not easy. It's not easy when you're going straight. It's not easy when you turn corners because the bags get caught in the front wheel, and it's certainly not easy to change gear or brake. I fell off three times, but somehow these problems didn't seem to affect Bike Buddy at all. How did he do that?

By 3.30pm we'd arrived. The owner was quite shocked to see us so early and the rooms weren't ready, but she was very friendly and invited us in for tea and cakes while we rested in the conservatory.

Despite having finished an enormous Sunday lunch only 90 minutes earlier, Bike Buddy tucked into the cakes as if he hadn't eaten for months. I took one cake and forced it into my stomach, not wanting to rebuff the owner's offer.

Despite having a very full stomach, I was a little disappointed to have finished so early again this morning. When we stopped I always felt we could have gone further, although while cycling I spent most of my time wanting to stop. Funny how your brain changes so quickly. The trouble was, I kept thinking one day we were going to get a shock and would rue the days we didn't keep going while we had the energy and the daylight. Either I would have calculated the miles completely wrong or we would take numerous wrong turns and end up cycling seventy or eighty miles in a day, and then we would be gutted that we hadn't take some miles out while we felt we could. Perhaps we were just getting fitter and the mileage was no longer enough to fulfil our physical capabilities. I looked at Bike Buddy. I didn't think so!

For another night the Bed and Breakfast surpassed our expectations. This one was a large modern farmhouse, surrounded by grazing paddocks and set amongst the jagged mountains. The air was fresh, the sky was blue, the birds were singing and life was good. We had single rooms again, and the loud drilling from Bike Buddy's mouth was slowly becoming a distant memory. Hooray, hooray, again I cry hooray.

Our single rooms gave us the use of a shared bathroom, which was just for Bike Buddy and I, and included lovely warm snugly towels. I buried my face in one towel shortly after we arrived, feeling the soft texture against my cheeks, until I realised I was in danger of becoming a woman. (Look when you've been out in the sun for more than two weeks, your backside feels like you've been sitting on a bed of nails for a month, your legs ache, your arms ache, your hands ache, you have flies in your hair, in your eyes, in your mouth, you can't straighten either leg and you walk like you've just filled your pants, believe me snugly towels are important. More than important, they are vital!)

I took my snugly towel from my room, walked across the landing and went for a soak in the bath. Despite living with the smell 24 hours a day, I realised I was starting to pong a little by this stage. I'd washed and scrubbed every night, but when I reapplied my smelly clothes it kind of ruined the effect. This afternoon, as

I'd done back in Tiverton, I bathed in my cycle clothes. I washed the same as if I had been naked, but scrubbed my clothes instead.

After washing my fabric-covered body, I peeled off my lycra and washed my naked body - a double douse today. At the same time I noticed the words on the back of my yellow t-shirt were starting to come off. I ran my finger over the rough letters, tutting slightly, but realised they would survive another week and that was all I required.

I dried myself on my snugly towel, dried my clothes with the same towel, then placed the towel around my waist ready to leave the bathroom. How do women get those towels to stay in place? Whenever I try to strap one round my waist the bloody thing always falls down. Today was no exception. With my freshly washed clothes in one hand, my toiletries in the other, I walked from the bathroom coming face to face with the owner. She smiled and asked if we had everything we needed. I smiled back, nodded slightly, and the movement of my head was just enough to unravel my towel and send it crashing to the floor. I was completed naked. The owner's eyes fell from my face to my crotch, I tried to cover myself but managed only to lose grip of my toiletries and juggled the deodorant, toothpaste and toothbrush in a frantic arm-swinging style reminiscent of an out of control windmill. All three items fell to the floor, resting gently upon the snugly towel and I was left with a pair of lycra shorts and a t-shirt to cover my embarrassment.

'I'll come back later,' said the owner.

'I don't blame you.' I replied.

I realised, when I finally got to my room, that my cycle clothes were almost dry enough to wear again already - amazing!

By 5pm Bike Buddy and I were starting to get hungry again. The owner offered to give us a lift to Aberfeldy for dinner, but we declined. I thought after my previous antics, she might want to drop us off in Aberfeldy and leave us there for the night. For some reason, when she spoke to me, the owner couldn't stop a tiny smirk appearing in the corner of her mouth. What was so funny? Was she laughing at my package?

The Bed and Breakfast had a separate lounge for guests, so after eating our bread, cheese and everything else Bike Buddy had found, we made ourselves comfortable and settled down to watch some television. I was comforted by the fact that downstairs Bike Buddy couldn't fall asleep, like he did in his bed. He would be forced to stay awake, keep me company, and avoid the drilling noise that always accompanied Bike Buddy during the night.

At least, that was the plan, but by 7.30pm he was snoring in the chair. I shook him vigorously, in a bid to wake him, and to release some of the pent-up frustration that was building within me thanks to my snoring companion. He wouldn't rouse so I shook him harder, and yet still he snored on. I couldn't hear the television, and the drilling noise was grating at my teeth and rattling my brain, so I punched him hard in the face. That worked, and he woke.

'Urgghhh, what was that?'

'Sorry,' I replied, 'my arm slipped.'

Having skin like a rhinoceros, Bike Buddy was just about to drift back off to sleep when I managed to suggest he take himself off to bed. He agreed, fell forward out off his chair and crawled on his hands and knees up the stairs to his bedroom.

I was alone again. Alone to think about how we were getting on, and alone to consider the most important aspects of my remaining life like, 'Whose cruel idea it was to put an 's' in the word 'lisp'?'

By 9.30pm I was deeply involved in a 'Who dunnit' on the television. I didn't very often watch who dunnits because I usually found I just didn't give a toss, but for some reason this one intrigued me. Besides when you watch a television near Aberfeldy you only get a choice of two channels - BBC1 or BBC2. No other channels work well enough to endure for more than a few seconds. ITV flickered continually, while Channel 4 rolled up the screen and Channel 5 didn't even exist as an option. There was no Sky, no Freeview and no Cable. BBC2 had some medieval dig program on, which I found even less appealing than the 'Who dunnit'.

By 9.36pm my eyelids were drooping, but I knew I had to try to fight my own tiredness. I was determined to find out who had actually dunnit. By 9.38pm, my right eye was shut. I often did this when I was tired. I hardly used my right eye anyway, it didn't work very well, so when I got tired I shut it. At least that way half my body could have a rest.

The program finished at 10pm. I remember being determined to stay awake. I remember telling myself to fight, to keep my one remaining eye open. I remember noticing that I could no longer see the television screen, and realising both my eyes had closed in my determination to keep one open, and then I remember waking up to see the end titles roll up the screen. I'd missed the last twenty minutes. Bollocks!

Disappointed with my lack of staying power, and frustrated with Bike Buddy for allowing me to fall asleep too early, I followed Bike Buddy up the stairs on my hands and knees. I could hear him snoring in his room, but tonight it didn't matter,

I had my own room. I crawled through the door, and into my bed. With the door shut, Bike Buddy's snoring was inaudible. Silence met me, and it made me smile. I relaxed in my snugly bed (which was almost as snugly as the towel), feeling the warmth engulf me as exhaustion took me slowly into dreamland.

And then I was awake. How did that happen? It had happened many times before, but I still didn't know how or why. I could be completely exhausted when I got to bed, but as soon as my head hit the pillow I was wide-awake again. Why was that? Most people go straight to sleep, not me! I sit and ponder things, and despite my lack of ability to watch television, tonight was no exception. I lay in bed and I thought about life, and how crap it really was when you took everything into consideration. Life is like an onion – it has many layers, but they all stink!

DAY 17: HAROLD AND HILDA – ABERFELDY TO NEWTONMORE

The day started in the best possible way. The owner of the Bed and Breakfast gave us a splendid breakfast, looked at my crotch, made us cheese and salad sandwiches to take with us, looked at my crotch, and when I went to pay she refused to take any money. She said the previous night had been one of the most enjoyable of her life, and could I keep the money and put it towards the charities. Unbelievable, she had never met us before, she had no idea who we were, but her kindness was remarkable. If only there were more people like her in the world, this world would be a much brighter place. I would have to get my tackle out more often.

As I set off on my bike the cold air instantly hit me. I had my long-fingered gloves on again, two shirts, a jacket, shorts and trousers, but I was still cold. My eyes started watering, and I found it impossible to see where I was going. Bike Buddy had to keep shouting out instructions so I didn't cycle into the hedge or miss a turning. I really did need to fit eye-screen wipers when it was this cold. Maybe I could invent them when I got home?

Today was the day we had been dreading, apart from all the other ones obviously. This was the day with the Sustran's warning; this was the day over Drumochter Pass. Bike Buddy had by now worked himself up into a real tiz. He was nervous, so much so, he was physically shaking when he looked at the pass on the map.

'We recommend you use the train,' kept reverberating through my mind.

'We recommend you use the train.'

They may as well have said, 'We recommend you go home a failure,' or 'We recommend you wimp out big boy.'

I'm sorry, but however bad this pass was, we had to cycle it. If Bike Buddy wanted to take the train, that was up to him, but I would make it all the way on my bike.

The air warmed up a little as the sun came up, which was just as well because my nose was running, my eyes were running and I could no longer feel my ears. We made reasonable time first thing and passed through Pitlochry, where we got told off for cycling across a footbridge. We didn't know it was a footbridge, otherwise we would have walked. Honestly! Still it didn't really matter, the moaning woman soon shut up when I cycled over her toes.

Pitlochry was a lovely town, beautifully set in open countryside. All the bridges leading to the town seemed to have a certain unique, individual character, as if someone had thought long and hard about each and every one.

From Pitlochry we wound our way to Killiecrankie and then on to Blair Atholl, where we decided to stop for mid-morning coffee in a large hotel. Blair Atholl was home to the Blair Castle. Tony had only been Prime Minister for a few years at the time and already had his own castle, unless this was the one owned by the Blair Witch.

Built in the thirteen century, Blair Castle was Scotland's most visited privately owned house. There didn't seem to be too many people visiting it today, and we weren't about to. I didn't want to see Tony anyway, besides Bike Buddy and I were too worried about our cycle up Drumochter Pass to take time out for a castle. Instead we sat in the hotel, warming our insides with caffeine and thawing out our ears.

As we drank the owners came over and told us the drinks were on the house. More generosity, and this time I hadn't even flashed them. I mean I'm not saying I wouldn't have done, if they'd asked me, I'm just saying I hadn't at that moment. I was starting to think we might get through the whole day without paying for anything.

We set off after our free coffee break and I started thinking about another poem. I needed to record something that told the story of our journey so far, but to get full impact from the poem, you have to picture Bike Buddy on his red bicycle, and me on my blue one. It also helps if you can remember the Milky Way advert:

Bicycle Race
The red bike and the blue bike had a race,
All red wants to do is stuff his face,

He eats everything he sees,

Covering everything in cheese,

But smart old blue, he puts less away.

Blue wants a meal that is wholesome and light,

Just enough to fill his appetite,

Yes, smart old blue, he puts less away.

Bike Buddy didn't find it amusing, especially after I'd been singing it non-stop for an hour and a half. But that didn't stop me, and it seemed a good way of getting Bike Buddy to cycle quicker – in his bid to get away from my incessant noise.

Bike Buddy's cousin, or was it second cousin, or was it second cousin twice removed. Anyway, Josh was going to join us for the day. We didn't know where and we didn't know when, but we did know he was going to be riding a motorbike. I'd never met the guy before in my life, so I wasn't going to recognise him, and Bike Buddy's reactions were so slow, he wouldn't notice a motorbike passing by until it was too late, so the plan relied solely on Josh finding us. The chances of this happening appeared to be slim – I mean we wouldn't even be cycling on the main road most of the day.

After our mid-morning break we joined the old A-road. What a delight. It was completely deserted, mainly because cars couldn't join it from the new road as there were bollards at every junction to make sure all cars stayed out. The road was fantastic for cycling on, slightly overgrown from both sides and therefore narrower than you would expect from an A-road, but still wide enough for two cyclists to ride side-by-side. The new main road was out of sight and out of earshot, and we started to feel close to nature once more. The birds could be heard, the bushes rustled as small mammals scuttled for cover, and at one stage I saw a slowworm slither across the road in front of me. For a beast known as a slowworm it was moving pretty damn quick, and I had to swerve to avoid turning it into two slowworms. A swerve that unnerved Bike Buddy, awakening him from his cycling coma.

Quietly at first, and then slowly building in volume, we heard the steady thud of a motorcycle engine behind us. I glanced over my shoulder, desperately trying to see who was invading our cycling heaven, and a motorbike suddenly appeared from the shadows behind us. The bike plodded up, gaining on us gradually, until the rider was within earshot and we heard a cheery, 'Morning!'

It was Josh. To this day, I still have no idea how he found us, it just didn't seem possible, but somehow he did, so we stopped our cycling for a quick introductory chat.

Josh was a paramedic (which will become very important later in the day). We knew the start of Drumochter Pass was just up ahead, and given the fear such a climb was creating in our stomachs, I suggested to Josh we met him at the summit. Although the climb was supposed to be up a dual carriageway, I was certain there would be somewhere for us to stop for lunch. Josh agreed and phudded off into the distance. I looked at Bike Buddy, who looked back at me. By our reckoning, the top of the pass was another ten miles further on. Hell started here!

The climb up Drumochter Pass was slow, and hard work. The wind was in our faces, which didn't help, but what did help was the fact Sustrans had kindly built a cycle track alongside the whole length of the dual carriageway. Looking at the road I was very glad we didn't have to cycle on it, otherwise the train idea might have been a good one.

Drumochter Pass was a dual carriageway, a very busy dual carriageway. If we'd cycled on the road I had a suspicion one of us would have died. Luckily, the cycle path wasn't even connected to the road. It ran five to ten yards away from the road, between trees and shrubs, which had been planted to make things look more picturesque. It actually worked! The cycle path was hillier than the main road, squeezed in a small gap between the road and the mountains, and kept dropping down to small wooden bridges, but apart from that it was very pleasant. I started to feel guilty for all the flack I'd spouted about Sustrans on this trip. They had done a bloody good job building paths for cyclists, and this one was a godsend. My only complaint remains the materials they choose to coat them.

The miles slumped past at a painfully slow pace, but things were nowhere near as bad as we had expected. Finally, as the road started to flatten off, we could see a black figure in the distance - it was Josh.

Unfortunately there was nowhere particularly safe to stop at the top of Drumochter Pass, so he'd decided to rest his motorbike against the grass verge, and jump the railings. We would be eating our lunch on the grass embankment of a dual carriageway. Not the nicest spot in the world, but a welcome rest nonetheless.

It was 1.00pm when we reached the summit of Drumochter Pass and were stopped by the man in black. We'd cycled a steady 33 miles in the morning, but were fairly hopeful that the hardest miles of the day were now behind us and life would be easier in the afternoon.

We pushed our bikes up against some trees and sat down on the grass. It was just as well the Bed and Breakfast owner had made us sandwiches because we wouldn't have found anything else to eat in this isolated spot. Josh recalled times he had driven up the pass in the winter, the biting wind blowing through the mountaintops, and snow covering the area. Drumochter Pass would not have been a nice place to be in the depths of winter. It was the highest point on the A9, and stood 452 metres (1,484 feet in old money) above sea level. It also housed the railway line between Perth and Inverness. In fact it was the highest point of any railway line in Britain and at one time required two engines to haul trains to the summit. The trains moved so slowly, passengers would alight and walk by the side of the track. (One has to ask at this point, how I had managed to fill my brain with so much useless information?)

Remember I told you Josh was a paramedic? Just after lunch I became very glad he was with us. Bike Buddy was looking tired, very tired. He stood up when we said it was time to go. As he reached for his bike, his right foot got stuck on a rock and he gradually fell forwards. It was like a comedy fall, his arms were by the side of his body, pointing straight down to his toes. He had his cycle helmet on, which was just as well, and he slowly collapsed like a ballet-trained sack of spuds, head first into a ditch. Funny thing was if we hadn't seen him fall we could have just walked over his back, because it was level with the grass surrounding the ditch, but what concerned me was Bike Buddy just lay there, completely still. To start with I laughed, then I realised he might be hurt, or worse still – had suffered a heart attack and died on the spot. Oh my God, I'd killed my father-in-law. My wife was going to be so angry.

Josh moved quickly. He reached Bike Buddy in a single stride (well he was only a yard away to start with), and checked his pulse. He was alive – halleluiah – and with Josh's help, Bike Buddy slowly rose from his ditchy grave.

Once vertical again, Bike Buddy explained how his foot had got stuck, how he'd collapsed forward and hit his head on a rock, but luckily his cycle helmet had saved him. See, it is always wise to wear a cycle helmet, even if you're not cycling at the time.

Josh gave Bike Buddy the once over, and made sure he had a steady pulse. Bike Buddy said he was okay, but would then complain of a headache for the next two days. He liked to have things to complain about. Without complaining Bike Buddy's life would have been empty.

We climbed back onto our bikes, and said farewell to Josh. How lucky we'd been to have him with us at the very time we needed a paramedic. Josh jumped on his motorbike and rode off towards the horizon. It was time for us to go. We were at the top of our journey, 452 metres above sea level, and it was time to come back down to earth.

Cycling after lunch was easy going. The cycle path continued gently downhill all the way to a small town called Dalwhinnie. Apparently Dalwhinnie was Gaelic for 'meeting place.' It was a barren and isolated spot, but was home to the highest distillery in Scotland, so if we managed to get cut-off from the outside world we could at least drink ourselves stupid while waiting for help. Perhaps that was where the meeting place was – in the distillery.

It was at Dalwhinnie we decided to stop for a coffee, and were joined in the café by a gang of Harley Davidson riders. They looked pretty 'ard to me. Bike Buddy just stared at them, I kept my eyes down, not wanting to provoke a fight. Don't look them in the eye. Don't look them in the eye. Of course I could do nothing but stare.

I watched as the bikers sat down in their leathers, removed their helmets and revealed a middle-aged lady and three gentlemen whose average age was around eighty-three. I stared even more. I couldn't take my eyes off them. How on earth did these oldies stay upright?

We drank our coffee, we talked about how old people managed to survive, and Bike Buddy nodded as if he was a youngster himself. I laughed, and suggested Bike Buddy looked like he should be sitting on the biker's table rather than mine. He tutted and ordered another drink.

After our coffee break I had my scary moment of the day. The road was narrow, and I saw a car in the distance, making its way towards me.

'Nothing wrong with that?' you might say.

True, but there was another car overtaking it at the time. This second car was on my side of the road, only a few metres before me and nearly removed my right kneecap as it sped past.

I screamed and wobbled the bike a bit with my body in an attempt to protect my leg. It was a pathetic effort, but all I could manage at the time because I couldn't break or steer to avoid him as I was using my left hand to hold a mobile phone to my ear. I realised, at that time, what a stupid thing it was to hold a mobile to my ear while cycling. I also knew I'd have to get a hands-free set when I got back. I wondered if they made them for bikes? Perhaps I could just use a heavy-duty elastic band!

The cycle from Dalwhinnie to Newtonmore was straightforward, and continued to be mainly downhill. We tazzed along at a good pace and soon passed the largest truck-stop café in the world. The building was immense, a huge shining silver fortress covering the land. Not a place two cyclists would be particularly welcome, so we cycled past and quickly arrived in Newtonmore.

Newtonmore, so I'm led to believe, was the central location for the filming of 'Monach of the Glen'. (Remember this point, it is very important in the next chapter.) The area was beautiful, set amongst the mountains, with secluded glens, flowing streams and green fields. Now we just had to find our Bed and Breakfast.

Thankfully, this one was fairly easy, and at 4pm we were knocking on the door. The Bed and Breakfast looked delightful. A recently build structure set amongst the trees in a secluded area of the town. Our bikes were put to bed in the garage overnight, safe and sound, and our rooms were clean, spacious and offered picturesque views across the valley.

However, there was one small problem - the owners reminded me of Howard and Hilda from Ever Decreasing Circles. If you've never seen Ever Decreasing Circles let me fill you in. Howard and Hilda always wore the same jumpers. Howard spoke very slowly and very precisely, ensuring he pronounced every syllable. He could talk for hours on the most meaningless and boring subject, and his voice was a monotone drone. Hilda always followed Howard wherever he went, and just smiled at him. She spoke quietly, always agreeing with her husband, but always in the shadows. The owners of the Bed and Breakfast were Howard and Hilda, the only difference was this Hilda had a very thick brown moustache.

After showering and allowing ourselves a quick relaxation we descended the stairs and made the mistake of asking Hilda where we could go for an evening meal. She panicked, like a rabbit caught in the headlights, not knowing what to do next. She looked around, searching out Howard for help, and he gratefully accepted her invitation to answer the question for her. Howard went into great detail of how to get to a lovely little Italian restaurant on the main road. He explained how we should walk out the front door, ensuring we carefully make our way down the two steps, not wanting to trip or slip on the concrete that could have got particularly treacherous after the rain a few nights previous. He explained the track back to the road, how it meandered through the trees, and would take us slowly, but safely to the main road. He described each and every possible obstacle that we could meet on our travels, including the normal location of cars parked along the track at this particular time of day. He explained other obstacle that would not normally be present, but just in case, he felt it was his duty to warn us of them. He explained how we should turn right on the main road, travelling past a number of shops and pubs (all of which he described in detail the history and purpose of, and how they all sat together to make the town the pleasure it had become), and how, eventually, if we were particularly careful we would finally arrive at the Italian restaurant.

Unfortunately I'd fallen asleep just after the steps. Bike Buddy kept nodding. He had an amazing concentration span when food was involved. After the explanation, and just as we wanted to leave to get our food, Howard continued to describe his bird-watching love, his collection of eighteenth century coins, his fascination of the variety of leaves that fell in the yard during the autumn, and his assortment of tourist attraction leaflets for the local area. The local area, according to Howard, covered the whole of Scotland, and Cumbria. Perhaps there just weren't many tourist attractions in this part of the country.

I made another mistake quite early on in the conversation, by asking if he had a mobile phone charger, which might fit my phone. This was now Howard's aim in life - to find me a charger. After two hours, forty-three minutes and sixteen seconds we escaped out the front door, in search of the Italian.

We followed Howard's instructions to the letter (which Bike Buddy had memorised). We turned when we were told to, we skipped when we were told to, and we jumped when we were told to. Eventually we arrived at the Italian restaurant, just as Howard had said. My God, he was good! Just one problem – it was Monday, and Howard had forgotten to inform us that the restaurant was always closed on a Monday.

Not wanting to see Bike Buddy fade away, we wandered back the way we'd come and went in a pub instead. They served food, and very nice it was too. After building up an appetite for Italian food, I ordered garlic bread and pizza, followed by chocolate sundae. Bike Buddy did the same.

After eating, we decided to continue our pool challenge. Actually, this was Bike Buddy's idea. I had a small problem, I had eaten so much food I was having difficulty moving my stomach around. As a result, I wasn't really in the mood for pool, but Bike Buddy was, and he gave me a real hammering.

When we left the pub Bike Buddy had a commanding 4-1 lead in the pool challenge series, and I realised there was only one way I would ever defeat him – I needed to get him absolutely rat-arsed drunk and then challenge him to a game.

On the way back to the Bed and Breakfast, Bike Buddy and I tried to formulate a plan. How could we get into our rooms without Howard cornering us, and talking us to death? I suggested we just opened the door slowly and silently crept in, making our way to our rooms without sound or smell. Bike Buddy said this was a crap plan, but then admitted he couldn't think of anything better. There was nothing else we could do - we had to just try it.

The door opened silently, we stepped through the porch, and quietly floated along the hallway. Just as we reached the stairs, Howard appeared by the side of us, like some paranormal vision. At first he didn't speak. We just said, 'Evening,' and tried to continue up the stairs in the vain hope that we could escape, but no! Howard opened his mouth and began the longest sermon the world had ever heard. This lecture explained how he'd been looking for a phone charger, but had failed, but he didn't accept failure very well. I tried to comfort him, but to no avail. Howard was inconsolable!

While Howard talked, Bike Buddy crept up the stairs unnoticed, and left me to my ultimate doom. I was going to die on those stairs, slowly whittled away by the monotone drone of Howard, the most boring person in the world. Sorry Howard, but you have got to get yourself a life.

At 12.34am, I managed to finally crawl away from Howard. By this time I knew his complete life history, as well as the history of Hilda, Hilda's family, his family, his brother's family, his brother's children's family, his friend from school's brother's cousins' friends' family etc. I was mentally exhausted, but I was free. I just needed to get through the morning without seeing him and I could enjoy the rest of my short life in relative peace.

As I lay in bed mulling over the cycle so far, and the distance travelled, I suddenly sat bolt upright and shrieked 'Eureka!' We'd done it! We had covered the distance from Lands End to John O'Groats. Unfortunately we hadn't cycled in a straight line, so our 932 miles (73 miles more than expected) was still 250 miles short of our final destination. We had spent more than 120 hours on our bikes, and quite frankly, I'd had enough.

DAY 18: STOP THIEF! – NEWTONMORE TO INVERNESS

I woke in a cold sweat in the morning. I was in fear for my sanity. I had to go down to breakfast, but I didn't want to see Howard again. I didn't want to spend the last few weeks of my life hearing Howard's drone. He would corner me like a cat playing with a mouse. I would be alone, and vulnerable, and I needed protection. I needed someone to talk to Howard for me and my only hope was Bike Buddy. Bike Buddy would be my saviour. I ran to his room and banged on the door.

At 8am we walked downstairs to breakfast like two men about to receive their final meal. (That's something I will never understand. Why do they insist on giving a condemned person a slap up meal before being executed? If it was me, I'm not sure I'd be particularly hungry! It's bad enough with a little stress, but knowing you're about to die would surely dissolve your appetite.)

'Even though I walk through the valley of the shadow of death, I fear no evil.' That's a lie. I was terrified! As I walked I slumped low and trudged slowly behind Bike Buddy, his incredible bulk protecting me from the evil that was Howard and Hilda.

When we arrived, I realised Hilda was alone in the breakfast room. That surprised me. She pointed to the menu without speaking. I stared at Hilda, although not in a 'corr she's gorgeous' kind of way, but in a 'how did she grow such a thick moustache' kind of way.

I'm sorry! I know that's really bad. Perhaps she had some kind of hair growing defect, which meant her facial hair grew ten times quicker than a normal man's. Perhaps she was allergic to hair removal cream, or shaving foam, or both, but despite all those words of sense running through my mind, I could not take my eyes off this large furry caterpillar lying on top of her lips. She had a thicker moustache than Bike Buddy, and he'd been growing his for forty years.

While staring up at Hilda, I moved my finger over the menu and, without speaking, pointed randomly at what I wanted for breakfast. Bike Buddy boldly quoted everything he wanted to eat. At the sound of each word Hilda physically shook, winced, and took a small baby step backwards. After Bike Buddy had finished his long list of requirements the room fell back into silence.

Having spent the evening listening to Howard, it was fairly obvious why Hilda was so quiet; she hadn't had the opportunity to speak since meeting him. Her tongue had completely seized up, perhaps even withered away to nothing.

Within minutes Hilda's moustache reappeared with our food, and I ate my boiled egg and toast. More food for Mr Strong!

We ate quickly. Even Bike Buddy stuffed the food away as if there was no tomorrow. We had to get away. We had to leave the breakfast room before Howard had an opportunity to corner us.

After our final morning rituals, we trudged downstairs to pay, but disaster; Howard was waiting in reception to accept our money, and to give us some last minute important information about his coin collection. If we hadn't forced our way past him, we would still be in that Bed and Breakfast now. God that man could talk!

The weather had taken a turn for the worse that morning. The rain was falling like a waterfall, and it was bitterly cold. Undeterred, and keen to escape the clutches of the damned, we cycled away from the Bed and Breakfast, on through Newtonmore itself and into Kingussie.

Kingussie, according to Howard, was Newtonmore's big rival in life. It stood at the foothills of two mountain ranges, and, like Newtonmore, also claimed to be the base for the filming of 'Monach of the Glen.' No wonder the two towns didn't get on!

As we meandered our way along the quiet main road (this far up the country every road seems to be quiet), we arrived in Aviemore. This amazed me; Aviemore was a ski resort in the winter. I couldn't believe we had cycled from the summer holiday resorts in the West Country up to ski resorts in Scotland. Yet there was no snow to be seen anywhere. Lots of rain, but no snow.

By now I was having difficulty feeling my fingers, my ears or my toes, so we stopped in Aviemore for some hot chocolate. We needed to warm up otherwise our bodies were going to seize up in the cold. No wonder Aviemore was a ski resort, it might not have actually been snowing, but it was certainly cold enough to freeze a lot of things – especially those bits furthest from the body core. I was amazed it could be this cold in Britain in the middle of August (even in a ski resort), although one good thing about the cold, wet weather was my bottom no longer hurt. I think that was mainly because without so much sweat, things stayed fresher, although after seventeen days non-stop in the saddle, perhaps my bottom had just given up the fight.

After defrosting our bodies, we went back out into the pouring rain to continue the trek towards Inverness. Little did we know of the difficulties to come.

From Aviemore we continued on the quiet main road to Carrbridge - a delightful village with the oldest stone bridge in the Highlands. The bridge was built in 1717 and was no longer used as a bridge, but could easily be seen from the road. When I saw it I was very glad it was no longer in use - a very slim stone arch that looked like it was struggling to hold itself up, let alone anything else. I wasn't sure how many more days Carrbridge would be able to make this oldest bridge claim – it could collapse at any time.

From Carrbridge we started the long hard climb up Slochd Pass. This pass was not quite as high as yesterday's Drumochter climb, but at around 400 metres (1,328 feet) above sea level, it was definitely enough to make us puff a little.

The weather wasn't really improving. The rain occasionally stopped its constant drain, and the warmth from the sun was finally beating its way through the clouds, but overall it was still wet and cold. As we reached the summit of Slochd Pass we decided it was time to take another breather. It was late morning, and after climbing to our highest point for the day, it seemed sensible to stop.

We came to a standstill at the top of the pass opposite Slochd Ski and Mountain Bike Centre. There were no seats to park our bums, but a couple of tree stumps made perfect chairs, so we propped our bikes up and sat down to share our water and chocolate. As we rested our weary legs, the owner of the Ski Centre came out in his van and asked if we were alright, or if we'd broken down.

'Broken down? With our bikes' we laughed. Did this guy not know who we were? We didn't break down, we were cycling masters, and nothing could stop us from our gradual ascent of the country.

He drove off into the distance and we continued to munch our way through chocolate. A few minutes later we were ready for the off, our bodies refuelled and our minds refreshed. Bike Buddy picked up his bike and cursed instantly. I thought he'd broken a bone or at least badly maimed himself, but no; he had another flat tyre.

This was the first flat with the new inner tubes, and quite unexpected. Unfortunately the problem with this flat was he'd also managed to split the beading of his tyre. (In case you have no idea what I've just said, the beadings on a tyre are the small strips of metal, which hold it to the wheel. If you split one you can't put the tyre on.) Bike Buddy was in trouble. If Bike Buddy was in trouble, so was I, and our tour was suddenly at real risk of ending in failure at the top of Slochd Pass.

Bike Buddy had been carrying a spare tyre at the start of our tour, unfortunately he had decided to leave it at home just over a week ago. Bike Buddy was carrying duct tape at the start of the tour, something we could have used to strap the tyre back together temporarily, unfortunately we had used the last of the duct tape to send our smelly clothes parcels back home a couple of days ago. Now we were in trouble!

You have to picture the scene. We were miles from anywhere on the top of one of the highest passes in Scotland. We had a mobile phone, but couldn't get a signal. We couldn't walk to get help because it was too far, we couldn't wave anybody down, because nobody was coming past. We were desolate, alone and with no means of transportation. A feeling of complete isolation. No back-up vehicle for help, nobody to rely on. Our tour was over, but, worse than that, even after accepting defeat, we had no way of getting home.

Suddenly I saw a brilliant light at the end of the tunnel, and nodded my head at the sign behind Bike Buddy - Slochd Ski and Mountain Bike Centre. To me it sounded like a place that might have some bicycle tyres.

We pushed our bikes down into the car park to have a look. Everything was locked up, the owner was not in. This didn't really come as much of a surprise since we'd already seen him drive off into the distance only moments earlier. We wandered round the side of the building and started peering through the windows.

The bike sheds were locked, the house was locked, and the garages were locked. However, lying against the wall of one of the sheds was an old racing bike tyre. This tyre was bright green, was not in good shape and had obviously been removed ready to be thrown away. However, this tyre would fit Bike Buddy's bike, and after much consideration we decided we had no alternative but to 'borrow' it.

Bike Buddy set to work changing the tyre over. He put the crappy 'borrowed' tyre on the front of his bike, and his remaining decent tyre on the back. Unfortunately when he removed the supposed decent tyre, it became fairly obvious this tyre wasn't going to last much longer either. While he stripped, rebuilt and pumped, I started to scribble a note to the owner on a page torn from my diary:

'Taken old racing bike tyre. Sorry for inconvenience, but are cycling Lands End to John O'Groats and have burst beading on tyre. Enclosed is £10 for tyre. Hope this is enough, otherwise you can contact us at our Bed and Breakfast tonight,' and then left him the phone number.

I grabbed ten pounds from Bike Buddy's wallet and pushed it into the torn page from my diary. Ten pounds was very generous for an old tyre that would never have be used again. The owner would probably return later and laugh. He would probably start chuckling, and chuckle himself stupid throughout the evening, 'Ten pounds for a worthless piece of worn rubber, hee hee hee!' From our point of view ten pounds was a small price to pay if it enabled us to complete our journey, and if it also made him happy, that was a bonus. The other bonus was, he might laugh so much it gave him stitch.

As we changed the tyre and wrote the note a police car drove past on the road above. We must have looked very suspicious. After all it can't be every day you see two men dressed in cycling clothes and cycle helmets mending bicycles in a mountain bike centre!

Okay, so despite the fact we should have blended in, the policemen seemed to think something was wrong. They drove back. Then a minute later they drove past again, very slowly. I waved - a proper wave, not an, 'I've still got my bow fingers' type of wave. I'm not sure that was the best idea in the world, but I did it anyway. They drove off into the distance.

I suddenly had a terrible thought; maybe they were after us for the attack on the farmers near Wilsontown. Maybe we fitted the description, and every policeman in the country was now out scouring the land for the two cycle criminals. Perhaps they'd pieced together the fact I had now killed eight people (at least I thought it was now eight, but that depended on whether the farmer was dead, or just in intensive care.) What did it matter? I had now killed more than a handful of completely innocent people, and maybe the police were on my trail. Oh shit!

I waited for the police to pass again, but nothing happened, and as the seconds ticked past I started to relax. My heart settled back down to a more normal rate, and I turned to Bike Buddy as he fought with his bike.

It wasn't long before Bike Buddy had the 'borrowed' tyre on his bike and we were ready to leave. One last look up and down the road just in case the owner was coming back, and then we tootled off towards Inverness. The policemen were obviously still suspicious because they had stopped just down the road, and watched as we cycled past. I felt guilty, I'm sure Bike Buddy felt even guiltier. After all, he was the one with the 'borrowed' tyre on, and he had no idea what I'd done on our trip up the country. I tried to be casual. I didn't want them to ask us any questions, but the more casual I tried to be, the more suspicious I must have looked.

By the time we passed the policemen, I was gripping my handlebars so tightly my knuckles were white. I was gritting my teeth, and my whole body was tense. I felt guilty and I looked guilty. I tried to relax, tried to act casual. I lessened my grip on my handlebars so that my knuckles returned to a more natural colour. I greeted the police with a cheery, 'Morning!'

They grunted back. Bike Buddy was also a little self-conscious. After all, he was the one with the bright green front tyre on his bike. The bright green tyre that looked completely out of character with the rest of his red bike. But, despite our guilt, the police didn't seem too bothered. Either they were tired of chasing cyclists, or they just didn't care. I thought they would at least ask us some questions, but no! Perhaps it was time for their tea break, so they let us go.

Up until that day I had never really believed in someone watching over us. I had never really believed in anything. I went to church every Sunday from the day I was born until I left to go to college, but I was never sure I really trusted everything I was told. I had studied science subjects all my life, and as a result I needed things proved to me before I could accept them. However, the day at the top of Slochd Pass was different. What were the chances of us bursting a tyre just fifty yards away from a mountain bike centre? What were the chances of the mountain bike centre having a single tyre propped up outside, and it being the size we needed? This tyre wouldn't have even fitted a mountain bike; it was a racing tyre through and through. Sometimes things happen, and you need to take time to think, 'Why?' The day at the top of Slochd Pass was one of those days. If you are up there Lord, all I can say is thank-you (oh yes, and I'm sorry I told my wife it was the cat who took a big bite out of the chocolate wedding cake she was making).

This newfound knowledge made me feel kind of warm inside, despite still being cold from the rain. Perhaps when I died, I would go to a better place, but then a thought suddenly hit me. If there was a God, he wasn't going to take too kindly to me murdering people as I cycled up the country, so I decided there and then to always refer to the killings as 'unfortunate accidents'. If I believed they were unfortunate accidents, then God would have to believe me when I took the lie detector test at the gates of heaven.

By now we were starting to get very hungry. It was an hour and a half since we'd consumed our chocolate, and we'd been prating around in the ski centre for most of that time. The fear of failure, the fear from being watched by police and the adrenalin needed to take something not belonging to us meant we had consumed our fat reserves despite not doing any exercise. It was now lunchtime.

The rain was still falling, and we were very wet. Cycling was certainly a chore rather than a pleasure, and the sooner we managed to stop the better. Half an hour after making the decision to find some food we came to a little village going by the name of Tomatin, and found a pub. I was encouraged slightly that, had we failed to find the tyre, it wouldn't have been too far a walk to call for help. Perhaps seven or eight miles. I could have walked it, even if Bike Buddy could not.

Tomatin was home to yet another Scottish Distillery. Anyone would think all Scot's did was drink alcohol, and Bike Buddy was starting to wish he'd been born in Scotland.

The pub seemed like a decent place, and with nothing else around for miles in any direction, we decided to stop. By now the rain was coming down in bucket loads, so we pushed our bikes into the porch, and propped them up against the wall. They wouldn't be in the way too much, and besides they needed a rest from the rain as much as we did. The landlord looked at us with disapproving eyes, but we just smiled and ignored him.

I ordered a rustic cheese and ham ploughman's and wanted it quickly. We needed to get to Inverness before five o'clock, to give Bike Buddy the chance to buy a couple of new tyres. He had by now decided, (what I had suspected for a long time) that neither of his tyres were any good, and if we were to complete the journey he would have to buy some new ones. Besides it was his wife who kept tight control of the purse strings, and she wasn't with us, so he could buy what the hell he liked. Never leave a cyclist alone in a bike shop; it's like leaving a small child alone in a shop full of sweets.

The rustic bread almost broke my jaw, but was soon washed down with a pint of orange juice and lemonade. I was ready for whatever the weather could throw at me, and stepped back out into the torrential downpour. It was days like this I wondered why we were touring on bikes. If we'd decided to do Lands End to John O'Groats in a camper van it wouldn't matter if it was raining. On a bike, it mattered big style! On a bike the wind direction determined whether we had a good day or a bad day. On a bike the rain could make us miserable. If I was miserable, Bike Buddy was suicidal. Rainy days and Mondays always get me down. Perhaps it should have been sung as, 'Rainy days and Tuesdays always get Bike Buddy down.' Although I'm not sure Karen Carpenter knew Bike Buddy at the time.

The afternoon cycle was extremely hard going. Bike Buddy was finding it difficult, and had decided to put his whinging head back on. He complained of a headache; a result of his sack of spuds fall the previous day. He complained about the rain, he complained about his tyres, his bottom, his waterproof jacket, which apparently wasn't waterproof at all, and he complained about the Sustran's route markers.

I felt some sympathy for him to start with. After all he had fallen headfirst onto a rock the previous day, and his head had a right to protest. It was raining, no argument there, but at the end of the day we were in Scotland, it always rained in Scotland. What did he expect - tropical sunshine? My bottom hurt as well, so he would get no sympathy there. Besides you didn't hear me complaining about my sore bottom. Had I even mentioned the two red blisters on my bottom on this journey? As for his waterproof jacket, really that was just tough.

I have a bit of a problem with sympathy. I'm quite good at it, but only for a short while. If my wife or children are ever ill I am always sympathetic and helpful. This lasts precisely until lunchtime, by which time the sympathy wears off. I start to think, 'Surely you feel better by now?' or 'Come on pull yourself together and stop moaning.'

Well, I'd reached the, 'Pull yourself together' stage with Bike Buddy. From now on he could moan alone. Having said that, we'd been following the Sustran's route again for a couple of days, and I had to agree with him on this one - they were bloody awful. Drumochter pass aside, I was not convinced Sustrans had chosen the easiest route anywhere.

The Sustran's route to Inverness took us in a big loop, and then another big loop. We circled our way to Inverness, never really getting any closer as if we were trying to creep up on the city without being seen, without it suspecting a thing. We followed the route like ants follow the line back home with their leaves. The trouble was, rather than being the leader, Bike Buddy acted like another worker-ant when he lost a route marker.

'What do I do, what do I do?' he would shout.

'Just keep going,' I would reply.

The circular route took us to a pile of stones in the middle of a field. These were very strange stones, each about the size of a baby's head. We stopped our bikes to have a closer look. The stones were designed in a circle, with a small walkway leading to the centre. I wandered in. Despite the many tourists viewing the stones, nobody else walked into the centre. I stood there, while Bike Buddy took a photograph. I then walked round inside the circle, picked up a stone, felt the weight in my hand, and then put it back. There must have been thousands of stones making up this circle, possibly even millions. After a few minutes, I walked back out, stepped to the side and read the notice posted up. The stones were the 'Balnuaran of Clava' - a complex Neolithic cemetery. A stone cemetery! I gulped. 'Do not enter the circle. Anyone who enters the circle will bring bad luck to himself and his Bike Buddy.' I gulped again. We left quickly.

Our next encounter was with a peculiar sign. We cycled along the road and there in brown and white was a five-foot sign shouting to the world the words, 'SECRET BUNKER 1 MILE.' Is it just me that finds this strange? If it is a secret bunker, why are they telling people where to go? I could imagine the secret scientist working on his secret invention, in his secret laboratory within the secret bunker. Suddenly the door would crash open and a dozen Japanese tourists would barge in taking photographs of everything inside. The scientist would try to hide, but the tourists were on him like a swarm of wasps around a barbecue. Before he knew what had hit him the tourists would whoosh back out like a tornado, leaving the scientist scratching his head and wandering how the hell his secret lair had been discovered.

A mile further down the road and the sign read, 'SECRET BUNKER NEXT LEFT.' I was dying to go and take a look, but Bike Buddy needed tyres, and we needed to get to Inverness. I would have to leave the secret bunker to my imagination. If anyone has found it, please let me know.

I had been looking forward to Inverness for a while. Inverness, the most northerly city in Britain, was sure to be a quaint little place. I couldn't imagine too many people living this far up the country.

There was one more surprise though, before we got to Inverness. The Sustran's route decided to take us into a forest on the outskirts of the city. I wasn't overly keen on the route through the forest. Pine needles weren't the best thing for cycle tyres, particularly Bike Buddy's dodgy back tyre and borrowed front one.

Bike Buddy kept looking down at his front tyre, certain it was deflating, but all my sympathy was used up, so I ignored him. We were only a couple of miles from Inverness, we could walk from here if it really became a problem (well I could anyway).

Out of the forest we reached the edge of the city, and I realised this wasn't a small quaint town at all. It was a heaving metropolis, like another Birmingham or Manchester. Inverness was the capital of the Highlands, and it certainly lived up to its name. I couldn't believe how many people were driving around the roads, and walking the streets. We hadn't seen anyone else for most of the day, and suddenly here they all were. Okay, so it was almost 5pm, and people were going home from work, but I didn't expect to see so many. 'Oh my God, it was almost 5 o'clock!' We needed to get to a bike shop, and quick.

We found a massive sports store, and were told they didn't sell tyres to fit racing bikes. (Why is it this country has large sports stores that don't actually sell anything useful for doing sports? Okay, you can buy fancy trainers, or designer sweatshirts, but you can't buy bike tyres. Come on! In France you can step into a supermarket and buy a bike tyre, or a chain, or new brakes, but in Britain you can't even get them in sports shops. What is cycling then, a separate entity all on its own? This country is a farce!)

We hurried on further, having received directions to a cycle shop. This one was much more helpful and suggested Bike Buddy purchase some Armadillo tyres. He didn't bother to ask the price (no wife around to stop him) and purchased, as recommended, the most expensive tyres in the shop. The owner must have seen how desperate we were and thought, 'Here's an opportunity to get rid of those gold rimmed bicycle tyres I've had in the window for thirty-six years.'

After re-mortgaging his house, selling one kidney, and half a lung, Bike Buddy strolled out with his new tyres. His borrowed tyre was still inflated, so we decided to get to the Bed and Breakfast before putting the new tyres to use. Besides it was still raining, and perhaps we could find a bit of shelter to change the tyres at our lodgings for the night.

Bike Buddy was still very depressed. He was becoming a fair-weather cyclist. That was not a good thing on a three-week long tour of Great Britain. Perhaps we should have been touring the Sahara Desert instead. Because of his depression, I carried the cycle tyres for him. I'd seen this done by many cyclists, they simply put them over their heads and rest them on one shoulder. This was easy, no problem, I could cycle with two tyres on my right shoulder. I could, that was, until I had to stick my right arm out to signal at a roundabout. Instantly the tyres started to slip down my outstretched arm and I couldn't move. I couldn't lift my left arm because it was the only one holding the handlebars. I couldn't move my right arm, because it was now the only thing holding the tyres up at all. The tyres slipped down further, until they were strapping my arm to my waist. I was stuck, I couldn't do anything but try to stop. I grabbed the brake lever with my left hand and the bike pulled sharply to the left. I hit the curb and came to an abrupt standstill. Luckily the tyres held me on my bike, and I just bounced delicately off the saddle onto the crossbar. 'Ouch!' In fact, more than ouch – 'arrggghhhh my balls!' The pain shot through me like a dagger. My balls, my balls, my balls! I was in agony. Bike Buddy didn't even notice, he didn't look behind him; he just carried on his way. They were his bloody tyres! I felt like throwing them on the road and cycling off without them, but I am a kind-hearted soul (honestly) and I simply hauled them back on my shoulder and carried on. I would be fine provided I didn't have to stick my arm out again and instead held the tyres on my shoulder with my right arm bent double.

We arrived at the Bed and Breakfast at around 5.30pm. The rain was still coming down, and we were drenched to the bone. I didn't like Inverness; it was too busy. I couldn't believe there were so many people living there. All this from a bit of oil.

The owners of the Bed and Breakfast were not friendly. They looked as if they really didn't give a damn, which, to be fair, they probably didn't. Bike Buddy was forced to change his tyres in the car park, and got even wetter. I didn't hang around, and instead watched him from my bedroom. I did check his front inner tube for punctures (from the comfort of my room), but the tyre seemed fine. We had come through the pine needles unscathed.

After changing the tyres, I joined Bike Buddy outside, and we walked our bikes to the shed and gave them a quick wipe down with a towel. We had to try to get some of the water off, before everything rusted up.

Our rooms were singles again tonight. I started to think I was actually missing Bike Buddy's drilling noise at night, and then I came back to my senses. I'd stick to the single rooms as much as possible.

After showering, we wandered downstairs and the owners very half-heartedly gave us directions to an Italian restaurant down the road. In a funny kind of way I was missing Howard, at least he gave good directions, although, perhaps this Italian restaurant might actually be open.

After another stint in the rain, we found the restaurant and were pleased to see it open. In a desperate bid to carbo load, I ordered Tagliatelle Carbonara with garlic bread. I needed pasta for energy.

After eating, buying a new disposable camera and sending the used one off in the post, we walked the mile back to the Bed and Breakfast in the still pouring rain. What a miserable day! Perhaps the weather would improve tomorrow, but somehow I doubted it.

It had been a tough day mentally. I thought we were going to give up today. I thought Bike Buddy had had enough. I thought the rain and the tyres had finally got to him, and he was going to just sit down on the side of the road and cry. I wouldn't have blamed him; he'd had so many punctures. Bike Buddy had now had eight punctures, and I still hadn't had any. Eight-nil, that's a hell of a record, and worse still he'd also broken his tyre. We needed an easy day tomorrow to raise our morale, but I had a suspicion we wouldn't get it. We were putting our faith in Bike Buddy's new Armadillo tyres; surely nothing could puncture those, and after tomorrow we would only be a couple of days away from our goal. Please let tomorrow be easy.

DAY 19: THE EASY ROUTE? – INVERNESS TO LAIRG

W hen we woke up in the morning it was still raining. The sky was dark grey, thick black clouds surrounded us in all directions, and it was chucking it down. It was the kind of day you looked at through the window, saw the misery outside and instantly wanted to crawl back into bed and pray for the rain to go away. Unfortunately we had some cycling to do. Unfortunately this cycling meant we had to go out in the rain, and unfortunately it meant we had to stay out in the rain all day.

Bike Buddy did not have a good morning, of which I felt partly responsible. Despite me checking the inner tube the previous night, this morning Bike Buddy's front tyre was flat. He replaced it, and found a very large hole in the inner tube. This was very strange since I'd checked it through water last night. I'm not a complete idiot. I did know what a hole looked like. I mean, I might have missed a small hole, but not one the size of a large furry mammal. Bike Buddy was not impressed. He tutted at me, looked at the inner tube and then tutted again. I'd pissed him off and we hadn't even had breakfast.

The puncture and the weather seemed to get Bike Buddy down even more than yesterday. By 7.30am he'd already moaned incessantly about his wet clothes, the terrible weather and his puncture and we hadn't even stepped outside. Somehow I knew today was going to be bad. Somehow I knew today was going to be the make or break for our trip, and Bike Buddy was going to have one of the worst days of his elongated life. I also knew we would both feel considerably better once we'd left the busy streets of Inverness and had regained the fresh air and pleasant cycling of the countryside. Perhaps today would be our last big test before succeeding in our goal? Let's hope so!

After breakfast, we set off from our dry rooms to the flooded roads and rain-soaked city. Making a fairly early start meant we could leave the busyness before the main rush hour, and hopefully reach peace and quiet when the rest of Scotland awoke into the oil-rich streets of Inverness.

The route out of Inverness took us first towards, and then over the Kessock Bridge. There was a cycle track along the side of the bridge, but the handrail was too low to be of any use if we did actually fall off our bikes. Despite my inability to enjoy heights, this bridge simply didn't bother me. I think because it seemed to be solid ground, and the bridge appeared stable, it was no problem. No problem for me anyway! Bike Buddy, who had spent half his life on scaffolding, was a different matter. He did not like this bridge. He did not like this bridge one bit.

I cycled merrily along, enjoying the view over the side. Peering at the murky water as it passed below us, and the mud-soaked banks on either side. Despite all the rain that had fallen on Bike Buddy and I, Inverness had obviously not received its full quota, because the river level appeared quite low. How much rain did this country normally receive? I didn't really want to hang around to find out.

The water was so brown I could see nothing within it. No fish, and no weeds, not even an abandoned shopping trolley or floating drunk who'd fallen in on his way home from the pub. The water was just muddy water, and I watched it alone.

After a few minutes cycling, I realised I'd reached the opposite side of the bridge. I looked back and saw Bike Buddy still at the start. I shouted for him to come across, but I don't think he heard me. He shouted back, and I just made out his murmurings of, 'How do you get to the other side?'

I looked up and down the river, then cheerfully replied, 'You're already on the other side.'

Bike Buddy did not appear pleased with my response, and set off slowly toward me. He was moving slightly slower than some of the slugs also present on the metal, creeping along at snail's pace. I also noticed he was leaning down over his handlebars. He was leaning so far forward his nose was almost touching his front tyre. I was puzzled by this sight. What was he doing? I then twigged it - he was trying to get his head below the height of the handrail. He was trying to get low enough to be safe. This had to be recorded, so in Bike Buddy's desperate hour of need, I simply took out my camera and took photographs of him.

Just before he reached me, Bike Buddy passed a man sweeping the track. I could hear the conversation they had as he slumped past.

'Good morning,' the man greeted Bike Buddy.

'You're wrong. You are very, very wrong,' replied a disgruntled Bike Buddy.

The man just stared, and then mumbled, 'Pleased to meet you, you stroppy old bugger!'

Bike Buddy just gave him a two-fingered salute, and cycled on. Oh, he was in a good mood this morning!

After Bike Buddy's pulse rate returned to a more normal level (well normal for him, please bear in mind he's on beta blockers), we followed the Sustran's route into the country. I should point out that when planning our route, this part of the journey had given me a choice; two routes marked by Sustrans; we could either take the summer route or the winter route.

The summer route was slightly further, and went via the Nigg ferry. To me, using a ferry was similar to using a train. Okay, this ferry only went about two hundred yards across the water, but it was still cheating, and as such I had opted for the winter route. As a result Bike Buddy had only prepared maps for the winter route, but now we had a problem. For some reason the winter route had not been sign-posted by Sustrans, and what's worse, we didn't realise this until we'd already missed a turn and were about four miles into the summer route.

One of the reasons for Sustrans creating two routes was because of the ferry. The Nigg ferry only ran in the summer. By this time, it was the end of August, but neither of us knew what Scotland considered to be the summer. Would the ferry still be running? Should we turn back, or continue? Bike Buddy and I met a postal deliveryman and stopped him to ask him about the ferry.

'Excuse me, do you know whether the Nigg ferry is running today?' I enquired.

'Aye, I should think so,' he merrily replied.

That wasn't as positive an answer as either of us had wanted, and after much deliberation, discussion about whether using a ferry was cheating, and considering that the mileage was longer anyway, we made the decision to continue on the summer route and just pray the ferry was running. Besides it was still chucking it down, and we had already done four miles on the summer route, four miles we would be forced to retrace if we decided on the winter route. So the summer route it was.

The summer route took us the long way up the Black Isle to Cromarty. We were now cycling blind. We were relying solely on the Sustran's route markers because

Bike Buddy's maps didn't cover this route. Take it from me; never trust Sustran's route markers unless you are prepared to be sorely let down.

Part way up the Black Isle we took another wrong turn and bumped into some genetically modified feed protestors. By this I don't mean the protestors were genetically modified, although some of them looked very strange. One was dressed as a skeleton, another as the grim reaper, and another like Michael Jackson. Not sure why Michael Jackson - probably because Jacko had, allegedly, been genetically modified a number of times.

We cheerfully waved at the protestors, who cheerfully waved back, but I couldn't understand what they were doing here. How many folk travelled this tiny back lane? I'd have been surprised if they'd met anybody else apart from the postman and us. Surely there were more prominent places to protest. Idiots!

At the town of Fortrose we decided we were so badly lost we should really ask someone for directions. I have to say though, all in all, Fortrose was not a bad place to get lost in. It was the main town on the Black Isle, and many of the houses were Victorian. Fortrose cathedral was a splendid sight, made from red sandstone in 1250 (although only a portion of the original building was still standing when we arrived). The city (it must be a city if it's got a cathedral) was quaint, and much more in line with what I'd been expecting from Inverness. Much better!

In search of some directions, we walked into the Tourist Information Office (which seemed like a good place to start), and met a lovely old lady who was happy to help.

'Can you tell us the way to Cromarty?' I asked cheerfully. Bike Buddy stood beside me in silence.

'Aye,' she said, 'you need to take the easy route.'

Now that was what I liked to hear - an easy route. Bike Buddy smiled for the first time in forty-three years, we wished the lady a pleasant day, waved, straddled our bikes and whistled while we cycled in the direction the lady had pointed, looking forward to a gentle jaunt to Cromarty.

Out of Fortrose the road lifted slightly, which we knew was going to come since we'd cycled down it only moments earlier. It wasn't steep, or particularly long, and was received joyfully in the full knowledge that this was going to be the last hill for a while. The easy route would surely be as flat as a pancake.

As we left the main road and headed in the direction instructed, the road rose violently towards the sky. We put our heads down and pumped on the pedals, the whistling gone, but hope still in our hearts. One short, sharp hill wouldn't be too bad bearing in mind the pleasant, easy cycling just round the corner.

Round the corner, the incline increased, as the road lunged towards heaven, and we could see the road continuing to rise into the distance. How could this be the easy route? If this was the easy route, what the hell was the other route like? Bike Buddy was getting demoralised, I was getting demoralised. Bike Buddy was getting tired, and started to moan. He hated hills, he was tired, cold, and wanted to go home. I hated Bike Buddy moaning, I hated hills, I was tired, cold and I wanted him to go home. All hope of a pleasant cycle had disappeared and we realised life on a bike didn't get much more miserable than this.

We dragged ourselves up the path leading along the south-eastern edge of the Black Isle, hardly moving, but edging forward in a desperate hope that the Nigg ferry would be running.

Drained and cursing the lady from the Tourist Office, we finally dragged ourselves to a signpost introducing us to a tiny village, going by the name of Eathie. I looked at the signpost, and looked at Bike Buddy. Bike Buddy looked at me. How could we have been so stupid? Now we knew exactly what the lady had said, 'Aye, you need to take the Eathie route.' Bitch!

After more climbing we reached a pinnacle giving views across the peninsular in both directions. The scenery was stunning, the weather was still wet, but our hopes lifted as we realised a ferry would have to leave from sea level, and therefore the cycle from now on had to be downhill.

Despite the wind blowing in our faces, our speed levels slowly rose and we whistled towards the town of Cromarty with the anticipation of a ferry to help us across the water. I knew I could swim it, if need be, but I also knew I'd struggle to do so while dragging my bike and panniers with me. I also knew Bike Buddy was non-amphibious, which meant he'd sink quickly.

When we arrived at the ferry terminal Bike Buddy was exhausted. It was coming on for mid-day, and we'd cycled more than 35 miles already, and when he looked at his map he slowly started to drift into a coma. Bike Buddy started shivering involuntarily, and quite violently. He was going into spasm, his eyelids flickered, and his pupils were unresponsive. Bike Buddy was dying on his feet. I went over to him and shoved some chocolate in his mouth.

'Stay with me Bike Buddy,' I cried. 'What is it? What has made you like this?'

Bike Buddy pointed to the map with his trembling finger, and then blurted out some words. To start with I couldn't decipher what he was saying, and then it hit me. He was telling me we had cycled further than we should, and based on the map he reckoned our total mileage today would be more than one hundred miles.

Holly cow, batman! Bike Buddy asked me if I could cycle one hundred miles today. I said I would if I had to. He then told me to leave him, to go on without him, to just leave him there to die.

I was determined to save Bike Buddy. Today was not a good day to die; it was raining. I needed him; he was the map-reader. And besides, who else would I be able to consistently take the piss out off on this trip?

I looked closer at the map and tried to decipher whether Bike Buddy was right. I asked another ferry passenger how far it was to Tain. He suggested it was only about five miles.

'There you go,' I said to Bike Buddy, 'that makes forty miles to Tain, and it's only about twenty miles from Tain to Lairg. A total of sixty miles, no worries!'

Bike Buddy wasn't convinced, but he did seem to cheer slightly.

The ferry itself was quite an experience. We were joined by two cars and a number of foot passengers. We were asked to hold our bikes until the ramp had been raised, and then we rested out bikes against it. We looked out across the water, viewing the large oil drills in the distance, and watching the birds skip across the surface. Bike Buddy remained quiet, not wanting to waste his energy talking, and I remained quiet, not wanting to admit that I still believed taking the ferry was cheating.

We found the Sustran's markers again as we left the short jump across the Cromarty Firth from the Black Isle to Nigg. Another amazing place name, but one I wasn't willing to speculate on.

From the ferry, it was no real surprise to find the Sustran's route took us the long way to Tain. We seemed to skirt all the way round the town without actually getting any closer. We visited Shandwick, the Hill of Fearn, then Shandwick again, but didn't get any closer to our destination. I'd taken the decision to cycle ahead from the ferry, but this tactic wasn't working and Bike Buddy was getting further and further behind. Once again I was literally dragging him up the country, and I wondered whether it would have been more humane to leave him to die in Cromarty.

My problem was when we got lost I cycled faster. It was like an inbuilt panic button. I had to go faster and faster until I found my way back onto the right track. Bike Buddy, on the other hand, got more and more demoralised and hence got slower and slower.

After ninety minutes of pure frustration, we got so fed up with the ever-circular Sustran's route, which kept forgetting to include route markers just when we needed them most and forgot to actually take us to the place it was supposed to, we decided on a new plan. We still had no maps and couldn't find any route markers, but we had found a signpost to Tain and made a beeline for the main road. Now we knew we were going the right way, it might not have been pleasant, but at least we would get to the Bed and Breakfast before nightfall.

The cycle for the last few miles into Tain were busy. The road wasn't packed, but the cars using it travelled quickly and had little respect for passing cyclists. Bike Buddy was in fear of his life, but I kept him motivated by the offer of food once we'd arrived in the town. Through this offer of a reward, we cycled forward and arrived in Tain at 2.45pm. We'd cycled 45 miles without a break (apart from the short ferry crossing), and were tired and very wet. We were also hungry and thirsty, and when I reviewed the map, realised it was another 30 miles to Lairg.

This was probably our lowest point of the whole trip. Bike Buddy was suicidal, and I was having real doubts whether we would make it through the day. We'd made the mistake of following the Sustran's route markers rather than our own maps, and with no maps to follow had continually got lost over and over again.

Pushing our bikes by our side, we walked slowly down the main street of Tain looking for somewhere to get lunch at such a late hour. It was at this point I realised Bike Buddy wasn't quite as bad as he was making out. Having found a café, Bike Buddy continued to walk, not content with a simple sandwich and coffee. Bike Buddy wanted an alcoholic drink, and he was desperately searching for a pub. In my mind, if he had enough energy to search for a pub, he certainly had enough energy to cycle a little further today.

Unfortunately he searched in vain, and I saw Bike Buddy start to panic. He needed food. I panicked when I got lost. Bike Buddy panicked when he might miss a meal. He started to run around the street like a headless chicken, not knowing what to do or which way to turn. He needed food. He needed a pint of beer. He was going to self-destruct in front of me, so I grabbed him by the arm, and tried to comfort him.

'Bike Buddy focus. Bike Buddy focus.' I said calmly.

Bike Buddy was hyperventilating. I had two options; I either found him a paper bag and got him to breathe into it, or I slapped him round the face. I chose the latter, it seemed more fun.

Once his breathing was back under control, I convinced him there was no pub for us to drink in, and we would have to settle for the café. He agreed, walked in holding his cheek and just sat down at a table. He couldn't even muster enough energy to stand at the counter and order food, so I ordered for him; jacket potato with cheese and coleslaw – obviously the same as me.

While waiting for the meal, with Bike Buddy sat in silence, I did a quick calculation and realised I'd eaten my way through thirty-six tonnes of cheddar cheese on this trip, and two tonnes of mozzarella. Although, I should add I didn't have a calculator with me, so that is only a rough estimate.

Tain was a thriving town. Its full name was The Royal Burgh of Tain, since it was given its first royal charter way back in 1066 (that year rings a bell, did something else happen then?), making it the oldest Royal Burgh in Scotland. Tain was a sanctuary, where people could claim the protection of the church. Bike Buddy would have preferred the protection of alcohol, but alas, he had to go without, and I knew he'd be like a bear with a sore head in the afternoon.

Lunch was a quick affair because we needed to get on. I made a vital decision over my jacket potato; it was time Bike Buddy took the lead. He was always quicker when he led, so I wanted to see what he could do.

With food in our stomachs, and a brief but welcome rest, Bike Buddy set off at a terrific pace. The route from Tain to Lairg was fairly straightforward, it was mainly on B roads, and kept us zipping along quite nicely without too many concerns about wrong turns. In fact, I soon realised, Bike Buddy was going so fast I was struggling to keep up. Surely this wasn't the same man I'd just dragged up the Black Isle.

The rain continued to be torrential. We'd received a brief respite while on the ferry (although sea water took the place of the rain), but now the rain was back with a vengeance. My hair was soaked, with the water dripping between the edges of my helmet and my head, slipping into my eyes and over my glasses. My legs were sodden, with no waterproof trousers to wear, and the water had infiltrated my waterproof jacket, making its way down my back. Actually, I couldn't determine whether the trickle of water running down my spine was rain or sweat. What did it matter, I was getting wet whatever the source. (Please note, I'm not complaining. I'd hate you to think I was complaining about my waterproof jacket not being waterproof. Did I mention my bottom was hurting?)

The speed was good, the road was quiet for a main road, and the scenery was pleasant enough – but the weather was appalling.

Bike Buddy's pace meant we quickly descended on Bonar Bridge, and I wondered what Bonar Bridge had been called before they built the bridge in 1812. Bonar, perhaps!

The place was deserted, just a bridge crossing the stretch of water known as Kyle of Sutherland and Dornoch Firth.

As we arrived at Bonar Bridge we thought about crossing the bridge and taking the A836 to Lairg. After our morning cycle, you'd have thought the A-road would have been the easiest option, but undeterred from our determination to stay away from main roads as much as possible, we opted to stay on the west side and make our way up to the Falls of Shin.

The road to Shin Falls wasn't quite as bad as I'd expected. I mean, the weather was horrendous and we couldn't see through the mist well enough to see the road ahead. The climb was long and hard going, and our tired legs resisted every turn, but we were moving. In fact, with Bike Buddy at the helm we actually made a decent pace, and, from what I could see, the falls were amazing. They were supposed to be a good place to watch salmon fling themselves upstream between April and November, but the rain meant we saw nothing.

Bike Buddy really was having a second wind. He fairly flew up the hill, and was throwing himself off the other side when I had a thought. By the top of the climb we were gently nestling within the rain clouds and visibility had reduced to virtually nil. I remembered I had a small LED light on the back of my bike and decided to switch it on; a bit of extra protection from cars taking me from behind.

We were soaked to the skin. Waterproof jacket or no waterproof jacket; after a while it didn't really matter. Rain was pouring in the neck at the top, and dripping down my legs at the bottom. My trousers didn't repel water, they attracted it. My legs were sodden, my shoes were saturated, and my feet squelched as I pressed down on the pedals, but despite the rain, I was actually having fun. We were cycling well, and looked like we would get to Lairg in good time. Today had been a test and I could suddenly see light at the end of the tunnel – we were going to pass this test after all.

Sustrans then outdid themselves. The route to get us back to the main road incorporated a grass bank - a very wet and slippery grass bank. Then, at the bottom of the grass bank was a flight of stairs - metal stairs - wet and slippery metal stairs. What a stupid thing to put in the middle of a cycle track! These stairs were lethal! We had to carry our bikes on our shoulders, down wet metal stairs in shoes with metal cleats on the bottom. Oh the fun!

At the bottom of the stairs was a metal footbridge and it was at this point I panicked. Bike Buddy was happy, the footbridge was very high in the sky, and very similar to scaffolding. He skipped along the bridge like a fairy on ecstasy. I was scared! I didn't like heights, and this bridge was high. I didn't like the fact I could see the floor beneath me, through the bridge. I didn't like the way the bridge creaked and clicked with every step, so I closed my eyes and kept walking quickly.

With my eyes shut tight, I suddenly walked headfirst into an immovable object. I thought perhaps I'd reached the other side so opened my eyes, but there standing in front of me was a mountain - Bike Buddy's arse.

Apparently Bike Buddy had thought it was time to get revenge for the Kessock Bridge incident and had decided to stop walking and make me stand on the bridge for as long as possible. He wanted me to cry. Bike Buddy was trying to make me cry. I wanted my mummy!

I pushed with all my might, but Bike Buddy could not be moved. Eventually, through my sobs, I heard him laugh quietly and then the bulk began to move forward once more. We were moving, and I nestled timidly against Bike Buddy's backside aching for protection.

Finally we reached the far side, and were met by another flight of metal stairs, which we slipped and clicked down, our bikes still hoisted high above our shoulders. At the bottom of the stairs we jumped the safety barrier and were safely back on the main road. Safe on a main road – what am I saying?

From the stairs to Lairg was nice easy cycling. Bike Buddy continued to lead, and continued to set a good pace. The rain was falling, but we were already soaked to the skin, and more rain just didn't matter.

The signpost arrived, and we sailed past into Lairg, which was a small picturesque village situated at the edge of Loch Shin. We cycled alongside the Loch for a while, and then turned up the main street into the village.

It was only a little after 5.30pm when we pulled up next to our Bed and Breakfast for the night; a pub. We'd cycled 30 miles in less than two hours in the afternoon, and this included a grass bank, metal stairs and the bridge from hell. We were soaked through, but we'd made it.

I rested my bike outside, walked into the pub and was greeted with a cheery, 'Afternoon.'

The pub already incorporated half a dozen drinkers and the barman, and one kind gentleman pointed out something I hadn't known. Something I wished he'd told me earlier in the day, something that could have saved me no end of heartache. He said, 'I wouldn't go out on a bike today, it's raining!'

Thanks mate!

The barman looked at me in a 'Please get out of my bar' kind of way. He obviously had a problem with me leaving a trail of water everywhere I went. I tried to be as considerate as possible. I walked in a straight line, and I walked back out along the same line I'd come in. I did, however, do a rather rapid twirl in the middle of the room, right next to Mr 'I wouldn't go out today' and soaked him with spray. Shame!

There was one other problem when the weather was wet and cold - it meant I didn't have anything to wear in the evening other than a pair of boxer shorts. Of course even these relied on my panniers remaining watertight throughout the ten-hour downpour. I wasn't sure the pub would be overly impressed if I went down for dinner in just my underwear, so I asked the barman if they had a tumble-drier. Alas, the owner of the Bed and Breakfast was out, and they couldn't use the tumble-drier without asking permission first.

To make matters worse our poor bikes had to spend the night outside in the pouring rain. We locked them up round the back of the pub, and covered them in Bike Buddy's cape.

When we entered our rooms, we found the radiators didn't exist and there was no hairdryer. We were soaked with no means by which to get dry and I found this very annoying. They were happy to take our money, but really didn't care if we were warm and dry. We'd met some fantastic people on this trip, some so kind you felt sure they couldn't be genuine, but they turned out to be just nice people. We'd also met some 'Don't give a damn' people. People who did the least possible to get by. This annoyed me! I'd always tried to go through life treating people the way I would want them to treat me. I know sometimes these ethics slipped a little, but at least I tried. I couldn't believe a Bed and Breakfast had nowhere for us to put our bikes out of the rain, and had no means by which we could get out of our wet clothes. I told them when I'd booked that we were coming by bike. Perhaps I should have asked if they had any drying facilities. At the time I just assumed they would. A kind of 'given' when you book a room, a radiator or heated towel rail etc. I had badly misjudged them. No wonder the tourist trade was dying in some areas of Britain. The service was so bad people didn't deserve to survive. Unfortunately it was because we kept putting up with it, that they got away with it for so long. Perhaps now was the time to start the fight.

I searched inside my panniers and found my boxer shorts had survived, miraculously. I also found my alternative luminous t-shirt, which had also remained dry. I had underwear and a t-shirt, so all I needed now was some trousers.

With no alternative, I opted for the 'gent's toilet hand-drier' approach and after many minutes standing under the hand-drier, casually greeting men as they came into the toilet, my trousers were dry. I could go to the ball; well, I could go get something to eat anyway.

Despite having dry trousers, I still didn't have dry socks, so I went into the restaurant bare foot. I didn't think anybody would notice, and quickly hid my feet under the table while ordering chicken curry and rice, followed by profiteroles. Unfortunately the waitress dropped her pen while taking our order, leant down to pick it up and caught a glimpse of my naked feet. I think she was a little turned on, because she came back up from under the table in a bit of a fluster.

'Excuse me sir,' she said, 'but you seem to have forgotten your shoes and socks.'

I looked at her, and then glanced below the table. 'Bloody hell! You're right,' I replied. 'But, I had them on when I walked in. I'm sure I would have noticed if I hadn't. Someone must have stolen them. Get me the manager, someone has stolen my shoes and socks.'

The waitress looked even more flustered now. Perhaps it was what I'd said. Perhaps it was because I'd raised my voice a little more than I should have done. Perhaps it was the fact that every person in the restaurant was now staring at us.

'I'm sorry sir, but the manageress is not here at the moment and she won't be back until tomorrow,' she replied.

'Then let me use her tumble-drier,' I blurted without thinking.

The waitress scribbled down our order, along with a little message to the chef to put something in my curry, and then she walked away.

After dinner, which was surprisingly good and creamy, I continued to dry my clothes on the hand-drier. I started with my socks and then moved on to my cycle shoes. I stuffed the shoes with paper towels and held them under the drier, but after a number of minutes I'd had enough. My hands were burning hot, but my shoes remained damp. Besides, I was fed up with talking to men as they took a leak. There are only so many conversations you can have in a toilet over a urinal, and I'd exhausted them all. What made it worse was I couldn't understand what they were saying anyway, they all had extremely strong Scottish accents. A man would walk in and our conversation would be something like this:

Him: 'Howzitgaun?'

Me: 'Fine thank-you'

Him: 'Wotchdaein' inna chanty?'

Me: 'Fine thank-you'

Him: 'Geesa fag'

Me: 'I don't smoke'

Him: 'Ya disnae smowke? Wotcha choob aw somin?'

Me: 'Fine thank-you'

Him: 'Ya drookit. It be stoatin aff the grun n the morra'

Me: 'Fine thank-you'

Him: 'Awayan'boilyirheid'

Me: 'Okay, bye.'

It didn't matter now anyway; my clothes were dry enough, and I was sure they'd be completely dry by the morning. Bike Buddy, on the other hand, had made no effort to dry himself off. He had more clothes in his panniers than I did, so he'd been fully dressed for dinner, but I wasn't sure he had anything dry to wear for cycling tomorrow. Honestly, sometimes he just needed to make a little effort.

Unfortunately, our accommodation was a twin room with en-suite so I was in no rush to get to our bedroom. I knew as soon as Bike Buddy got in the room he would start snoring, probably even before his head hit the pillow. Therefore I decided we should stay in the bar for a while, and suggested to Bike Buddy we continue our pool challenge.

At this stage of the pool challenge I was 4-1 down, but still had my newfound ace to play. I bought Bike Buddy three more pints of beer, watched him down them one-by-one and then stepped up to the pool table. Life was easy this evening, Bike Buddy couldn't hit diddly, and I raced to a 4-0 lead on the night and 5-4 lead overall. The trophy was mine, provided we didn't go anywhere near another pool table over the next couple of days.

The inevitable happened, soon after I took the overall lead in the pool challenge, Bike Buddy decided to retire to his bed. There was nothing left for me to do, but to climb the stairs to the room of drills. I was not going to get much sleep tonight. Bike Buddy was exhausted and I knew he would snore like he'd never snored before.

I lay in bed at 11pm, with the drill going off beside me. My legs were exhausted, my arms were exhausted, and my face felt like it had been sand blasted for weeks, but my mind was still active. I couldn't sleep with Bike Buddy snoring in the next bed. I would have to stop him. I switched on the television. Bike Buddy half woke up, grunted, turned over and went back to sleep. It worked again – result.

What a day! We'd managed to get through the day with just one puncture - first thing this morning, which was probably just as well or Bike Buddy might have just laid down in the middle of the road and gone to sleep never to wake up again if he'd had anymore. Bike Buddy now led 9-0 in the puncture competition, and quite frankly I thought my effort was starting to get a little embarrassing.

Today had been one of our longest on the saddle. We'd cycled 72 miles, which was 16 more than we thought it would be, and very hard going. What's more, it had rained all day, and we were knackered, but we'd done it.

I was excited about the coming day. After all, we only had two days cycling left and it really looked like we were going to complete this journey after all. I would achieve my one main aim and go into the record books as someone who'd had actually cycled the longest distance between two points in mainland Britain. I was finally going to make a name for myself and with my name recorded, I would in some way live forever. Perhaps we would break the world record for taking the longest route from Lands End to John O'Groats on a bike. Perhaps we would make it into the record books for the most wrong turns on a single cycle trip. I wondered how many other people had cycled from Lands End to John O'Groats. I wondered how long it would take us to cycle to the moon. I wondered if Neil Armstrong was the first man to walk on the moon, who it was videoing him? And slowly I drifted off to sleep.

DAY 20: THIS IS GETTING TOO EASY – LAIRG TO BETTYHILL

I woke at 2 am with both my legs in complete limb-numbing cramp. To start with I thought someone had sliced my legs off and I was just feeling the burning pain of my limbless stumps. I threw myself out of bed, half-expecting to land on my leg-less torso, but was relieved to semi-consciously see my limbs were still intact. I tried desperately to push my feet against the floor, to free the muscles.

I occasionally had cramp in the night, but never before in both legs at the same time. I always tried not to complain too much about cramp at home, because my wife always said, 'You should feel the cramps you get when you're having a baby,' and it was therefore probably best to just let it lie.

I was standing in the corner of the bedroom, with my hands against the wall, pushing with all my might. My legs hurt so much, but the pain was going, when Bike Buddy opened one eye, grunted, and went back to sleep.

'Thanks for the help,' I snorted.

Once the cramp had subsided I climbed back into bed, but soon remembered how much I hated this period. My legs still ached, and I kept thinking the cramp was coming back so lay there twiddling my toes, and moving my legs back and forth, trying to get comfortable; trying to make sure my legs stayed crampless through the remainder of the night.

I think I got another couple of hours of sleep before Bike Buddy woke me with the sound of plastic bags. I tried to ignore him, and continued to lie in bed with my eyes still shut, trying to avoid the inevitable.

Finally I opened my left eyelid, just slightly and took in the full glory of Bike Buddy in his underpants. Urgh!

The first thing I wanted to know was about the weather.

'Is it still raining?' I enquired.

'Nope,' came Bike Buddy's quick response.

'Hooray!'

We wanted to take it easy today, so decided to set off a little later, resting after yesterday's mammoth ride. This was just as well because we needed to wipe our bikes dry first, and clean off some of the gunk that had built up during the course of the previous day.

I got to the bikes first and tried to remove Bike Buddy's cape, which had acted like a water butt in the night and had saved a few gallons of water within its folds. Unfortunately, as I removed it, I only managed to pour more water all over his bike. He'd tied the cape round his seat and handlebars, so I quickly replaced it and waited for him to arrive and remove it himself.

When Bike Buddy turned up he was quickly into complaining mode, 'Someone's moved my cape.'

'Really,' I replied, 'how do you know?'

Somehow the minuscule movement I'd made was enough to trigger an alarm in Bike Buddy's brain, which informed him of the cape movement. Like when you sneak a biscuit out of the cookie jar at home, and your wife instantly knows because the cookie jar has moved at least a millimetre from the place she'd left it. Like when you borrow someone's pen at work while they are away for the day, and they know as soon as they step back in the office. It's strange, but perhaps it is the little folk quietly whispering in their ears.

After drying our bikes, we made our way back in for a good Scottish breakfast to set us up for the day ahead. My efforts with the hand drier seemed to have paid off, and all my clothes were dry. Unfortunately my shoes were still damp, and quickly soaked my socks when I placed them on my feet. Undeterred, I packed my odds and ends in my panniers and was ready for some breakfast. (I wonder what my odds and ends would be called if I got rid of all but one of them?)

Bike Buddy's clothes were still wet, which put him in a bad mood instantly, but I didn't care. It was his own fault for being such a lazy bastard.

The waitress from the previous night served us our breakfast and I waved my feet at her and told her I'd found my shoes and socks.

'Some bugger had left them in the urinal,' I bleated. 'Still I've wiped them on the tablecloth and they seem to be okay.'

She smiled in a 'thank God you're leaving today' kind of way and left.

At 8.30am we were on our way and I was in a good mood. Today would be a great day! It should be shorter than the hell of yesterday, and tonight we would be at the north coast of Britain. Tonight we would celebrate.

My newfound joy partly evaporated just a few miles down the road. The sky was overcast, but remained dry. I was just thinking about how glad I was I'd spent so long drying my clothes last night, and merrily avoiding the puddles, when a 'friendly' chap in a black Volkswagen Golf overtook me. He overtook me on a narrow stretch of road, and did so just at the point when he could drive through the biggest puddle you were ever likely to see. He hit the water at breakneck speed, and fired a tidal wave over my body, from head to toe. I was soaked, completely and utterly soaked. So much water poured over me I couldn't see where I was going for a few seconds until the wave cleared. I was livid! I was livid because he had been so inconsiderate. I was livid because all my hand drying had gone to waste, but I was mainly livid because he'd driven so quickly I hadn't even had time to show him how livid I was. What a git!

Bike Buddy, who was taking the lead again, heard my cries of anguish, and asked over his shoulder if I was alright. I said yes, and shook my fists at the driver, but it was too late, Mr Volkswagen had already disappeared into the distance.

I was determined this soaking wasn't going to dampen my spirit for the celebration ahead. Regardless of inconsiderate drivers, today was still going to be a good day.

Everywhere we turned we got the same view, miles and miles of open countryside, rolling hills and very scruffy looking sheep. The sheep were only scruffy because their coats were so long. They need to be long to keep out the biting wind, which whipped over the hills.

The route through the Highlands was fairly straightforward. After all, there were only a couple of roads, so it was difficult to make a wrong turn. We followed the A836. At least I was told it was an A road, but to be perfectly honest, I doubted it. It was a single-track road, with just the occasional passing place. This wasn't really a problem, we only saw about a dozen cars all day, and most were courteous enough to wait at a passing place to let us through.

The lack of turnings and resting places meant we cycled along at a fair pace, and didn't have to keep stopping to check the map. As a result we arrived at an inn mid-morning, and decided it would be wise to stop for a break. It was unlikely there would be many more places to stop and get a drink between here and Bettyhill, and Bike Buddy didn't want to take the risk of going without a drink. What was more, parked outside this inn was the black Volkswagen that had soaked me earlier in the day, and my mind was already starting to plan my revenge.

The only problem with pubs and inns is they are never open when you need them. Luckily many of the owners we'd met were more than happy to open up just for us. The door was ajar, so we wandered in. The owner was welcoming, told us he was always open to weary travellers, and invited us in for a cup of tea.

We'd pushed our bikes up against the wall outside, but there seemed little point in locking them. After all we'd seen hardly anybody apart from Mr Volkswagen all morning, and just because he was a git didn't mean he was a thief. In fact, locking them seemed to be disrespectful to the locals. It would be a sign that we didn't trust them, and if we didn't trust them, why should they trust us?

We stumbled into the bar area, our legs still numb from the day before, and fell onto some wooden benches. The owner brought us a pot of tea and some cakes, and then offered to make us some sandwiches for the remainder of our journey. He suggested we wouldn't find anywhere else to get some food between there and Bettyhill. We accepted, and were presented with a large box of sandwiches and cakes.

As we sat drinking our tea, Bike Buddy noticed a map on the wall, and asked the landlord what the B873 to Bettyhill was like. The landlord stretched behind the bar and pulled out a contour book. This was an amazing book, small enough to fit in a pocket, and showing every road in Scotland. At the back of the book he showed us the contour for every road in the Highlands of Scotland. It just so happened that our planned route, the route suggested by Sustrans on the National Cycle Network, the A836 to Tongue, was not only further but also much, much hillier. The road undulated all the way to Tongue, and the coastal road from Tongue to Bettyhill wasn't much better. The landlord suggested we took the B873. It was flat, ran alongside the rivers and lochs, and was a good three or four miles shorter. The plan was set - we would cut right at Altnaharra.

Outside, our bikes were still propped up against the wall. Nobody had stolen them, nobody had nicked the panniers, nobody had nicked the mileometers. Finally a place where we could trust our fellow countrymen.

I looked at the black car next to us, and wondered if it was the publican's. He'd been kind to us, and I didn't want to make him suffer, so decided I would be kind to the Volkswagen owner just in case. He was a lucky man.

With our lunch packed away in the panniers, we remounted and set off down the road. The cycle to the inn had been a gentle rise higher and higher. As a result the trip the other side was a lovely gentle decline all the way to Altnaharra.

Altnaharra really was just a couple of houses, nothing more. Completely isolated, but in an area of outstanding beauty. I looked around for a small shop, or Post Office, but there was nothing. Where did these people go to get food? Where did they go if they wanted a newspaper? More importantly, where did they go for a drink?

In the middle of the village (i.e. between the two houses), we turned right onto the B road and took the gentle climb up the other side in our stride.

This road was wonderful - fairly flat cycling alongside Loch Naver. The peace and tranquillity surrounded us, not a single sound other than the birds in the trees, and the gentle trickle from the streams.

Part way along the B road we noticed fishermen in the river with their heads covered in netting. The midges must have been annoying them – which Bike Buddy and I found highly amusing, because they hadn't really bothered us at all. No midges had attacked us. Perhaps these Scottish folk weren't as tolerant as us hardened Englishmen. Perhaps Scottish midges preferred the taste of Scottish flesh. All those thoughts ran through my mind, until we decided to stop to eat our lunch. Suddenly the sky turned black with humming insects and we were descended on by a buzzing, heaving mass of midges.

I have never eaten so quickly in my life. Within five minutes, with our mouths still full of food, we were back on our bikes and pedalling down the road. The midges didn't have a preference for Scottish flesh, the Scots weren't intolerant to insects, it was just that midges preferred to hit stationary targets. We were okay provided we kept moving!

As we cycled, the midges amused me. I decided, in my own mind, that we had to keep above ten miles per hour, because below ten miles per hour we would explode, engulfed in a midge-bomb.

From then on, at every junction, I took pleasure in shouting to Bike Buddy, 'Stay on or get off? Stay on or get off? Don't drop below ten miles per hour. Stay above ten.'

Bike Buddy just tutted.

Bettyhill arrived very quickly. Soon the signpost read, 'Two miles', and a glance at my watch told me it was only just after 1pm.

The last two miles to Bettyhill were, as you might expect from the name, upwards. It was a long drag up to the village, but it had been an easy day's cycling, and one small hill wouldn't change that.

If I'd known we could cycle this distance so easily I would have given us a little further to go. It was a shame to stop really. It was raining again, but still a shame to stop. We were so close to the finishing line, we just wanted to keep going. Unfortunately I wasn't sure we could cycle all the way to John O'Groats in the afternoon, so there was no real reason to carry on. We could rest our limbs and set off fresh tomorrow for the final showdown.

Bettyhill was a reasonably new settlement. The original village, called Farr, was a mile east of Bettyhill. The village itself was small, with amazing views over Torrisdale Bay, but I imagined Bettyhill could be a very isolated place in the winter.

We got to the Bed and Breakfast by 1.30pm, the earliest ever, and too early for the owner. She very timidly opened the door, and then informed us that our rooms weren't ready. Never mind, we could sit in the lounge.

The rooms were singles with a shared bathroom, and I started to dream of a night without the drill. We sat with a cup of tea in the lounge watching television, and then decided to walk around the village. However, before we could take a stroll we needed to put our bikes in the peat shed, to keep them out of the rain. I kept thinking how bad it would be to collect our bikes in the morning only to discover them covered from wheel to saddle in peat. I hoped she didn't have another peat delivery today, otherwise we would need to dig them out before we cycled off.

We wandered around the village, which didn't take long, so wandered around again. On the second circuit we managed to find our way into a school playground, although I'm not sure how. The children were at school, and stared out the windows at us, until the teacher came to the door and waved her arms above her head. To start with I thought she wanted us to go and see her, perhaps to give a presentation to the children about what we were doing. I mean, after all, we'd reached celebrity status by now, having nearly cycled from Lands End to John O'Groats. I was sure the children would want to hear our tales of courage and physical accomplishment, but as I began to walk towards the school, Bike Buddy grabbed me by the arm, 'She wants us to go,' he said.

'She wants us to go. She wants us to go where?' I replied. 'Oh, you mean, she actually wants us to go.'

Fine, we won't tell the children our exciting story, they can buy the bloody book like everyone else.

Round the corner from the school we caught sight of the road out of Bettyhill; the road we would take the next morning. This road looked steep. A dramatic fall towards the sea followed by an equally steep climb up the other side. I didn't like steep descents, particularly in the morning and this hill started to play on my mind so much that I wanted it out the way that evening. I wished we hadn't seen it. In fact, what I really wished was it wasn't even there. Perhaps a fairy could come down in the middle of the night and magic the hill away, making the road out of Bettyhill completely flat. So flat, they had to rename the town Flatbetty. I wasn't sure my wish would come true, and I wasn't sure Betty would appreciate the name change, but I continued to wish it nonetheless.

By 4pm we'd crawled to the local hotel for dinner. It was not the greatest place on earth, but pleasant enough. As we settled into our chairs for the evening, I couldn't help thinking about what we had done. We'd cycled from the south coast of Britain to the north coast. Surely, it was time to celebrate. I ordered a beer, and joined Bike Buddy in a celebratory drink – my first beer for three weeks.

Unfortunately the hotel had a pool table. Bike Buddy wanted revenge for the previous night, and challenged me to a continuation of our game. I had no choice but to accept, and we played five or six games to while away the time. At the end of the first five games neither of us could remember the score. There probably wasn't a great deal in it, and we decided it was probably a seven all draw. Now it was time for one final game. One game to decide the winner; to determine the greatest end-to-end pool player ever.

I broke; slamming the cue ball into the pack with such venom the ball hit the front of the pack, lifted off the baize, flew off the end of the table, bounced twice on the floor and disappeared out the open doorway. I looked in horror, and looked at Bike Buddy. Bike Buddy looked at me, but apart from us, nobody else seemed to have noticed. I peeked out the door and looked down the hill that led to the sea. The ball had gone, and it wasn't coming back!

We potted the remaining balls nonchalantly, pretending we were still playing properly, then with all the balls safely slotted into pockets we replaced the cues and sat back in our chairs. Seven-all draw it is then!

What a day's cycling. It had been easy. I told you we were going to have a good day, and the joys of the previous few hours raised my spirits to new levels and I had this overwhelming feeling we had finished. I drank beer with Bike Buddy; although soon realised it was not good to drink beer with Bike Buddy. Starting at 4pm, drinking through the afternoon, and with nothing to line my stomach since the rapidly eaten lunch, I very gradually felt rather tipsy. It was time to order some food.

At 5.30pm a lad called Lee walked in. He had a natural way of depressing us. Having nodded at him, he nodded back, and after he left the bar to find himself a room for the night, he reappeared to have a chat. It just so happened that Lee was doing the same journey as us, so he sat down and joined us for a bite to eat and a drink.

It was nice to meet a fellow nutter, but Lee looked like the kind of lad who'd told his parents he was popping out for a quick bike ride and had just kept going. Although he was pleasant enough, I kept thinking he was making a mockery of our achievements. Where were his lycra shorts? Where was his luminous cycling top? How could he just pop out for a ride and end up cycling nine hundred miles? Lee just looked as if he wasn't making an effort, and that made me feel like the effort I'd put in wasn't really that much of an achievement after all.

As we ate and drank, two more nutters walked in; a whippet and his lip pierced girlfriend. They too were cycling Lands End to John O'Groats, this time on a tandem, and they seemed to think it was a race.

The Tandemeers didn't arrive back in the bar until much later; they were obviously enjoying each other's company somewhere else in the hotel. Perhaps the whippet got one of his legs caught in his girlfriend's pierced lip.

We sat with Lee, as he told us how he'd raced the Tandemeers up the country. As he spoke I kept thinking how we had to beat them to the finish line. Tomorrow had now turned into a race. 'Just popping-out' Lee and the Tandemeers may not be aware of it, but Bike Buddy and I would certainly be doing our utmost to reach John O'Groats before them. I would also be making some slight adjustments to their wheel bolts to make sure they made a poor start.

Wanting an early night so we could get cycling before our competitors, we were about to say our farewells and leave the hotel when I told Bike Buddy I was going to the toilet. Instead, however, I searched outside for the bikes of our rivals.

It didn't take me long to spot the tandem propped up against the side of the building, and Pop-Out Lee's bike was next to it. Luckily both had quick release wheel bolts so I quickly released the ones holding the front wheels. I then fastened them back up, but very loosely. From first look, the bolts would look fine, but the front wheels would definitely fall off as they pushed the bikes out of the pub. With any luck the wheels would roll down the hill, and it would take them an hour or more to retrieve them from the sea. I could be such a bastard when I wanted to be, especially when I was drunk.

I went back to Bike Buddy and he gradually staggered to his feet. We left Pop-Out Lee and the Tandemeers to their drinks, and walked back to our Bed and Breakfast. Okay, that's not quite true. Bike Buddy hobbled back to the Bed and Breakfast, and I stumbled. I swayed back and forth, travelling twice the distance required. The road was wobbling around me and the stars were revolving in the sky. I was drunk! I was drunk and I hadn't got to John O'Groats yet. Oh, I was going to be in good shape in the morning.

As we staggered along the road, I remembered something that had been playing on my mind for the last couple of days. How come Bike Buddy couldn't keep up with my leisurely average speed of 10-12 miles per hour when I was leading, but managed to consistently travel at more than 17 miles per hour when he led? This was very strange. Normally people found it easier to follow. Perhaps Bike Buddy's brain had been screwed in the wrong way round. Perhaps I had such a nasty looking backside it was putting him off. Come to think of it, why didn't Bike Buddy's backside put me off? Why was I thinking about another man's backside? Oh my God, I'd spent too much time in another man's company.

When we arrived back at the Bed and Breakfast the little old lady had finally made up our beds and our rooms were ready. It was just as well, by then it was nearly 10pm, and I knew Bike Buddy could literarily drop to sleep at any time. Much better for him to do this lying in his bed than standing up.

I also needed my bed; my head was aching. I think I did a good job in pretending I was sober, and staggered past the little old lady to my room. I lay back in my bed and looked up at the ceiling. It was revolving, so I closed my eyes, but then my eyeballs started to revolve instead.

I knew my head was going to hurt in the morning, and I knew my body would cramp in the night, but there was nothing I could do about it. I knew I'd been stupid drinking so much before we reached our goal, but it seemed so close now. We were on the north coast – how hard could the last day's cycle be?

Through my drunken state I thought about what we had achieved. We'd cycled from the far tip of Cornwall up to the north coast of Scotland. We'd cycled more than one thousand miles. In fact we'd clocked up 1,106 miles instead of the 1,018 it should have been. There was only one day remaining for us to complete our challenge; a challenge we could then be proud of forever and which meant I would achieve my lifetime goal and could die in peace. Meeting the other cyclists had annoyed me, and deflated my exhilaration slightly. I mean, I wanted to complete this cycle ride to become famous, and yet other people who had no right to achieve such a thing were also doing so.

Despite these slight doubts, I thought about the day ahead. I thought about what John O'Groats would be like; the residents out on the street to cheer us across the finish line, the owner of the last pub in Britain offering to buy us a drink in celebration. Tomorrow would be a wondrous day. A day to celebrate again, a day to remember! I passed out!

DAY 21: DAY AT THE RACES – BETTYHILL TO JOHN O'GROATS

We wanted to get away early today. We had a race to win against Pop-Out Lee and the Tandemeers. I'd woken at 2am with a stonking headache. By 4am it had subsided a little, and then between 4.30am and 5.15am I suffered with continual leg cramps. After the previous night's troubles, my legs decided to alternate cramping. This kept me busy for 45 minutes, before I eventually drifted off to sleep again – but only briefly. I spent the rest of the early morning worrying about the steep fall and hill we would face first thing, and as a result I was awake early, sweating, and sitting on the toilet.

At 7.45am we were dressed, fed and watered. We stepped out of the Bed and Breakfast and dug our bikes out of the peat shed like a couple of criminals reclaiming stolen property, from a coal mine.

The first part of the day involved the death drop we'd seen the previous night. Not something I'd been looking forward to because I was fairly certain we would miss the bend at the bottom and just end up in the sea. However, the death drop and climb out of Bettyhill weren't anywhere near as difficult as they'd appeared the night before. Perhaps we were just getting fitter, or perhaps our eyes had just deceived us.

One thing I'd learnt on this tour was not to judge a hill by its contours. Some hills appeared very steep as we approached them but turned out to be fairly easy. Others looked easy, but became complete nightmares. After twenty days in the saddle I'd finally worked out the reason. Hills looked steeper when we approached them on a downhill stretch. Then when we reached them the momentum from the downhill helped lift us up the other side. If you see a hill when you're already cycling uphill, you can bet your life it will be a bitch.

Despite this pleasant surprise, the remaining route to Thurso was hilly with long climbs and long falls, but somehow I didn't mind hills when I could whiz back down the other side without having to use my brakes. These hills were good hills, happy hills.

All the way to Thurso we looked over our shoulders. Where were Pop-Out Lee and the Tandemeers? There was no sign of them, but we were convinced the Tandemeers would be quicker than us. Pop-Out was probably not quicker than us, but you could never tell. I just hoped that my delaying tactic had worked.

By the time we reached Thurso none of them had appeared. I was starting to think maybe they'd escaped from Bettyhill before us, and were already in John O'Groats congratulating each other on a fine victory. Surely nobody got up earlier than Bike Buddy!

The original plan had been to get to Thurso for lunch, however, with the exceptionally early start we'd made this morning, and our better than expected progress we arrived in Thurso at just after 10.30am. We'd cycled 30 miles in less than three hours, so decided to take a major risk and stop for a mid-morning coffee and cake. Not wanting to be unknowingly overtaken, we decided to find a café overlooking the main road.

Thurso was a bustling little town; one of only two main towns in Caithness. The town used to be the centre for production of Caithness Flagstone, and was also a fishing village but both these industries have left it now. Thurso was, however, the most northerly town on mainland Britain, with numerous shops, hundreds of people and a lively buzz about it.

We found a suitably placed café, chose our seats in the window, and tucked into our light snack. Bike Buddy and I didn't speak throughout this pit stop; we just looked out of the window, but there was still no sign of them.

After a quick coffee break we went in search of some lunch, and purchased some triple combination sandwiches from the supermarket. The Post Office was inside the supermarket, so while Bike Buddy got the food, I got our books stamped as quickly as possible. No time to waste, we needed to get going rapidly.

By the time we'd eaten our cakes, drunk our coffee and purchased our lunch over an hour had passed. Surely the Tandemeers and Pop-Out had overtaken us by now? If not, we were certain to be victorious.

We cycled out of Thurso and joined the final road to John O'Groats. It was disappointing to find this road so busy. Tourists were obviously driving up to John

11228

868

36202421911322323934

O'Groats just to have a look. This made the cycling quite stressful, but we were on a high so it didn't really matter.

Ten miles from Thurso and we saw a tandem propped up against the wall of a restaurant. The Tandemeers had overtaken us, probably while we were in Thurso, but they'd stopped for lunch. Now we'd got them! Bike Buddy and I suddenly had renewed energy in our legs. We stamped down on our pedals and shot past the restaurant. If you'd seen us you wouldn't believe we'd cycled more than 1,100 miles already. Victory would be ours!

Before starting our cycle ride, Bike Buddy and I had talked about going to Dunnet Head en-route to John O'Groats. John O'Groats is not Britain's most northerly point, for that claim goes to Dunnet Head. We'd discussed going to the Lizard in Cornwall too, so we could say we'd been to the most southerly and northerly points in Britain, rather just Lands End to John O'Groats. This conversation re-emerged on the final stretch. Bike Buddy was not bothered either way, and I pointed out that we hadn't visited the Lizard in Cornwall, so why should we bother with Dunnet Head? Besides we had a race to win. As a result, we didn't bother.

We continued as fast as we could until we were only eight miles from John O'Groats; still no sign of the Tandemeers coming after us, and no sign of Pop-Out Lee, so we decided to stop and eat our sandwiches. There was nowhere to sit, but we didn't care. We were in a rush anyway, so just propped our bikes up against a telephone exchange box, and tucked in.

This broke the record for the fastest lunch I had ever eaten - faster than the midge-infested one from the previous day. There was no time to worry about indigestion. We kept staring down the road, waiting for the tandem to appear, or Pop-Out to just pop-out, but nothing. We ate, we weed, we got on our bikes and fleed.

Eight miles to victory! Bike Buddy and I thumped harder on the pedals. We were flying. Just one mile to go and we decided to stop so Bike Buddy could exchange his thick woollen jumper for his 'Lands End to John O'Groats' luminous t-shirt. Personally I'd worn mine all the time, night and day. I was surprised when he suggested the change, because I couldn't believe cold-blooded Bike Buddy could possibly have warmed up enough to just wear a t-shirt like me. It was therefore no surprise when he put the t-shirt on over the top of this long-sleeved top. While Bike Buddy changed I kept lookout, continually watching for the Tandemeers or Pop-Out, but there was still no sign of them.

As we merrily jaunted along the last mile, I took my song and poem writing skills to a new level. The jubilation I felt had to come out, and the only way was for me to sing it out. I changed a few words in my mind, and then belted out the words to one very famous Queen song. Our own cycling anthem:

We are the Champions

I've let out some howls,
When hurting my balls.
I've had pain and torture and everything that goes with it,
And cursed them all.
It's been no bed of roses,
No pleasure cruise,
I've had my share of gravel under my tyres,
But I've spun through.
We are the champions, my friends.
We kept on cycling to the end.
We are the champions,
We are the champions,
No time for losers, 'cos we are the champions.
Of the world.

I've clicked in my shoes,
Time after time.
I've swallowed some midges,
But passed them through fine.
And bad mistakes,
I've made a few,
I've had my share of water splashed in my face,
But I've come through.
We are the champions, my friends.
We kept on cycling to the end.
We are the champions,
We are the champions,
No time for losers, 'cos we are the champions.
Of the world.

The weather was perfect for the last couple of miles - the sky was blue, the sun was beating down and we felt like we were in heaven. Those last miles to John O'Groats were the best miles I had ever cycled in my life. I felt overjoyed at what I'd accomplished and overjoyed at what Bike Buddy had accomplished. I remembered the last three weeks, the hard times, the good times, the high times and the low times. I remembered the heat in Cornwall, and the cold in Scotland. I remembered the generosity of people on the way. I remembered the gravel tracks, and the grass banks, the mudslides and the metal staircases. But more than anything else I remembered how Bike Buddy and I had dealt with them all ourselves. Nobody else there to carry our luggage, nobody else there to point us in the right direction. At the end of the day we had done it all ourselves. Bike Buddy and I - the greatest cyclists in the world, the best tourers ever, the kings of the universe.

As we zipped along to our finish point, we looked north out across the Pentland Firth and took in the sight of the Island of Stroma just a few miles offshore. What a fantastic view to finish a cycle ride!

We rolled into John O'Groats at 1.30pm having beaten the Tandemeers, and having beaten Pop-Out Lee. We would be modest in our victory. After all they didn't even know they'd been in a race.

Our first port of call was to have our photos taken at the sign. We stood waiting while another cyclist had his photo taken. There he stood with his racing bike, grinning at the sign. He was celebrating with his family, who had followed him up in the car. That had to be a thankless task - sitting in a car for a fortnight watching your old man cycle his bike - yippee! The son was not a happy bunny. He had a green face, and a sulky mouth. He sat by the side of the road holding his head in his hands. Either he was ill, or just pissed off. I think he was probably a bit of both. After all he'd been sitting in a car for a fortnight watching his dad's lycra clad backside wiggling about in front of him. Enough to make anyone sick.

After the photo shoot, we cycled across the official finish line together. I shook Bike Buddy's hand and congratulated him on a job well done. He may have nearly snored me to death, and he may have been extremely slow when he followed behind, but he had become a very good friend, and I could think of nobody else I would have rather shared the moment with.

We then entered the John O'Groats House Hotel for a celebratory drink. I strode in and triumphantly announced what we'd done.

'Do you know, we've just cycled from Lands End to John O'Groats?'

'Aye,' came the short reply, 'sign the book.'

I said, 'Did you not hear what I said? I said, we've just <u>cycled</u> from Lands End to John O'Groats.'

'Aye. You're the fourth today, just sign the book.'

What a bastard!

What was disappointing was that almost everyone in John O'Groats seemed to go out of their way to show us how unimpressed they were with our achievements. I realise they must have seen a lot of nutters doing the same thing, but a smile and a, 'Well done' would not have hurt them and would have gone a long way to making us feel good.

This reaction caused me major concerns. I had wanted to do this cycle so I could be famous for it, yet so many other people had already done the same, and were still doing so, I wasn't going to be famous for cycling up the country. I was just another idiot who had too much time on his hands.

We signed the book, although I felt a little strange signing the book as an end-to-ender. I was still not comfortable with the term. Nonetheless, we signed, wrote a short description of our journey, and bought a couple of pints of best ale. Halfway through my ale, and I did what so many people must do when they go to the last pub in Britain - I used the telephone to phone home.

There was probably more to see at John O'Groats than at Lands End. Recent investment in the area meant we were no longer greeted with a windswept car park, but instead saw a visitor's centre, many craft shops, and a real harbour. No silly fairground rides, but just a neat and tidy area to mark the end of the world.

It was amazing how many other cyclists got to John O'Groats the same day as us. I counted eight in total, including ourselves. Again, the number of other cyclists lowered my achievement further. The Tandemeers turned up about an hour after we did. Bike Buddy and I nodded to them to say, 'Hi'. The Tandemeers looked unhappy, they looked almost desperate. We wandered over, and checked they were okay.

'You alright?' I asked, with a tone that suggested I had no reason to think they shouldn't be.

'Only just,' replied the bloke, 'some bastard sabotaged our bike. Undid the bloody wheel nuts and the bloody wheel fell off as we cycled out of the car park. Luckily we were almost at a standstill when the wheel fell, and we managed to get away with just cuts and bruises. Not like poor old Lee.'

I looked quizzically at them, encouraging them to continue.

'He left the pub about an hour before us, and we were just in time to see the ambulance carry him away. It didn't look good. I think maybe the same thing had happened to him, because his bike was on the side of the road, but the front wheel was missing. Lee had fallen over the side of the cliff. They had to drag him up on a stretcher, but I don't think he made it. He was a hell of a mess. Poor sod! What kind of a sick bastard would do such a thing?'

I looked at Bike Buddy and shook my head. What kind of a sick bastard would do such a thing? Exactly!

Looking at the other cyclists, I have to say I respected the Tandemeers, and poor Pop-Out Lee at that moment. The five of us had all carried our own equipment. The other three cyclists we met at John O'Groats that day all had back-up vehicles and were celebrating with friends and family who had driven the journey with them. Despite the delight of having friends there to celebrate I still believed the true adventure was completing the journey unaided. The freedom and isolation we felt when we were doing everything ourselves made the journey both exhilarating and scary at the same time. We were never sure whether we would make it until we crossed the finish line. There were many occasions when Bike Buddy and I were very close to giving up, and I'm sure if we'd had a back-up vehicle we would have got in it and gone home, but, because we were on our own, we didn't have that luxury. We had to get by on what we had in our panniers, or in the case of the borrowed tyre, what we could find at the scene. Besides, we now had another celebration to look forward to, the one when we get home.

After congratulating the Tandemeers we set off for the Bed and Breakfast, which was only a quarter of a mile up the road. This Bed and Breakfast was probably one of the biggest disappointments of the whole trip.

The owner's first comment to her daughter as we arrived was, 'Guess where these two have cycled from and to'.

Her daughter just grunted and walked away.

That annoyed me more than anything else. These people made their livelihood out of people like us, the very least they could do was try to make us feel special even if they didn't really believe we were. When we'd arrived at Bettyhill we felt like we'd made it, and in some ways that celebration was better than the real one. My big achievement was being devalued everywhere we turned. I hadn't become someone, I was still a nobody and I would be dead in a few months.

Our celebration meal in John O'Groats ended up being haddock and chips at the Bed and Breakfast. There was nowhere else to go. We ordered wine for our 'posh' dinner, but had to ask three times for them to bring it out. A bit of a damp end to a glorious three weeks, but nothing could dampen the warmth we now felt inside. We'd cycled 1,159 miles from one end of the country to the other. We'd sat on our bikes for 143 hours, and we had finally reached our destination.

Our last night with our bikes was in a twin room. I thought the snoring wouldn't bother me now, but I was wrong. Bike Buddy and I sat and chatted about our adventure into the night. We felt good, and our bikes felt pretty good as well, lying in relative luxury in the laundry room, but something kept gnawing away at me. Had this really been a big achievement?

To begin with as I tried to drift off to sleep I could hear the comforting sound of a drill vibrating through the room. Slowly this pleasant noise increased in volume and started to shake my bed. The bed shaking started to unnerve me and soon my head was spinning with thoughts and problems. I had cycled up the country. I'd finished the one thing that I'd wanted to do before I finally reached my doom. Had it been worth it? Had I achieved what I'd set out to achieve? I wasn't sure I had. I'd wanted to become someone, but the last two days had put doubts in my mind. Cycling Lands End to John O'Groats didn't make me famous, it was just another stupid waste of time like the rest of life.

I still didn't want to die, and desperately craved everlasting life. Cycling from Lands End to John O'Groats hadn't changed that, and it hadn't solved the problem. I was still dying from a Colonic Worm Infestation, and there was nothing anyone could do about it. I was still going to die a nobody. Okay, I'd given life to my children, but I wanted more. I wanted to live forever, in people's minds at least. Cycling up the country was an amazing achievement, but other people did it every day. I wasn't someone special. The people in John O'Groats had gone out of their way to make sure I knew that. I needed another plan. How could I live forever?

The answer hit me. In fact, I believe it had probably been with me for weeks. The only people who live on forever are those who do hideous, horrendous crimes. Think about the names you know from history. Okay there are kings and queens, but there are also murderers. The greatest criminal minds in the world. I had murdered perhaps nine people on this cycle trip. All of them had been hideous mistakes, and I probably wouldn't go down for murder even if caught; I was certain manslaughter was the most I could be convicted for.

Manslaughter; unless I admitted that I had killed them on purpose. If I owned up to the murders, I would become a mass murderer, and my illness would mean a sentence spent in a hospital, not a prison. What's more I could sell my story and make a fortune. I could leave enough money for my wife and children to be safe and happy forever. I just needed to admit to the murders. I needed people to be aware of what I had done, and I needed one final piece of my jigsaw to be put into place. I needed to find a finale, my way of signing off and, with the thought of eternal fame surging through my body, I lifted my pillow and placed it firmly over Bike Buddy's face. His snoring softened, his breathing subsided and slowly Bike Buddy drifted off for his everlasting sleep.

EPILOGUE

There isn't really an epilogue, but if reading Matthew and Bike Buddy's adventures have inspired you to undertake the same trek, the following pages may be of interest. They include hand-drawn maps of the routes taken, as well as a guide to the road surface and route profile.

I cannot guarantee the complete accuracy of the information contained within the next few pages, although I will guarantee, if you use them, you'll get lost. So use them wisely.

Day 1: Penzance to Lands End and Return

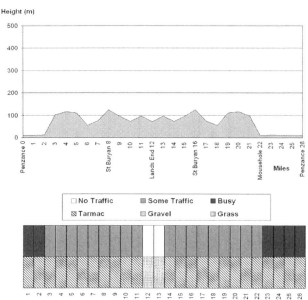

Day 2: Penzance to St Column Major

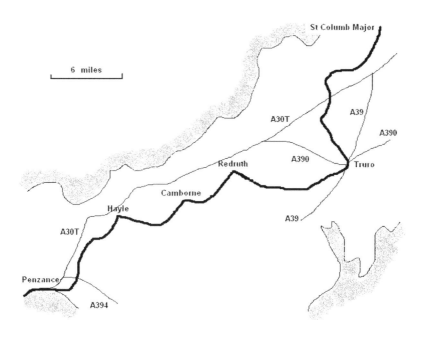

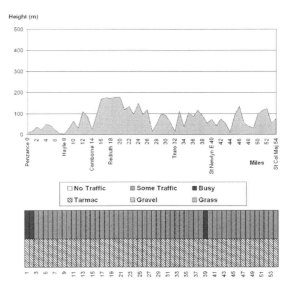

Day 3: St Columb Major to Pyworthy

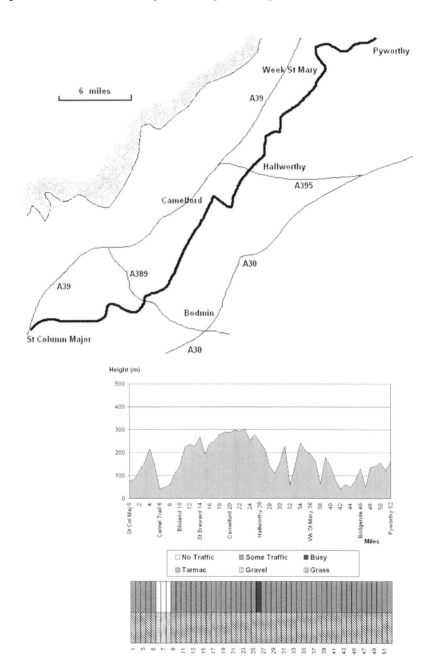

Day 4: Pyworthy to Tiverton

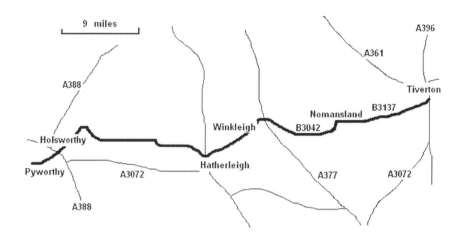

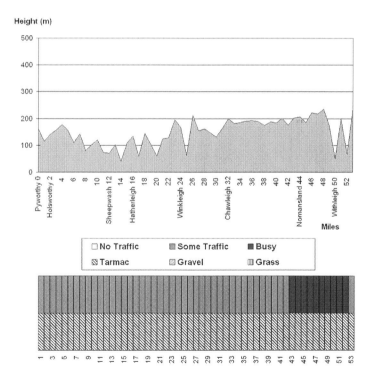

Day 5: Tiverton to Glastonbury

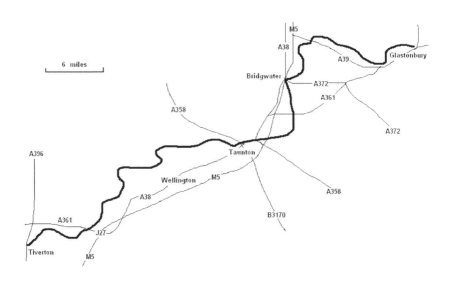

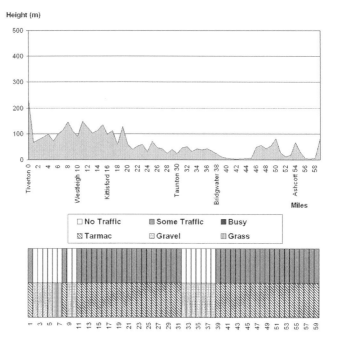

Day 6: Glastonbury to Tetbury

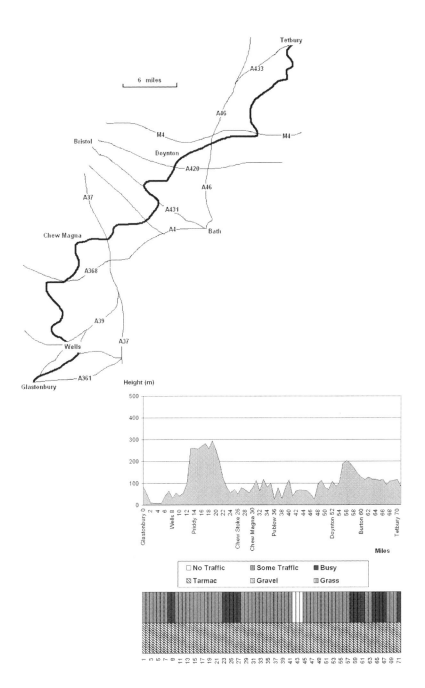

Day 7: Tetbury to Wyre Piddle

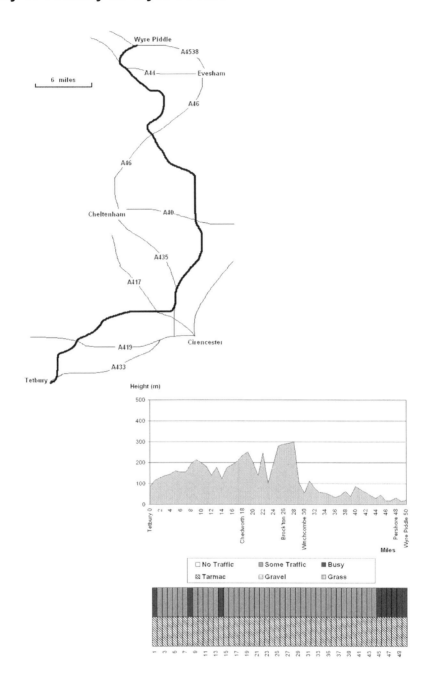

Day 8: Wyre Piddle to Wellington

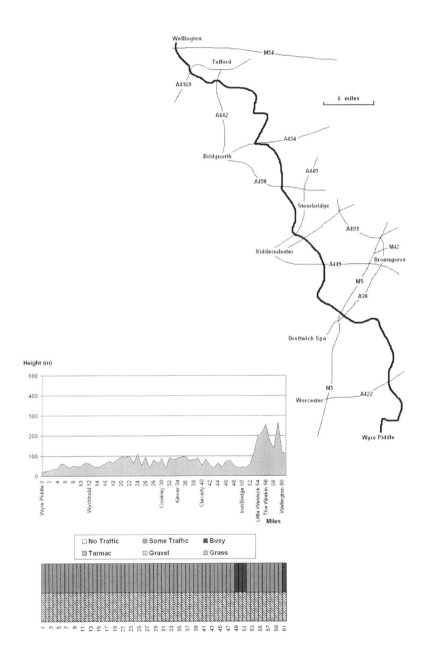

Day 9: Wellington to Middlewich

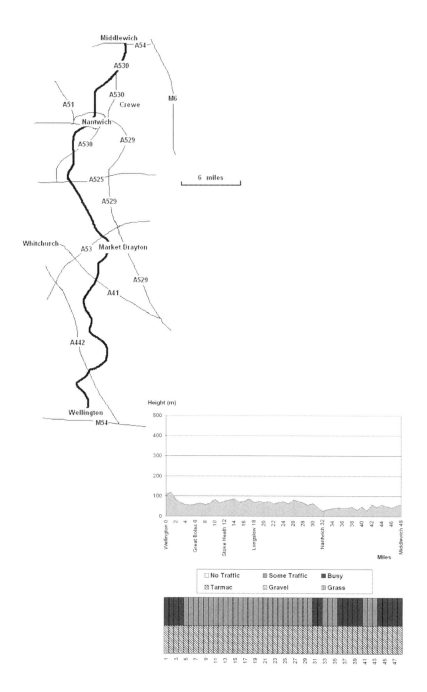

Day 10: Middlewich to Clayton-le-Dale

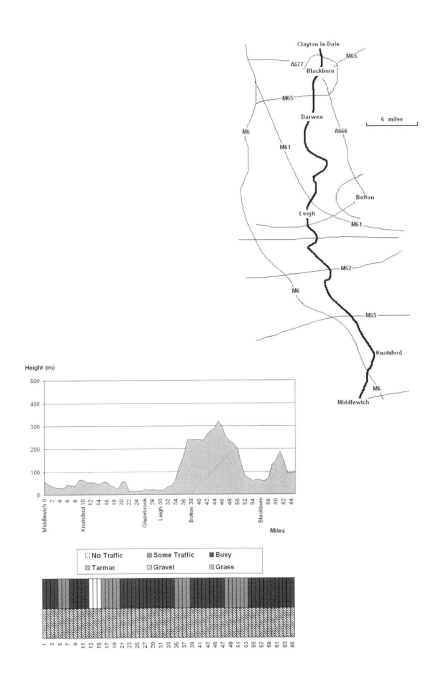

Day 11: Clayton-le-Dale to Sedbergh

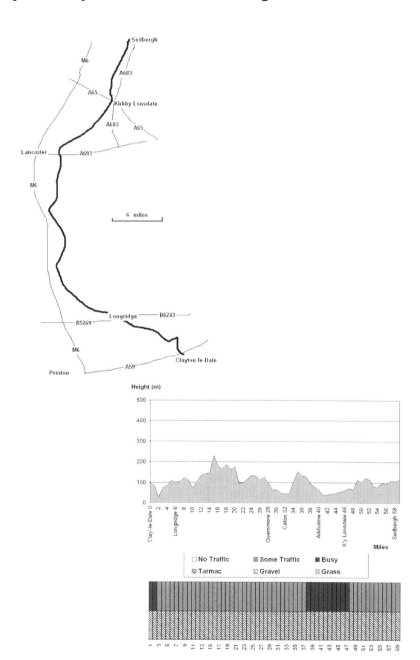

Day 12: Sedbergh to Castle Carroch

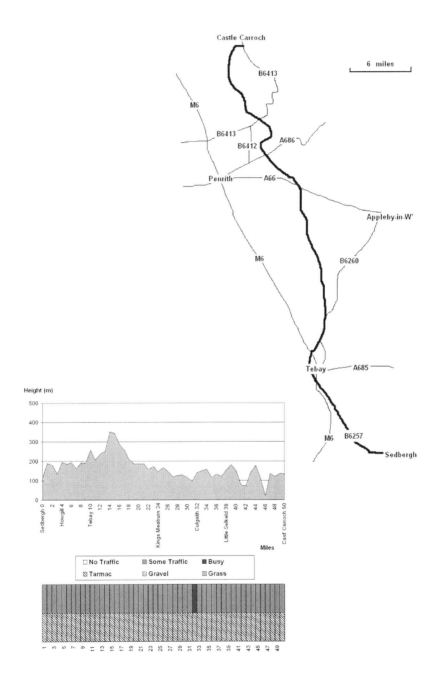

Day 13: Castle Carroch to Ettrick Valley

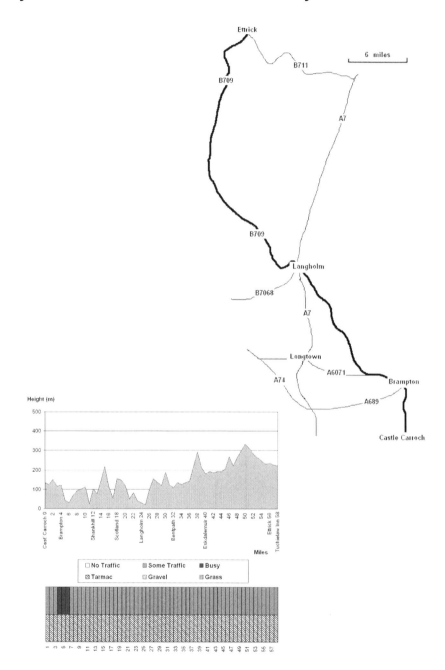

Day 14: Ettrick Valley to Wilsontown

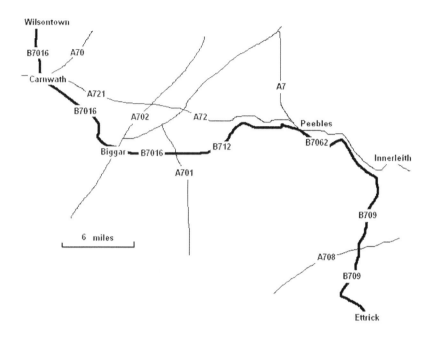

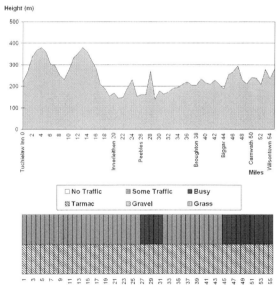

Day 15: Wilstontown to Callander

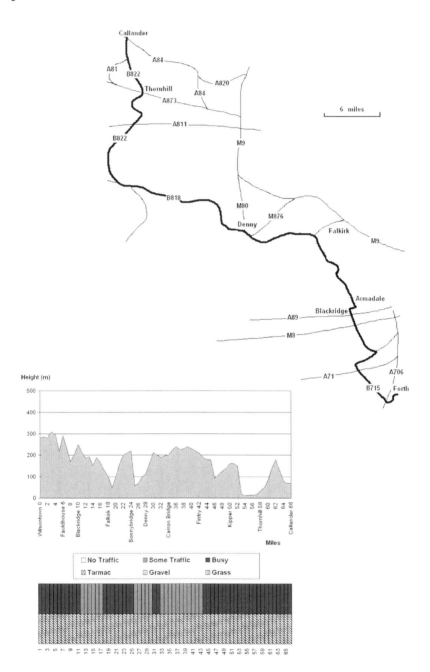

Day 16: Callander to Aberfeldy

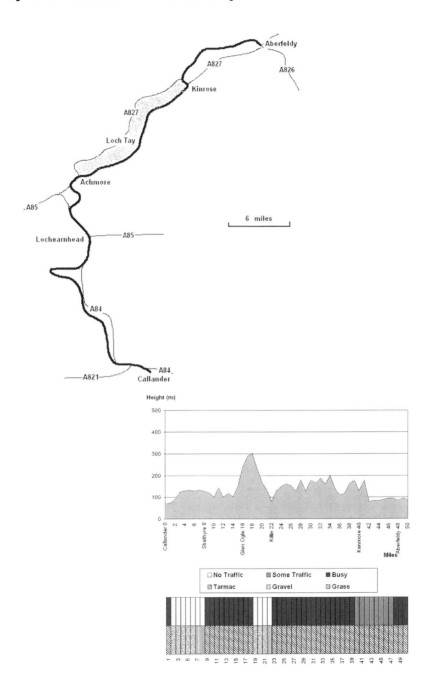

Day 17: Aberfeldy to Newtonmore

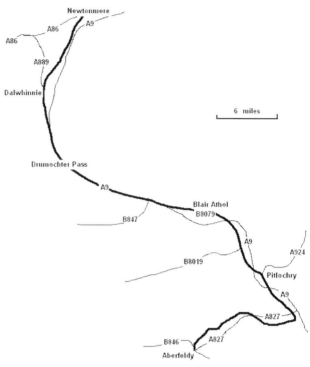

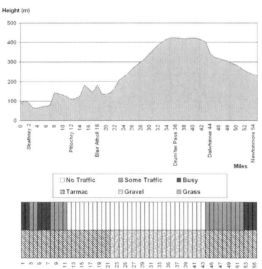

Day 18: Newtonmore to Inverness

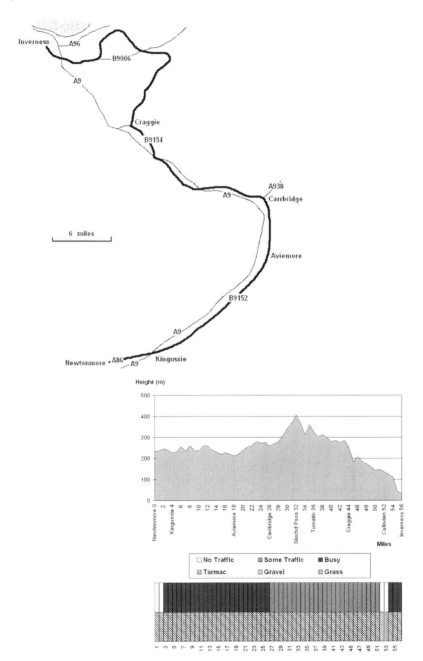

Day 19: Inverness to Lairg

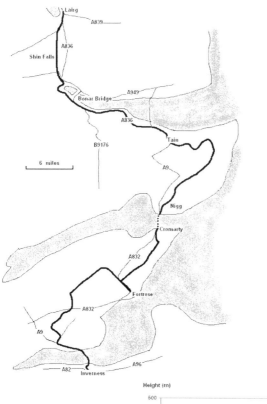

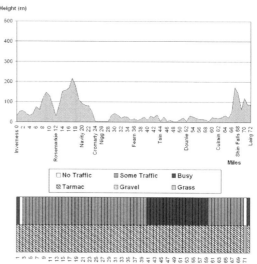

Day 20: Lairg to Bettyhill

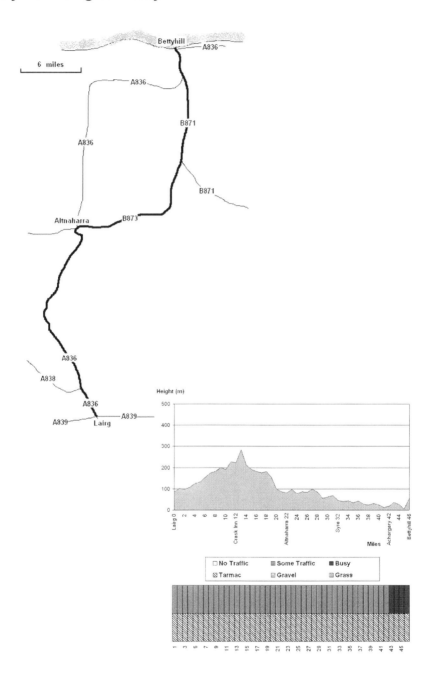

Day 21: Bettyhill to John O'Groats

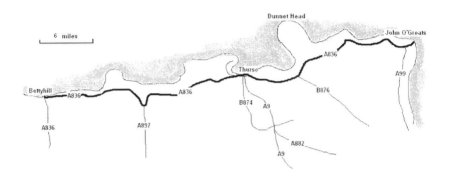

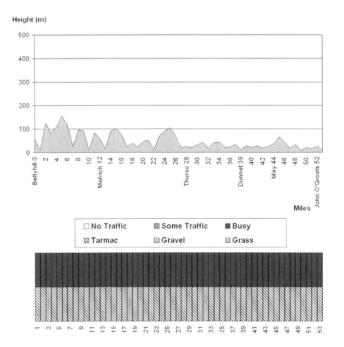

33495527R00151

Printed in Great Britain
by Amazon